On your Side

Edition : 2005
ISBN : 81-7008-484-9
Economy Edition Price : Rs. 125.00
Series : *On Your Side*
Title : *Excel 2002*
FOY–2770–125–OYS–EXCEL 2002

Published by **FIREWALL MEDIA**
(*An Imprint of Laxmi Publications Pvt. Ltd.*)
22, Golden House, Daryaganj,
New Delhi-110002
India
Phone : 011-23 25 25 74
Fax : 011-23 25 25 72
E-mail : colaxmi@hotmail.com

Branches

- **Bangalore** (*Phone* : 080-26 61 15 61)
- **Chennai** (*Phone* : 044-24 34 47 26)
- **Cochin** (*Phone* : 0484-239 70 04)
- **Guwahati** (*Phones* : 0361-254 36 69, 251 38 81)
- **Hyderabad** (*Phone* : 040-24 75 02 47)
- **Jalandhar City** (*Phone* : 0181-222 12 72)
- **Kolkata** (*Phones* : 033-22 27 37 73, 22 27 52 47)
- **Lucknow** (*Phone* : 0522-220 95 78)
- **Mumbai** (*Phone* : 022-24 46 39 98)
- **Ranchi** (*Phone* : 0651-230 77 64)

http:/www.laxmipublications.com

C—9586/04/12

On Your Side Collection directed by Corinne HERVO
English edition by Adrienne TOMMY

*This is a book for anyone who uses **Excel 2002** (the version of Excel included in the Office XP suite).*

It is designed so that you can look up the task you want to perform and find a clear description of how go about it.

The screens illustrated throughout these pages add to the efficacy of the explanations, by showing the dialog box corresponding to a particular command, or by giving a precise example.

This book is made up of ten parts.

Excel 2002 *p. 1 to 21*	A basic overview of the Excel workspace and tips on how to move around it and select items within it.
Managing documents *p. 22 to 43*	How to open and save documents and manage workbooks and sheets.
Entering and modifying data *p. 44 to 76*	The various ways in which you can enter, modify, copy or transfer data and manage named ranges.
Calculations *p. 77 to 108*	How to perform the more common calculations, including advanced calculations such as arrays and how to use the worksheet auditing features.
Presentation of data *p. 109 to 136*	Commands for modifying row and column layout, formatting data and tables and for managing styles and outlines.
Printing *p. 137 to 148*	Description of all the possibilities for printing (page setup, headers and footers), including views and reports.
Charts and objects *p. 149 to 187*	All the options for creating and working with charts and graphic objects (including clip art).
Lists of data *p. 188 to 206*	How to manage and filter lists efficiently and how to prepare pivot tables and pivot charts to analyse list data.
Group work *p. 207 to 127*	Techniques for using shared worksheets, including protecting data and setting access and data entry conditions.
Miscellaneous features *p. 228 to 257*	Deals with other Excel features, such as using smart tags, importing data, creating macros and managing Web pages.

FOREWORD

A useful list of shortcut keys can be found in the ***Appendix****. You can find techniques and commands more quickly by using the comprehensive* ***index*** *at the back of the book.*

Typographic conventions

To help you find the information you require quickly and easily, the following conventions have been adopted.

These typefaces are used for:

bold showing which menu option or dialog box to use.

italic giving an explanation of the command you are following, or of any changes on the screen.

[Ctrl] showing which keys you should press. When two keys are displayed together they must be pressed simultaneously.

The following symbols indicate:

♦ An action you should perform (activating an option, clicking with the mouse).

❑ A general comment on the command being used.

A useful tip.

A technique which involves the mouse.

A keyboard technique.

A technique which uses options from the menus.

TABLE OF CONTENTS

EXCEL 2002

MANAGING DOCUMENTS

TABLE OF CONTENTS

CALCULATIONS

PRESENTATION OF DATA

TABLE OF CONTENTS

CHARTS AND OBJECTS

TABLE OF CONTENTS

GROUP WORK

MISCELLANEOUS FEATURES

Starting and leaving Excel 2002

Starting Excel 2002

♦ Click the **Start** button.

♦ Move the mouse onto the **Programs** option.

♦ Click **Microsoft Excel.**

❑ *If you have a shortcut to Excel on the Desktop, double-click the icon to start the application.*

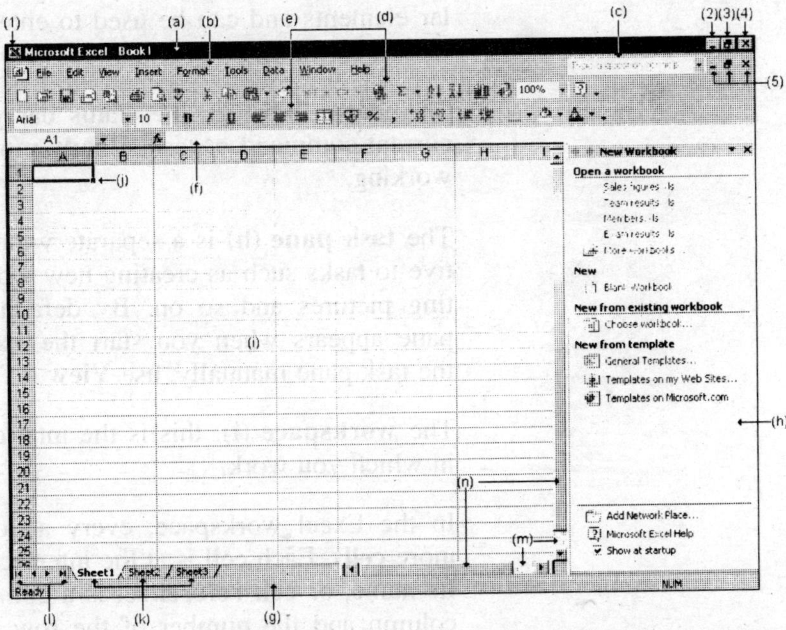

The **title bar** (a): on the left there is the button which opens Excel's **Control** menu (1). Next to it is the name of the application (Microsoft Excel) and the active workbook. On the right there are the **Minimize** (2), **Maximize** or **Restore** (3) and **Close** (4) buttons for the Excel 2002 application window.

Below this, the **Minimize, Restore** and **Close** (5) buttons for the workbook appear.

The **menu bar** (b): this contains all the Excel menus as well as the **Type a question for help** text box (c) in which you can type questions or keywords to search the Excel help for.

The **Standard toolbar** (d) and **Formatting toolbar** (e): these tools carry out common commands instantly and apply formatting. Double-click the move handle on its left edge to undock the toolbar and transform it into a floating toolbar.

The **formula bar** (f): this bar displays information about particular elements and can be used to enter and modify data (text, values or formulas).

The **status bar** (g): the status bar gives information about the current command or task. **Ready** mode means you can now start working.

The **task pane** (h) is a separate window containing options relative to tasks such as creating new workbooks, finding text, inserting pictures and so on. By default the **New Workbook** task pane appears when you start the Excel application. To display the task pane manually, use **View - Task Pane**.

The **workspace** (i): this is the interior space of each worksheet, in which you work.

In the Excel workspace, every action is performed on one or more **cells**. Each cell is at the intersection of a row and a column. Its name, or **cell reference**, is a combination of the letter of the column and the number of the row in which it is situated. For example, a cell in column C, at row 11 is called C11.

When you click a particular cell, the cell becomes **active** and its reference appears at the left of the formula bar.

Up to 256 columns and 65536 rows can be used in Excel 2002. The black square at the bottom right corner of the active cell is called the **fill handle** (j).

Worksheet **tabs** (k): a book consists of several **sheets** (three by default). Excel identifies them by **tabs which** appear at the bottom of the book window. The name of the active sheet appears in bold type on a white tab.

The **tab scroll bar** (l): use these buttons to display the first sheet, the previous sheet, the next sheet or the last sheet.

The **scroll bars** (m): these are used to move across or up and down the active worksheet. The rectangles that can be seen on the scroll bars (n) are called **scroll cursors** or **scroll boxes**.

Leaving Excel 2002

♦ **File** **Exit**	Click [X] in the application window	♦ Alt F4

If you cannot see the full list of options in a menu, click [»] at the bottom of the menu or double-click the menu name; the complete list of options will open (it opens automatically after the menu has been on screen for five seconds).

♦ If you have left any documents unsaved, save them. The **Yes To All** option saves all open documents.

Using help

First method

You can access directly the Microsoft Excel Help window.

♦ **Help** **Microsoft Excel Help**	♦ F1

*This command either opens the Microsoft Excel Help window or displays the Office Assistant. If the Office Assistant appears and you wish to deactivate it, click the **Options** button in the Assistant's yellow search box and, on the **Options** page, remove the tick from the **Use the Office Assistant** check box.*

*You can also show the help window by clicking the **Microsoft Excel Help** link at the bottom of the **New Document** task pane.*

♦ To search for a help text in the Contents, click the **Contents** tab in the Microsoft Excel Help window. Expand the hierarchy of the contents by clicking the plus (+) sign next to the **Microsoft Excel Help** category. Click the plus sign on the book icon that corresponds to the category you wish to see (or double-click the book icon); continue clicking the plus (+) sign on each sub-category until you arrive at the help topic that interests you. Click the question mark icon on that topic to display its text in the right pane.

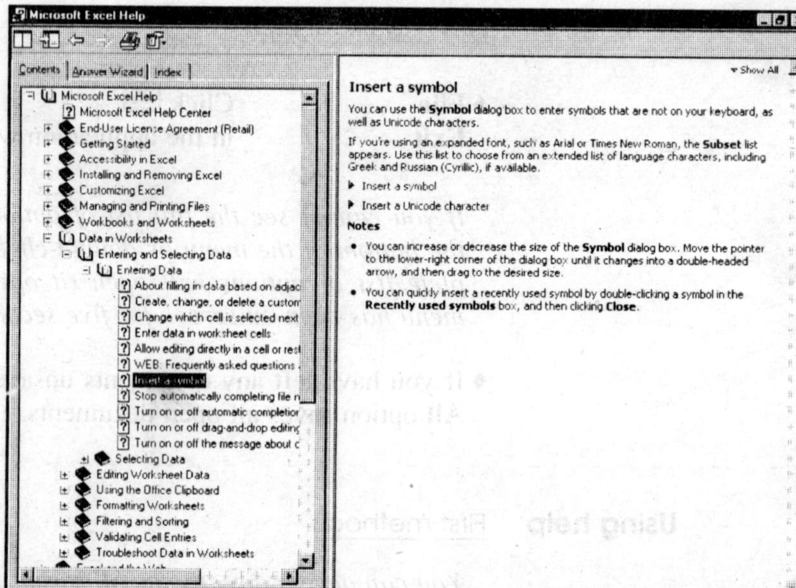

♦ To show a list of topics that corresponds to a particular request, click the **Answer Wizard** tab and enter your question in the **What would you like to do?** text box. Click the **Search** button then select the topic you require, to display the help text in the right pane.

*The **Search on Web** button starts your Web browser and connects to the Microsoft Internet site to find more help on the question you asked.*

♦ To look for a help text using the **Index**, start by clicking the **Index** tab. In the **Type keywords** box, enter the first letters of the keyword you require then click the **Search** button. You can also double-click one of the suggested keywords displayed in the **Or choose keywords** list box. Select the help topic you require to see its text in the right pane.

♦ To hide the left pane of the help window, containing the **Contents, Answer Wizard** and **Index** tabs, click the button. The button can be used if you wish to reopen this part of the window.

♦ To see the last help text visited, click the button and the button to advance forward again.

♦ The buttons on the left either arrange the help window and the application window in a tiled manner ( ) or place the help window over the application window ( ).

♦ To print the displayed help text, click the button. Define the print settings in the **Print** dialog box then click **OK.** When you print a text displayed with the **Contents** tab, you will be asked if you wish to **Print the selected topic** or **Print the selected heading and all subtopics**. Make your choice and click **OK.**

♦ Close the **Microsoft Excel Help** window by clicking its button.

Second method

*You can also get help using the **Ask a Question** box.*

♦ Click the **Ask a Question** box Type a question for help on the right end of the menu bar, enter your question or a keyword and press Enter.

*The topics corresponding to the search subject appear. The **See more** option, when it appears, shows additional lists of topics.*

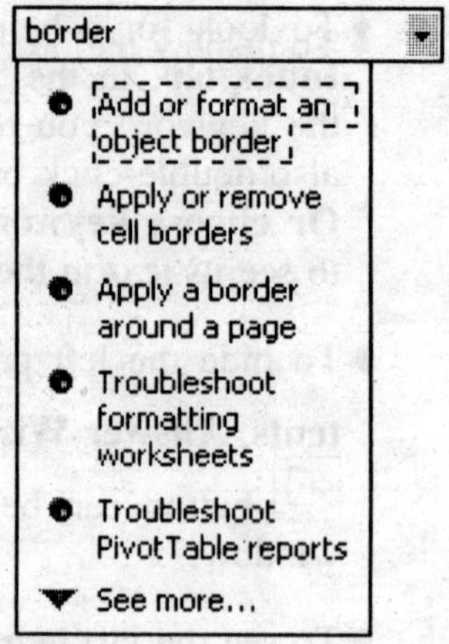

♦ Click the help topic of your choice to display the corresponding text; the **Microsoft Excel Help** window appears on the screen.

♦ Consult the help text. If you wish to search for further items in the **Microsoft Excel Help** window, click the button to show the pane containing the **Contents**, **Answer Wizard** and **Index** tabs (cf. above).

♦ Click the button to close the help window.

❑ *You can also get help from the Office Assistant. Show the Assistant with the* ***Help - Show the Office Assistant*** *command, click the Assistant then enter your question or keyword in the text box. Click* ***Search*** *to start searching.*

❑ *To hide the Office Assistant, use the* ***Help - Hide the Office Assistant*** *command or right-click the Assistant and choose* ***Hide****.*

❑ *To deactivate the Assistant, use the* ***Help - Microsoft Excel Help*** *command (or F1) if the Assistant is hidden or click the Assistant if it is on the screen. Click the* ***Options*** *button, deactivate the* ***Use the Office Assistant*** *checkbox and click* ***OK****.*

> *You can also search for further help on the Microsoft site by using the* ***Help - Office on the Web*** *command.*

Managing the task pane

♦ To display the task pane, use the **View - Task Pane** command.

The task pane is anchored to the right of the application window.

*If you click the **View** menu again, you can see a tick now appears next to the **Task Pane** option.*

♦ To change the contents of the task pane, click the button on the pane's title bar and click the option that corresponds to the task you wish to perform.

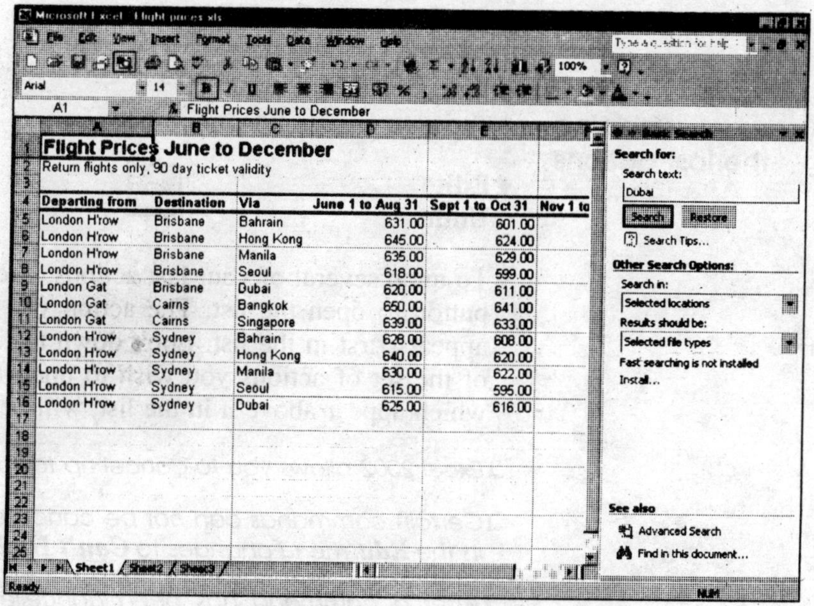

Here, the task pane shows options for finding text.

♦ To see the previously displayed task pane, use the and/or buttons on the task pane's title bar.

To detach the task pane, point to its title bar and drag it away from the side of the application window, or double-click its title bar. It then becomes a floating task pane.

To dock (or reattach) the task pane, double-click the pane's title bar or drag it by its title bar towards the right edge of the application window again.

♦ To close the task pane, use the **View - Task Pane** command again or click the button on the pane's title bar.

Repeating your last action

♦ If necessary select the item concerned.

♦ **Edit Repeat** ♦ Ctrl Y

❑ *When the last command can not be repeated, the* ***Repeat*** *option is replaced by* ***Can't Repeat*** *(in grey).*

Undoing the last actions

♦ To undo your last action, use:

♦ **Edit Undo** ♦ Ctrl Z

♦ To undo several of your last actions, click the arrow on the button to open the list. The action you performed most recently appears first in the list. Look down the list, and click the earliest of the set of actions you wish to undo (this action, and all those which appear above it in the list, will be undone).

❑ *Excel 2002 allows you to cancel up to 16 of your last actions.*

❑ *Certain commands can not be cancelled. In this case the option in the* ***Edit*** *menu changes to* ***Can't Undo*** *(in grey).*

❑ *After a command has been cancelled, you can restore it by clicking the button.*

Moving around on a sheet

There are several ways of moving around a worksheet: some involve the mouse, others make use of the keyboard.

♦ Use the scroll bars to reach the cell you want to activate:

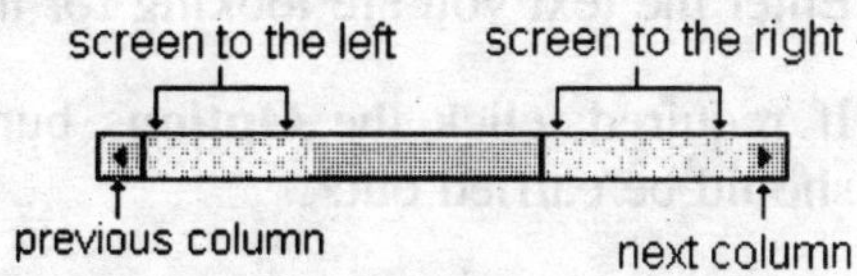

♦ Use the keyboard as follows:

cell to the right	→ or Tab
cell to the left	← or Shift Tab
cell above	↑ or Shift Enter
cell below	↓ or Enter
screen to the right	Alt Pg Dn
screen to the left	Alt Pg Up
screen above	Pg Up
screen below	Pg Dn
column A in the active row	Home
cell A1	Ctrl Home

Going to a specific cell

♦ Click the box on the formula bar where the reference of the active cell is displayed (the **Name Box**).

This selects the reference of the active cell.

♦ Type in the reference of the cell required.

♦ Press Enter.

Finding a cell

By its content

♦ If you wish to search the whole worksheet or all the worksheets in the workbook, activate a single cell. If you wish to search a section of the active sheet, select the corresponding range of cells.

♦ **Edit**
Find ♦ Ctrl F

♦ Enter the text you are looking for in the **Find what** box.

♦ If required, click the **Options** button to define how the search should be carried out:

Within	in the list, choose whether to search in the current **Sheet** or in all the sheets in the **Workbook.**
Search	in the list, choose in which direction the search should be carried out.
Look in	choose whether Excel should search for the item in the **Formulas**, the **Values** or the **Comments** of the cells.
Match case	tick this option if you want Excel to distinguish between upper and lower case characters in the search.
Match entire cell contents	tick this option if you want Excel to search for cells containing the whole search text and only that text.

♦ To search cell by cell, click the **Find Next** button. If the cell found contains what you were looking for, click the **Close** button, if not click **Find Next** to keep searching.

♦ To search all cells simultaneously, click the **Find All** button. When you do this, a detailed list of the cells found appears in the bottom part of the dialog box.

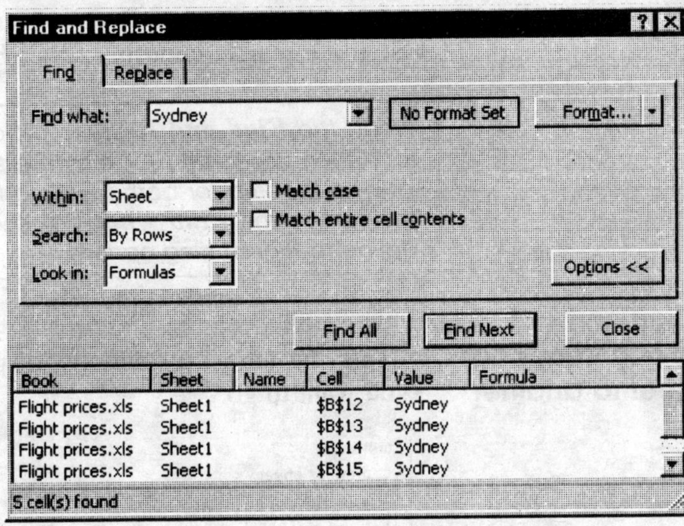

♦ Click one of the values in the list to select the corresponding cell. Click the **Close** button.

Finding a cell by its formatting

♦ Activate a single cell or select the part of the sheet in which you want to search.

♦ **Edit**
Find

♦ Ctrl F

♦ If necessary, click the **Options** button to show the full range of search options.

♦ Delete anything that may be still in the **Find what** box.

♦ Click the **Format** button and in the **Find Format** dialog box, select the options for the required format.

*The **Choose Format From Cell** button automatically retrieves all of the selected cell's formatting attributes.*

♦ Click **OK**.

♦ Start the search, choosing either **Find Next** or **Find All**.

> *When the **Find and Replace** dialog box is closed, you can perform the last search made by pressing* [Shift] [F4]*.*
> *You can search for both text and formatting simultaneously: enter the text in the **Find what** box then click the **Format** button to define the formatting options.*

Moving from one sheet to another

♦ Using the tab scroll buttons, display the tab of the sheet where you want to go:

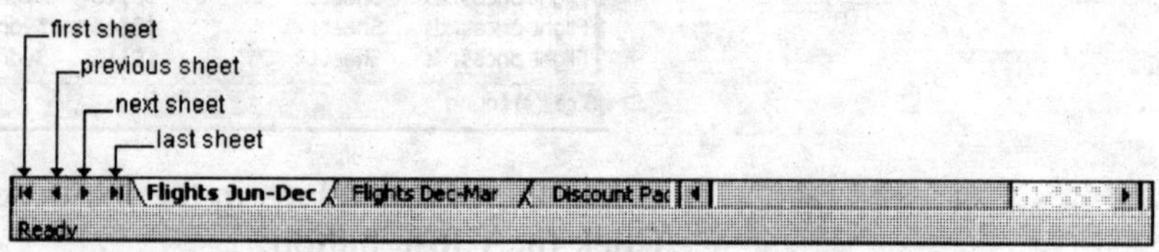

♦ To scroll the tabs quickly, hold down the [Shift] key as you click ◄ or ►.

♦ To open the worksheet, click its tab.

♦ On the keyboard you can use [Ctrl] [Pg Dn] to move to the next sheet or [Ctrl] [Pg Up] for the previous sheet.

> *You can increase or decrease the space reserved for sheet tabs by dragging the tab split bar situated to the left of the horizontal scroll bar.*

Freezing and unfreezing titles on the screen

When a table is too big to be visible all at once on the screen, freezing columns or rows is a way of bringing together data at opposite ends of the table.

♦ To freeze the row titles, make sure that the columns containing them can be seen at the very left of the screen. To freeze the column titles, display the corresponding row at the top of the screen.

♦ To freeze the row titles, select the next column. Select the next row to freeze the column titles.

♦ **Window**
Freeze Panes

	A	B	C	D	E	F
1	**Discount Packages**					
2	*Destination*	*Airline Code*	*Description*	*Insurance Inc*	*Adult Rate*	*Child Rate*
14	Crete	AEG	..\OneStop Travel\Pa	Yes	259	189
15	Crete	AFR	..\OneStop Travel\Pa	No	289	200
16	Cyprus	AEG	..\OneStop Travel\Pa	Yes	365	269

Rows 1 and 2 have been frozen, which makes it possible to display row 14 underneath row 2.

❑ *To release the titles you have frozen use **Window - Unfreeze Panes**.*

❑ *You can also display two different parts of the worksheet simultaneously by splitting the window. To do this, drag the split bar located at the top of the vertical scroll bar and/or the split bar located at the right end of the horizontal scroll bar, depending on whether you want to split horizontally or vertically. This action produces two separate panes, each of which can display a different area of rows and/or columns, allowing you to work on two distant parts of the same worksheet. To remove the split, use the **Window - Remove Split** command.*

Changing the magnification

♦ **View**
Zoom

The standard zoom value is 100%.

♦ In the **Zoom** dialog box, choose a factor of magnification or activate **Custom** and enter a value.

♦ Click **OK.**

❑ *You can also select a zoom value from the* 100% *list.*

The ***View - Full Screen*** *command gives over pratically all the space on the screen to displaying the document.*

Hiding/ displaying zeros

All the zeros in the worksheet

♦ **Tools**
Options
View tab

♦ Deactivate/activate the **Zero values** option under **Window options.**

♦ Click **OK.**

In specific cells

♦ Select the cells containing zeros that you do not want to see.

♦ **Format**
Cells
Number tab

♦ Choose **Custom.**

♦ In the **Type** box delete everything and enter **0;0;**.

♦ Enter.

❑ *To display hidden zeros activate the **Zero Values** option (in **Tools - Options**), or apply any other format to the cells concerned.*

Displaying values in Euros or another currency

♦ If necessary, display the **EuroValue** toolbar with the **View - Toolbars - EuroValue** command.

♦ If the toolbar is unavailable, the corresponding add-in has not been loaded. To load it, choose **Euro Currency Tools** in the **Add-Ins available** list (**Tools - Add-Ins**). If the add-in does not appear in the list, click the **Browse** button to find it and load it. If a message appears, to advise you that the component is not installed, insert the Excel 2002 or Office XP CD-ROM, if necessary and click **Yes** to install the required component.

♦ Open the 

list on the **EuroValue** toolbar to select the type of conversion required, from a currency into Euros or from Euros into another currency.

ISO Code	Currency Unit
ATS	Schilling (Austria)
BEF	Franc (Belgium)
DEM	Deutschmark (Germany)
ESP	Peseta (Spain)
FIM	Markka (Finland)
FRF	Franc (France)
IEP	Punt (Ireland)
ITL	Lire (Italy)
LUF	Franc (Luxembourg)
NLG	Guilder (Netherlands)
PTE	Escudo (Portugal)
EUR	Euro (Member states of the euro zone)

The above example shows how to convert Irish pounds into Euros.

♦ To convert a cell value and display the result in the first box on the **EuroValue** toolbar, click that cell.

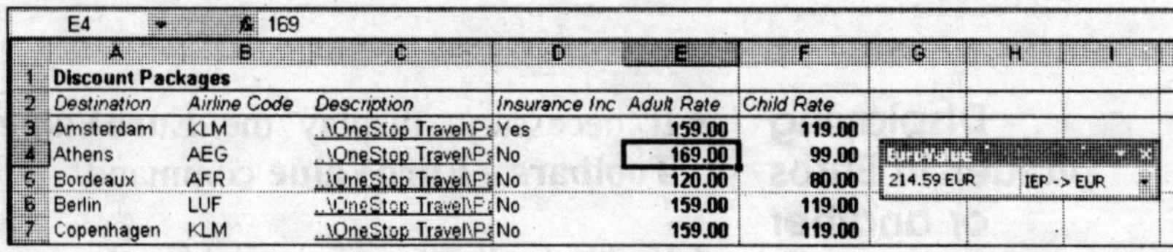

♦ To show the converted sum of the values of a range, select that range of cells.

Docking/ undocking a floating toolbar

When a toolbar is displayed as a window it is said to be ***floating****. A toolbar which appears as a bar at the edge of the window is a* ***docked*** *toolbar.*

♦ To dock a floating bar, double-click its title bar or drag it to one of the edges of the Excel window.

♦ To float a toolbar again, double-click one of its edges, or drag it away from the edges of the window.

Displaying/hiding a specific toolbar

♦ **View**
Toolbars

♦ To hide or display an individual bar, click its name.

❑ *You can also right-click one of the toolbars then click the name of the bar to display or hide.*

❑ *To hide or display several toolbars at once, use* ***View - Toolbars - Customize****. On the* ***Toolbars*** *page, activate or deactivate the names of the toolbars concerned then click the* ***Close*** *button.*

Click [button] *to display or hide the* ***Drawing*** *toolbar.*

Managing tools in a toolbar on the screen

♦ **View**
Toolbars
Customize

Deleting a tool button

♦ Back on the workscreen, drag the tool button you want to delete off the bar.

As soon as the button is moved away from the bar, it disappears.

♦ Close the **Customize** dialog box.

Adding a tool button

♦ Click the **Commands** tab of the **Customize** dialog box.

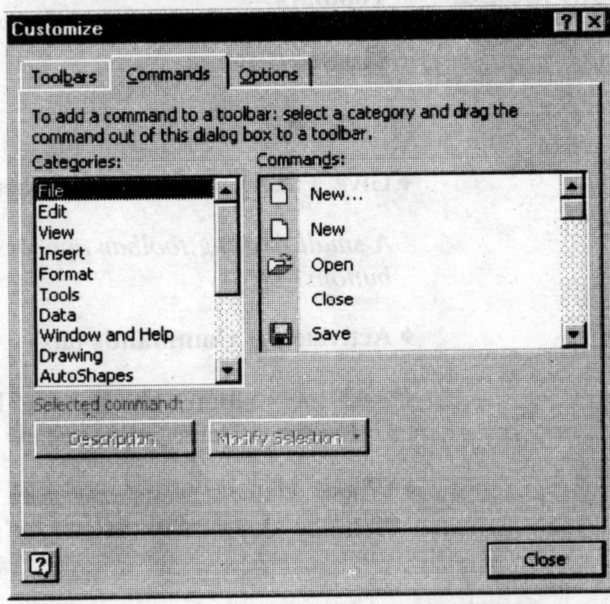

♦ Select the category containing the tool button you want to add.

♦ Select a tool button from the **Commands** list and drag it onto the bar in the window.

♦ Click the **Close** button to finish.

❑ *A new tool button stays where you positioned it. If you are not satisfied with its position, open **View - Toolbars - Customize - Commands** tab, then drag it to a new location on the toolbar.*

❑ *Click the button on the far right of some toolbars to add or remove buttons.*

> *Once a toolbar has been customised, you can retrieve the original version by clicking the **Reset** button in the **Customize** dialog box (**Toolbars** tab).*

Creating a custom toolbar

♦ **View**
Toolbars
Customize
Toolbars tab

♦ Click **New**.

♦ Give a name for the toolbar, then enter.

A small floating toolbar appears on the worksheet: it has no tool buttons yet.

♦ Activate the **Commands** tab.

♦ Add tool buttons to the new bar by dragging them from the **Commands** frame onto the new toolbar.

♦ When all the buttons you want have been added to the toolbar, click the **Customize** dialog box's **Close** button.

Selecting a range of adjacent cells

♦ There are three ways to select adjacent cells:

dragging	point to the first cell of the selection, hold down the mouse button, and drag over the others. When you are satisfied with the selection, release the mouse button.

Be careful not to drag the fill handle (the black square in the bottom right-hand corner of the active cell).

Shift-clicking	Click the first cell to be selected and then point to the last cell concerned. Hold down Shift and click; release the mouse button before the Shift key.
Using the keyboard	Hold down the Shift key while using the appropriate arrow keys.

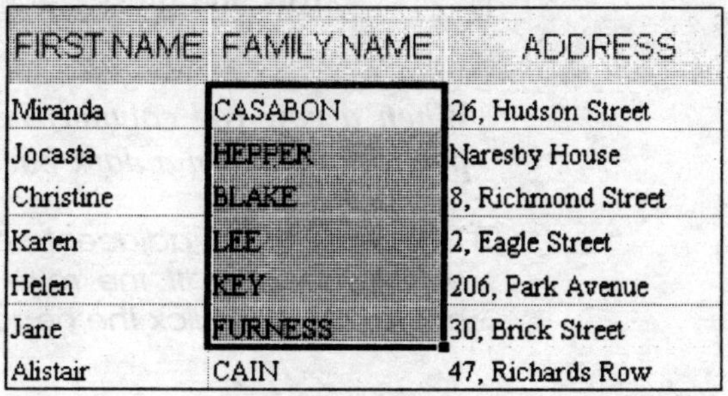

FIRST NAME	FAMILY NAME	ADDRESS
Miranda	CASABON	26, Hudson Street
Jocasta	HEPPER	Naresby House
Christine	BLAKE	8, Richmond Street
Karen	LEE	2, Eagle Street
Helen	KEY	206, Park Avenue
Jane	FURNESS	30, Brick Street
Alistair	CAIN	47, Richards Row

*A **range** of selected cells appears darker on the screen except for the active cell, which appears as usual.*

❑ *The status bar automatically displays the sum of the selected cells, providing at least one of the cells contains a numerical value.*

Selecting non-adjacent cells

♦ Select the first cell or range of cells.

♦ Point to the next cell, or the first cell of the next range.

Do not click at this stage.

♦ Hold down the [Ctrl] key and click. Drag if necessary, to select a range of cells.

♦ Release the mouse button, then the [Ctrl] key.

❑ *In a formula or a dialog box the selected, nonadjacent cells (or ranges) are separated by commas. For example: A5:A10,L5:L10 refers to the ranges of A5 to A10 and L5 to L10.*

Selecting rows and columns

♦ Use the mouse or the keyboard:

	Row	Column
	click the number of a row to select it.	click the letter of a column to select it.
	activate any cell in the row and press [Shift] [space].	activate any cell in the column and press [Ctrl] [space].

When a row (or column) is selected, its number (or letter) appears in white on a dark background.

❑ *To select several adjacent columns or rows, drag over the column or row headers. If the rows or columns are not adjacent, hold down [Ctrl] and click the header to select each row or column.*

Selecting the entire worksheet

♦ Click the button in the top left corner, where the column containing row numbers meets the row containing column letters or
press [Ctrl] [Shift] [space] or [Ctrl] **A.**

Selecting cells according to content

♦ **Edit**
Go To

♦ [F5] or [Ctrl] **G**

♦ Click **Special.**

♦ Indicate the type of cells to be selected.

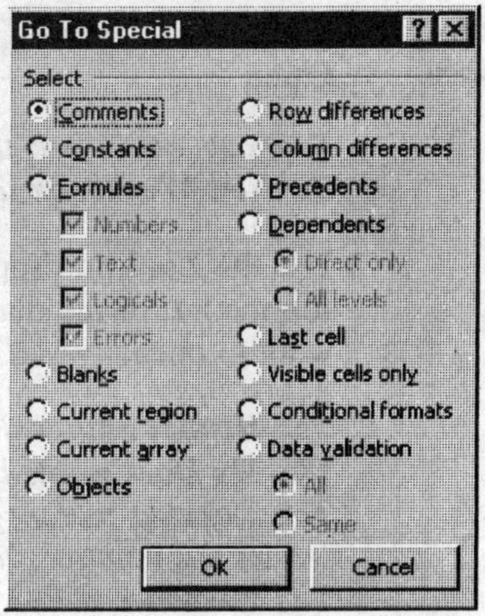

♦ Click **OK**.

Personal notes

Opening a workbook

♦ **File Open** [open icon] ♦ Ctrl O

*You can also click the **Workbooks** or **More workbooks** link in the **New Workbook** task pane.*

♦ Use the **Look in** drop-down list or the buttons on the **Places Bar** (on the left of the dialog box) to help you find the workbook you want to open.

*The **History** button shows the last 50 folders/documents used.*
*The **My Documents** button opens the My Documents folder.*
*The **Desktop** button goes to the shortcuts and documents installed on the Windows desktop.*
*The **Favorites** button opens the Favorites folder.*
*The **My Network Places** button takes you to your network.*

*The **Look in** list contains all the drives accessible on your computer (the floppy drive (A:), the hard drive (C:), perhaps a CD-ROM drive) and on your local network (**My Network Places**).*

♦ Click the drive in which the workbook is stored (A:, C:, D:...), or click **My Network Places** to choose a drive on another workstation.

♦ Go to the folder containing the workbook you want to open by double-clicking its icon; open any subfolders in the same way.

♦ Click [up-folder icon] to open the folder above.

♦ To return to the folders you visited previously, click [back icon].

♦ Open the [views icon] list, then click [details icon] to see a detailed list.

*The first column displays the **Name** of each workbook. The **Size** of each workbook and the date and time it was last **Modified** appear in other columns.*

♦ To view the properties of a workbook, open the [views icon] list, click [properties icon] then select the book whose properties you want to see.

Certain properties such as the title, subject, or comments only appear if details of the workbook have been entered in the ***File - Properties*** *dialog box -* ***Summary*** *tab.*

♦ To preview the workbook, open the list, click , then select the workbook.

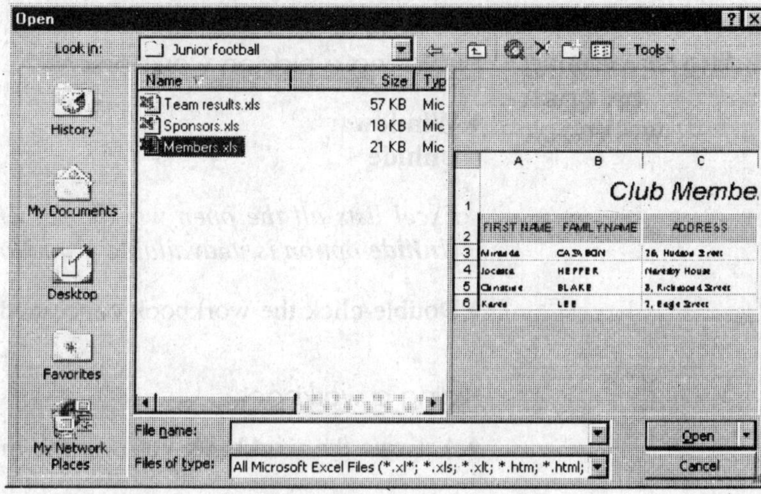

A preview picture of the selected workbook appears on the right, provided you activated the ***Save preview picture*** *option in the* ***File - Properties*** *dialog box -* ***Summary*** *tab the last time you used and saved the workbook.*

♦ To display only the names of the workbooks and their associated icons, open the list and click to use a list presentation style. Click to show the list of workbooks with large icons or to show them with small icons.

♦ To open a workbook, double-click its name.

❑ *To activate another open workbook, click its name in the* ***Window*** *menu (the active workbook has a tick by its name). If the* ***Windows in Taskbar*** *option is active in* ***Tools - Options - View*** *tab, a button appears on the taskbar for each open workbook; click the button to activate the workbook.*

> *To open one of the last four workbooks used, open the **File** menu and click the name of the workbook in the list at the bottom of the menu. You can also click the link to the workbook that appears in the **New Document** task pane. The **Recently used file list** option in **Tools - Options - General** tab defines the number of files listed (from 1 to 9); you can modify the number of **entries**.*

Hiding/displaying an open workbook

Displaying a hidden workbook

♦ **Window**
Unhide

*Excel lists all the open workbooks which have been hidden. The **Unhide** option is unavailable if no workbook is hidden.*

♦ Double-click the workbook concerned.

Hiding a workbook

♦ Activate the workbook you want to hide.

♦ **Window**
Hide

Saving a workbook

Saving a new workbook

♦ **File**
Save

♦ Ctrl S

♦ Using the **Save in** list or the **Places Bar**, choose the drive where you want to save the workbook.

♦ Open the folder (and subfolder if necessary) in which you are saving the workbook by double-clicking its icon.

♦ Double-click the **File name** box, then give a name for the workbook. You can use up to 255 characters, including spaces.

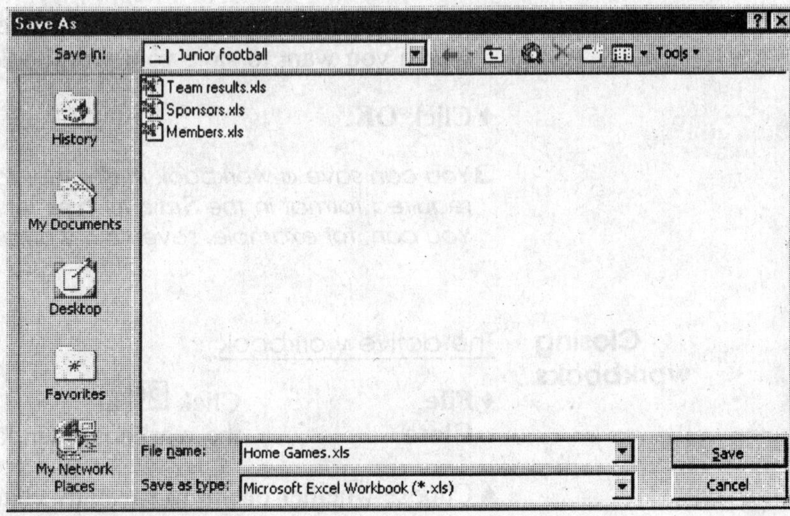

♦ Click **Save**.

The workbook's new name appears on its title bar. Excel files have the extension .XLS (this extension may be hidden).

Saving an existing workbook

♦ **File**
Save

♦ Ctrl S

> *When you close a workbook or leave Excel, you may, before saving, wish to activate the cell that must be active the next time you open the workbook; Excel will save this information.*

Choosing the default file location

This folder will be proposed automatically when you are saving or opening a workbook.

♦ **Tools**
Options
General tab

♦ In the **Default file location** box, give the path of the folder in which you want to save your workbooks.

♦ Click **OK**.

❑ *You can save a workbook in another format. To do this, select the required format in the **Save as type** list in the **Save As** dialog box. You can, for example, save your workbook in XML format.*

Closing workbooks

The active workbook

♦ **File** **Close**	Click  in the workbook window	♦ Ctrl F4 or Ctrl **W**

♦ Choose whether or not to save any changes made.

All open workbooks

♦ Hold down the Shift key, as you open the **File** menu.

*The **Close** option is replaced by **Close All**.*

♦ Click **Close All**.

♦ Choose whether or not to save any modified workbooks (the **Yes To All** option saves all the workbooks).

Creating a new workbook

♦ **File** **New**		♦ Ctrl **N**

♦ Click the **Blank Workbook** link in the **New Workbook** task pane.

*If the **New Workbook** task pane is already on display, simply click the **Blank Workbook** link, without using the **File - New** command.*

*A new workbook called **Book[number]** appears.*

Creating a workbook based on a template

♦ If necessary, use the **File - New** command to show the **New Workbook** task pane.

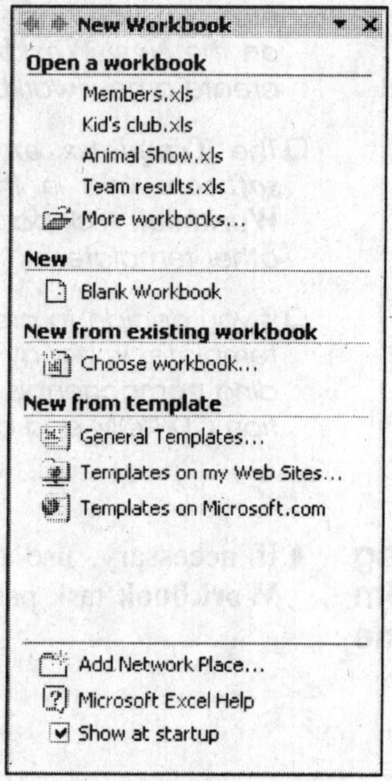

♦ Click the **General Templates** link in the **New from template** section.

*The templates located in the **Templates** folder appear on the **General** page.*

♦ If necessary, click the tab corresponding to the folder containing the template.

♦ Double-click the template name.

When you open a template, Excel copies its content into a new workbook; the new workbook takes the template's name followed by a number.

♦ Enter the information you wish into the new workbook.

♦ Save this new workbook as you would save any other.

❑ *When you have created a workbook from a template, the template's name appears as a link in the* ***New from template*** *section on the* ***New Workbook*** *task pane. You can now click the link to create a new workbook based on that template.*

❑ *The* ***Templates on my Web Sites*** *and* ***Templates on Microsoft.com*** *links in the* ***New from template*** *section on the* ***New Workbook*** *task pane take you to Web sites so you can download other templates.*

❑ *If you decide to create a workbook based on a predefined Excel template, you may see a message telling you that the corresponding component is not installed. If this happens, insert the installation CD-ROM and click* ***Yes*** *to install the component.*

Creating a workbook from an existing one

♦ If necessary, use the **File - New** command to show the **New Workbook** task pane.

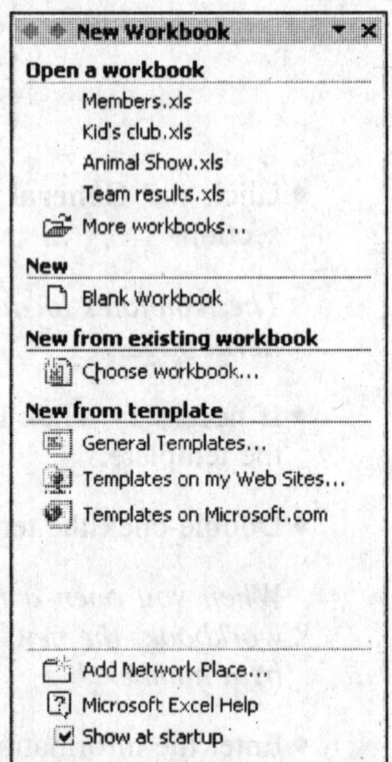

♦ Click the **Choose workbook** link in the **New from existing workbook** section.

♦ Select the workbook of your choice.

♦ Click the **Create New** button.

Excel opens a copy of the chosen workbook, giving it the same name followed by a number.

♦ Save this workbook as you would save any other.

Setting up a hyperlink with another workbook

♦ Select the cell where you wish the hyperlink to be placed.

♦ **Insert**
Hyperlink   ♦ Ctrl K

♦ If necessary, activate the **Existing File or Web Page** shortcut in the left part of the dialog box.

♦ Make sure the **Current Folder** button is active. Use the **Look in** list to choose the drive where the workbook is located then double-click the folder (and subfolders) containing the workbook.

♦ Select the name of the workbook with which you want to set up a link.

This can be a file on your own computer or on your network or an Internet address.

If the workbook you are looking for is one of the last workbooks used, you can find it by clicking the ***Recent Files*** *button.*

♦ To go straight to an exact point in the workbook, use the **Bookmark** button and select or enter the item to be accessed.

You can use a cell reference, the name of a sheet, a named range of cells and so on.

♦ If you wish, modify the name of the link that will appear in the cell, using the **Text to display** box.

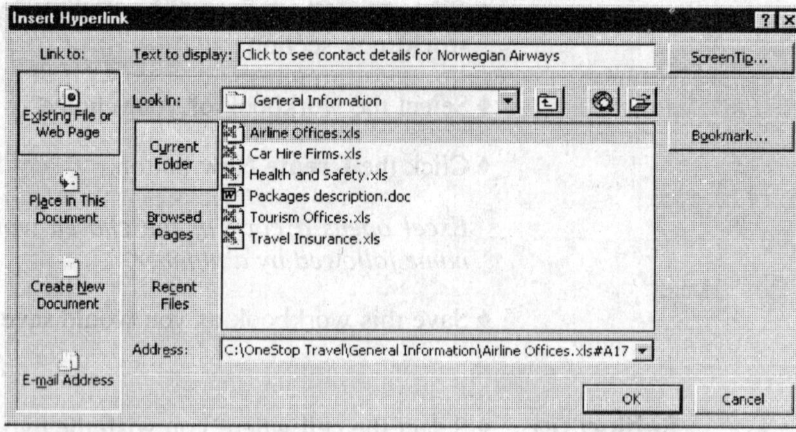

♦ Click **OK** to create the link.

♦ To open the document associated with the link, point to the link and when the pointer takes the shape of a hand, click.

*The linked document appears on the screen, along with the **Web** toolbar (if not, you can show the toolbar using **View - Toolbars - Web**).*

Both documents remain open.

❑ *Once you return to the workbook after having consulted the linked document, the hyperlink text becomes purple. To delete a hyperlink, select the cell containing it and press the* Del *key.*

Finding files, items or Web pages

Carrying out a basic search

You can search for the names of files or items or for specific text within them. From Excel 2002 you can search for Office files (made in Excel, Word, PowerPoint or Access), Outlook items or Web pages.

♦ If the task pane is not open, display it using the **View - Task Pane** command. Click the ▾ button at the top of the pane or select the **Search** option and if necessary, click the **Basic Search** link at the bottom of the pane.

*You can also click the tool button to open directly the **Basic Search** task pane.*

♦ In the **Search text** box, enter the required text.

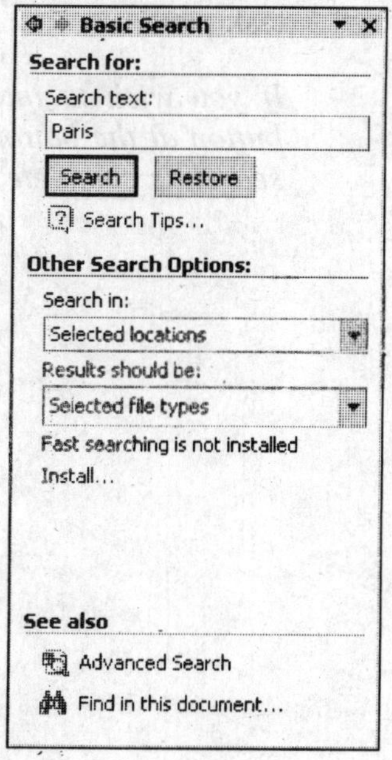

♦ To specify where the search should be carried out, expand the **Search in** drop-down list and make your choice. The plus (+) sign expands the hierarchy while the minus (-) sign collapses it. Select (or deselect) a location and everything it contains by adding or removing a tick in its checkbox. To choose only selected sublocations, tick the corresponding check boxes: the tick will disappear from the main location's check box.

*You can also enter the file path for the search location into the **Search in** box.*

♦ To specify the type of files sought, expand the **Results should be** list and activate (or deactivate) the types of items to include (or exclude).

♦ Click the **Search** button.

*You may see a message telling you that the corresponding component is not installed. If this happens, insert the installation CD-ROM and click **Yes** to install the component.*

♦ The list of items found appears gradually in the **Search Results** task pane.

*If you wish to interrupt the search in progress, click the **Stop** button at the bottom of the task pane. If you stop a search or the search is complete, the **Modify** button appears instead.*

♦ To open one of the items found (a file, Web page or Outlook item), click its name.

When you point to an item, an arrow appears to the right of it. If you click the arrow, you open a list containing options so you can open the item in its application, create a new item from that one, copy the link into the clipboard or show its properties.

♦ To start a new search, click the **Modify** button to return to the **Basic Search** task pane.

♦ When you have finished all your searches, you can close the task pane by clicking its [X] button or deactivating the [search] tool.

❑ *You can install a component that accelerates the search speed. To do this, click the **Install** link in the **Other Search Options** section.*
*The options within the **Basic Search** task pane can also be found under the **Basic** tab in the **Search** dialog box (**File - Open**, open the **Tools** list and click the **Search** option).*

Carrying out an advanced search

*You can search for files or items with the help of one or more search criteria defined in the **Advanced Search** task pane. As with the basic search feature, you can look for Office files, Outlook items or Web pages.*

♦ If the task pane is not open, display it using the **View - Task Pane** command. Click the [▼] button at the top of the pane or select the **Search** option and if necessary, click the **Advanced Search** link at the bottom of the pane.

*You can also click the [search] tool button then click the **Advanced Search** link.*

♦ To set each search criteria:

– Open the **Property** list and select the characteristic to include in the search.

– Set the search **Condition** in the corresponding box.

– If required, enter a comparative value in the **Value** box.

– Click the **Add** button.

– If there are no other conditions, click the **Search** button.

– If you wish to set another condition, select an operator: **And** if all the conditions must be met simultaneously or **Or** if one or the other can be met.

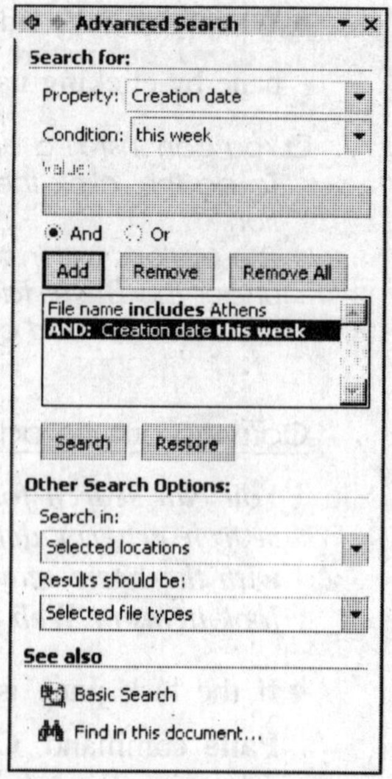

The criteria shown here will find all files with the word "Athens" in the file name and which have been created in the past week.

♦ The **Remove** button deletes the criterion selected in the list and the **Remove All** button deletes all the current criteria.
As for a basic search (cf. above), use the **Search in** list to define where the search should be carried out and indicate the type of items sought in the **Results should be** list.

♦ Click the **Search** button.

*You may see a message telling you that the corresponding component is not installed. If this happens, insert the Excel 2002 or Office XP CD-ROM and click **Yes** to install the component.*

*The list of items found appears gradually in the **Search Results** task pane.*

*If you wish to interrupt the search in progress, click the **Stop** button at the bottom of the task pane. If you stop a search or the search is complete, the **Modify** button appears instead.*

♦ To open one of the items found (a file, Web page or Outlook item), or to start a new search, proceed as for a basic search (cf. above).

♦ When you have finished all your searches, you can close the task pane by clicking its button or deactivating the tool button.

❑ *The **Restore** button on the **Advanced Search** task pane displays the previously defined search criteria.*

❑ *The options within the **Advanced Search** task pane can also be found under the **Advanced** tab in the **Search** dialog box (**File - Open**, open the **Tools** list and click the **Search** option).*

Using the Favorites folder

The Favorites folder stores shortcuts to frequently used workbooks or folders (it does not store the actual items). These shortcuts allow you to access the workbooks or folders concerned quickly and easily.

♦ **File**
Open

♦ Ctrl O

♦ To add a workbook or folder to the **Favorites**, select it and click the **Tools** button then choose the **Add to Favorites** option.

♦ To use the **Favorites** folder, click the **Favorites** button on the **Places Bar** on the left side of the **Open** dialog box.

*All the workbook or folder shortcuts contained within the **Favorites** folder appear.*

♦ Double-click the required shortcut to open the associated workbook or folder.

Using e-mail

With Excel, you can send Excel data by electronic mail as long as you have an e-mail application (such as Outlook or Outlook Express) installed and an Internet and/or intranet connection for your computer.

Sending a worksheet as the body of a mail message

This technique allows the recipient to read data produced with Excel, even if he/she does not have the application installed on his/her computer.

♦ Open the workbook then activate the sheet you want to send.

♦ **File**
Send To
Mail Recipient

The first time you use this command, a dialog box appears and prompts you to specify if you want to ***Send the entire workbook as an attachment*** *or* ***Send the current sheet as the message body****. You should choose the second option.*

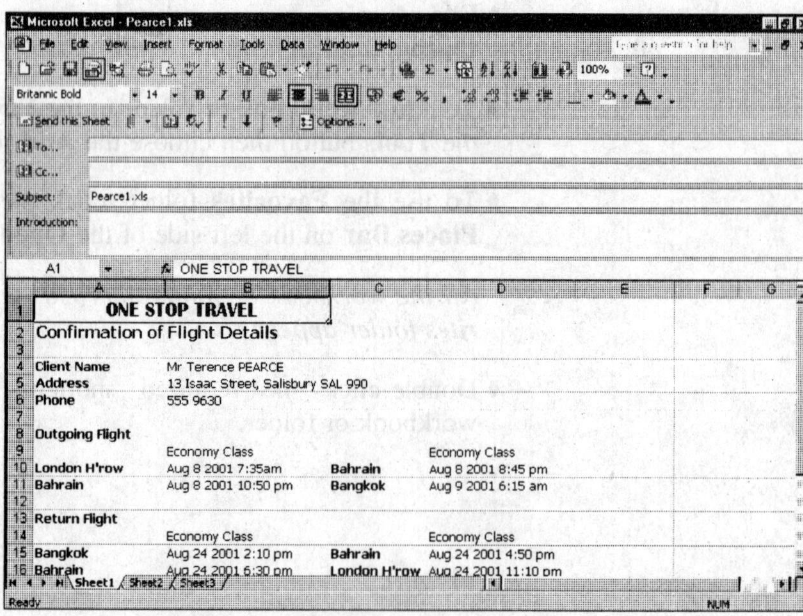

This screen may differ depending on the e-mail software used by default.

♦ In the **To** box, indicate the e-mail address(es) of the recipient(s) by typing them in (use a semi-colon to separate each address from the next) or by pressing [To] and selecting them from an address book.

♦ In the **Cc** box, indicate any addresses to which you want to send a carbon copy of the message.

♦ In the **Subject** box, change the message title if necessary; by default, the workbook name appears in this box.

♦ Click the **Send this Sheet** button.

A copy of the active worksheet is sent to the mail recipient. This sheet will make up the body of the message.

❑ To close the e-mail window without sending the message, click the button on the ***Standard*** toolbar again.

Sending a worksheet as an attached file

Using this method implies that the recipient already has Excel installed on his/her computer.

♦ Open or create the worksheet you want to send.

You can send only a whole worksheet and not a part of one.

♦ **File**
Send to
Mail Recipient (as Attachment)

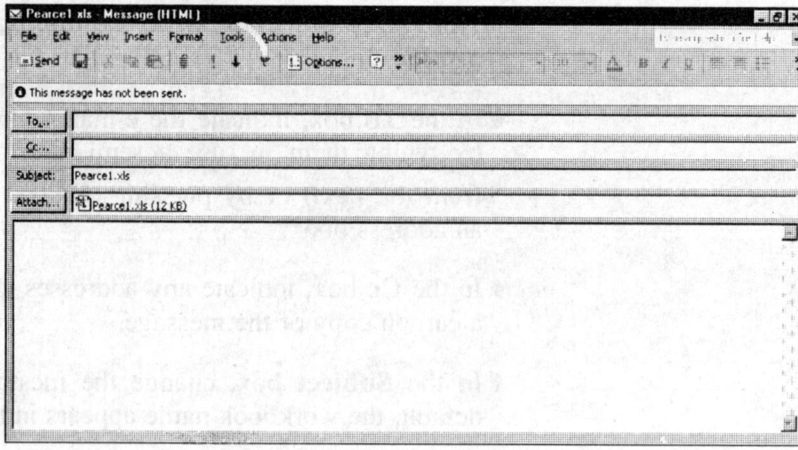

The e-mail application (Outlook 2002 in this example) opens a new mail message window. The attached file usually appears as an icon either in the lower part of the window or in the message header. Depending on the file format used (rich or plain text) the lower part of the window may be divided into one or two panes.

- ♦ In the **To** box, indicate the address(es) to which you want to send the message, separating names with a semicolon or click the To: button to select the names in an address book.
- ♦ If you want to send any copies, enter the addresses in the **Cc** box.
- ♦ In the **Subject** box, if necessary, change the title of the message.
- ♦ If sending a message with the attachment, click the space provided for the body of the message and type your message in.
- ♦ Click the **Send** button.
- ♦ To open or change an attachment, the recipient must open the message then double-click the attachment's icon. Opening this file will start the Excel application automatically.

❑ *To close the e-mail window without sending the message, click the* ☒ *button.*

❑ *If you made any changes to the message, Excel prompts you to save the document. If you click **Yes**, the document will be saved in the **Drafts** folder, or in the **Inbox** depending on your software; You can send it at a later time.*

. . . . . Personal notes . . . .

Naming a sheet

The name of a sheet appears on its tab.

♦ Double-click the tab of the sheet you are going to name.

♦ Type the new name over the former one in the **Name** box.

This name can be up to 31 characters long, spaces included. It should not be written inside square brackets nor include the following punctuation marks: colon (:) slash (/) backslash (\) question mark (?) or asterisk (*).

♦ Enter.

Selecting sheets to create a workgroup

There are two main objectives when you select more than one sheet. Firstly you can group the sheets to make actions common to all of them (copying, deleting etc) and secondly, changes made to one of the sheets, such as entering or editing data or changes to the page setup, can be carried over to all the sheets in the selection.

♦ To select several adjacent worksheets, click the first sheet's tab, hold down the ⇧Shift key and click the tab of the last sheet required.
To select several nonadjacent sheets, click the first sheet's tab, hold down the Ctrl key and click the tab of each other sheet you require.
To select all the sheets in the workbook, right-click one of the sheet tabs and choose the **Select All Sheets** option.

♦ To select a single sheet again, deactivating the workgroup, click the tab of a sheet that is not in the selected group or right-click the tab of one of the selected sheets and choose **Ungroup Sheets**.

When all the sheets in the workbook are selected, moving to another sheet will cancel the selection.

Changing the colour of the worksheet tabs

♦ Go to the sheet concerned, or if necessary select several worksheets.

♦ **Format**
Sheet
Tab Color

♦ Click the colour of your choice.

♦ Click **OK**.

The colour of the selected sheet(s) appears on the tab as a coloured line beneath the tab's name.

Copying/moving a sheet from one workbook to another

♦ Open the workbook from which you want to copy or move, and also the destination workbook.

♦ Activate the sheet to copy or move, or select the sheets in question.

♦ **Edit**
Move or Copy Sheet

♦ Open the list entitled **To book** and click the name of the destination workbook.

♦ Indicate the sheet in the destination workbook in front of which you want to insert the sheet transferred.

♦ If appropriate, activate **Create a copy**.

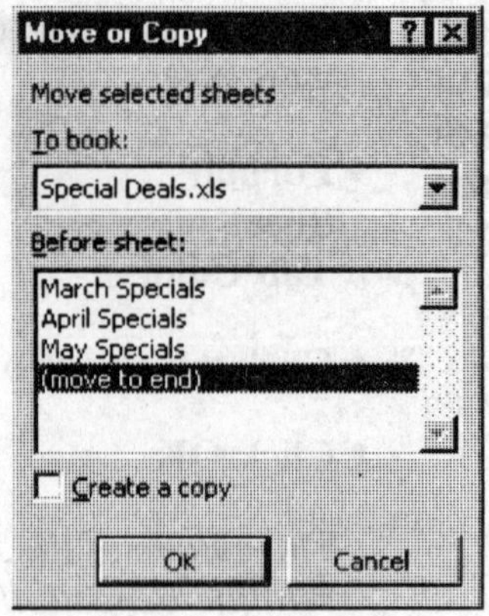

♦ Click **OK**.

❑ *The destination workbook becomes active.*

Moving one or more sheets in the active workbook

♦ Click the tab of the sheet you want to move, or select several sheets.

♦ Drag the sheet(s) to the new position.

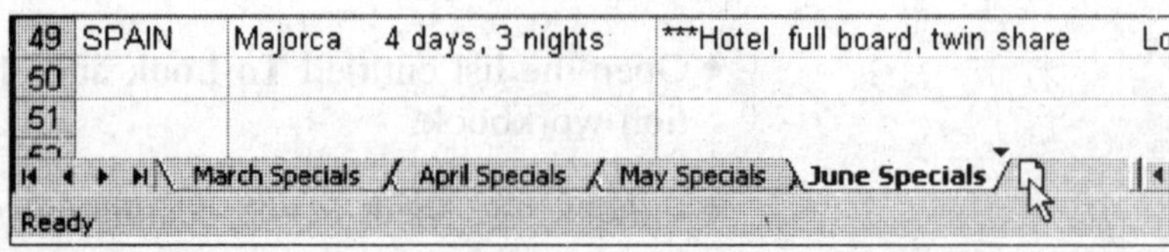

♦ When you are satisfied with the position, release the mouse button.

Deleting worksheets

♦ Activate the worksheet, or select the group of sheets, that you wish to delete.

♦ **Edit**
Delete Sheet

If the selected sheet(s) contain(s) data, the following message appears.

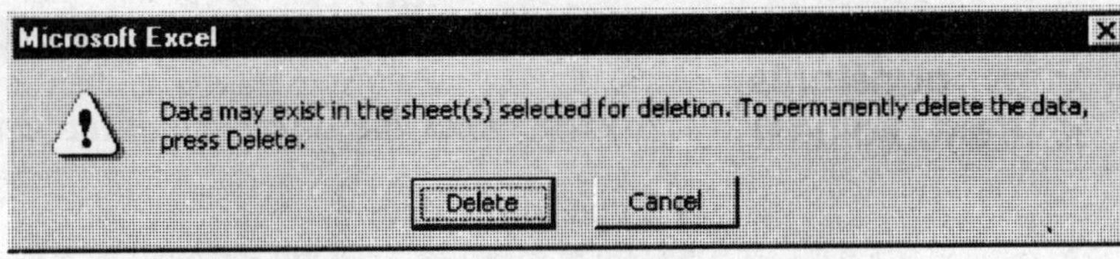

If the Office Assistant is active, this message may appear in the Assistant's yellow message screen.

♦ Confirm your deletion by clicking **Delete**.

Inserting sheets

♦ Select the sheet in front of which you want to insert the new one.

♦ To insert several sheets at once, select as many tabs as you wish to insert new sheets.

♦ **Insert**
Worksheet

.... *Personal notes* ....

Entering constants (text, values)

♦ Activate the cell where you want the data to appear.

Always check the reference of the active cell on the formula bar.

♦ Type in the data.

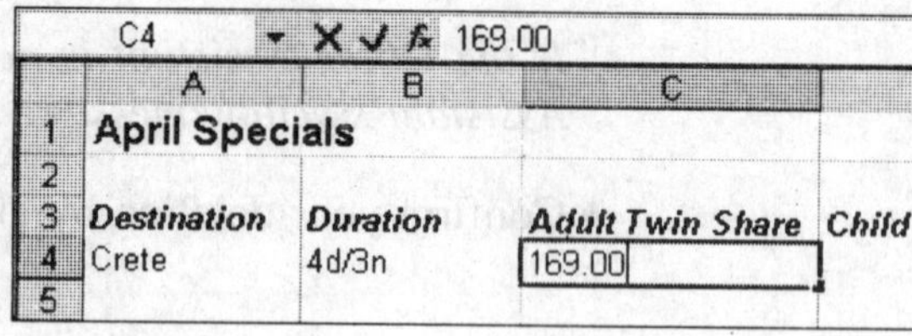

As soon as the first character is typed, two buttons appear on the formula bar.

 To cancel what you have typed in (equivalent to Esc).

 To enter what you have typed in (equivalent to Enter).

At the same time, the word "Enter" appears on the status bar; only data entry can currently be made.

♦ Activate the next cell that you want to fill in.

*Activating a new cell confirms what you have typed in the previous cell. As soon as a new cell is activated (with the mouse or direction keys) Excel returns to its **Ready** mode, and the*  *and*  *symbols disappear.*

Once entered, text is aligned on the left of the cell while numerical data (or dates) are aligned on the right. Dates are formatted (for example 03/03 becomes 03-Mar).

*Until you validate (or cancel) the data you are typing, Excel will not return to **Ready** mode.*

❑ *When entering data keep these observations in mind:*

- *you can type up to 32000 characters in each cell.*
- *with numerical data, be careful to type in the number 0 (zero) and not o (the letter).*

- negative values can be indicated either by preceding the value with a minus sign (-) or by putting the value between parentheses.
- If you add your local currency sign to a number, Excel converts to a currency format (e.g. £10000 becomes £10,000). This depends on your regional settings.
- To enter a percentage, type the % sign immediately after the number.

❑ When entering dates using only the last two figures to represent the year, Excel interprets the year as follows:

- from 00 to 29 as the years 2000 to 2029,
- from 30 to 99 as the years 1930 to 1999.

❑ If you are using Windows 2000 or later, these settings can be modified under the **Date** tab of the **Start - Settings - Control Panel - Regional Settings** menu.

Preventing Enter from activating the next cell

If this option is deactivated, pressing Enter will not automatically move the pointer to the next cell.

♦ **Tools**
Options
Edit tab

♦ Deactivate **Move selection after enter**.

♦ Click **OK**.

❑ By default, pressing Enter activates the cell below. If you would prefer the cell above, or to the left or right to be activated instead, change the **Direction** option under ***Move selection after enter***.

Inserting symbols

This technique inserts symbols that do not appear on your keyboard. A symbol can be inserted in an empty cell or within text while you are entering it.

♦ **Insert**
Symbol
Symbols tab

♦ In the **Font** list, select the font that contains the character you want to insert.

♦ Select the required character.

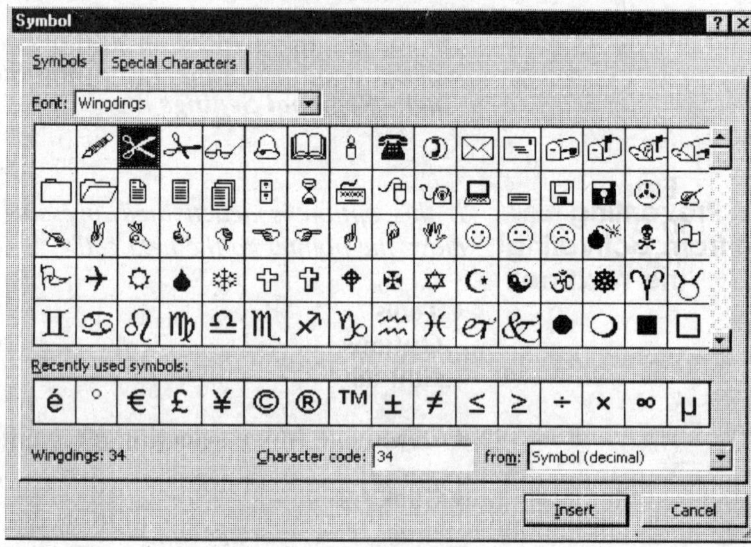

♦ Click the **Insert** button.

♦ Close the dialog box with the **Close** button.

♦ Finish entering your text, if necessary and confirm it.

❑ *The options on the* ***Special Characters*** *tab can be used to insert a range of characters such as non-breaking spaces/hyphens, copyright and trademark symbols etc.*

Inserting the current date into a cell

♦ Activate the cell where you want to display the date.

♦ There are three ways to insert the computer's current date:

=TODAY()	The current date is updated each time the sheet is opened.
=NOW()	The current date and time are updated when the sheet is opened.
Ctrl ;	The current date is not changed automatically.

♦ Enter.

❑ *If the date shown is incorrect, correct the system date of your computer.*

Entering data in a particular range of cells

By selecting the range where you are going to enter data, you can work more quickly.

♦ Select the cells that you want to fill in.

♦ When typing in a row of data press Tab after each cell to move to the next. When typing in a column of data press Enter after each cell.

♦ If you need to return to the previous cell press Shift Tab or Shift Enter.

❑ *Be careful: using any other method to move between cells will cancel your selection.*

Using the AutoComplete feature

When you start entering characters in a cell, Excel may attempt to complete your entry using an existing entry from the same column (providing there is no more than one blank cell above the one in which you are working).

♦ If you wish to use the entry proposed by Excel, enter. Otherwise, to display a list of the entries available, press Alt ↓.

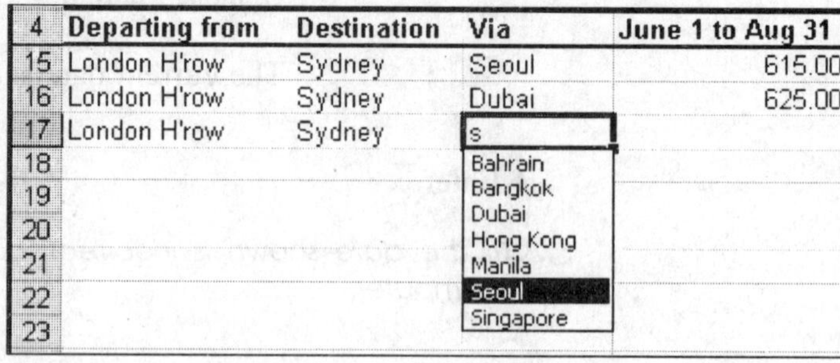

*The list of the existing entries in that column appears. You can also display this list by right-clicking the cell and choosing the **Pick From List** option.*

♦ Click the entry you require. If you do not want to use any of the entries, just type your text as usual.

❑ This feature is only available if the ***Enable AutoComplete for cell values*** option in the ***Options*** dialog box is active (***Tools - Options - Edit*** tab).

Entering the same data in several cells

♦ Select the range of cells concerned.

♦ Enter the formula or text common to all these cells.

If you are entering a formula, enter it as it should appear in the active cell of the selected range.

♦ Validate with Ctrl Enter

This technique enters and copies the data simultaneously.

Entering several lines of text in the same cell

♦ Activate the cell where you want to type the text.

♦ Enter the text, pressing Alt Enter when you want to change line.

♦ Enter.

Creating a series of data

A series is a logical progression of cell values. You can create a series of dates, times, months, days or a combination of text and numerical values.

Creating a simple series

A simple series shows a list of values, incrementing each time by one value.

♦ Enter the first value in the series.

♦ Drag the fill handle from the bottom right of that cell to the last target cell for the series.

♦ When you reach the end of your series, the **Auto Fill Options** button appears to the bottom right of the series. If you click this button, you can (depending on the type of series, and your needs) choose an option to modify the way the values are copied or incremented.

Creating a complex series

With this type of series, you can define the interval between each value.

♦ Enter the first two values, to give an indication of the interval you want to use.

♦ Select these two cells.

♦ Drag the fill handle.

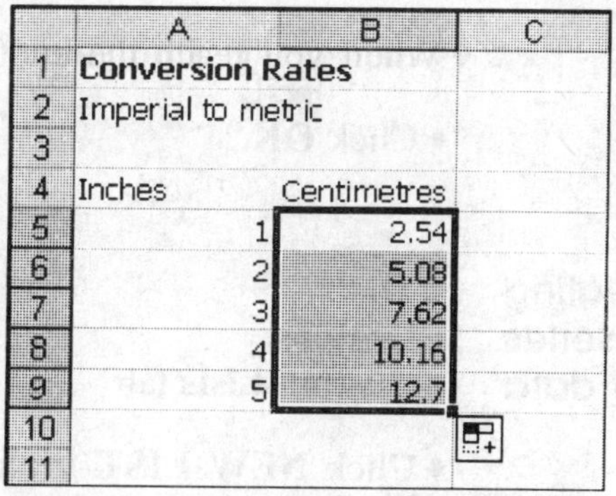

Here, the interval value of 2.54 is repeated over the whole series.

- Enter the first value in the series then select the cell containing that value.
- **Edit**
  Fill
  Series

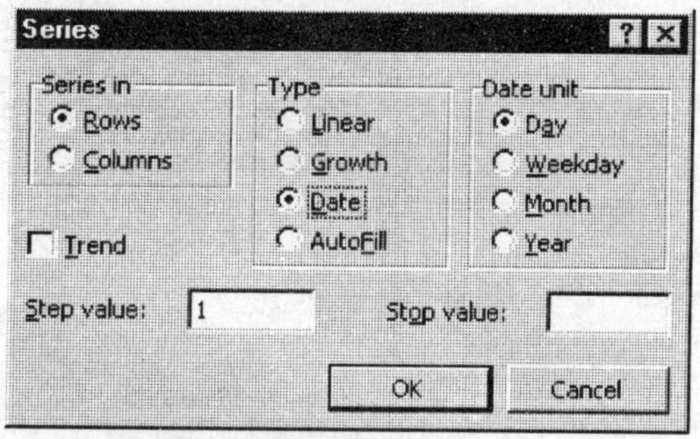

- In the **Series in** frame, indicate whether the series should be inserted in **Rows** or **Columns.**
- In the **Type** frame, specify the type of series you are making.
- If you choose a **Date** type, give the **Date unit** in the right hand frame.
- Modify the **Step value** as necessary.

♦ Indicate the **Stop value** (the last value) in the series.

♦ Click **OK**.

Creating a custom series of data

♦ **Tools**
Options
Custom Lists tab

♦ Click **NEW LIST** in the **Custom lists** box, even if this choice has already been selected.

*The insertion point appears in the **List entries** box.*

♦ Enter the data in the **List entries** box, pressing Enter to separate each entry:

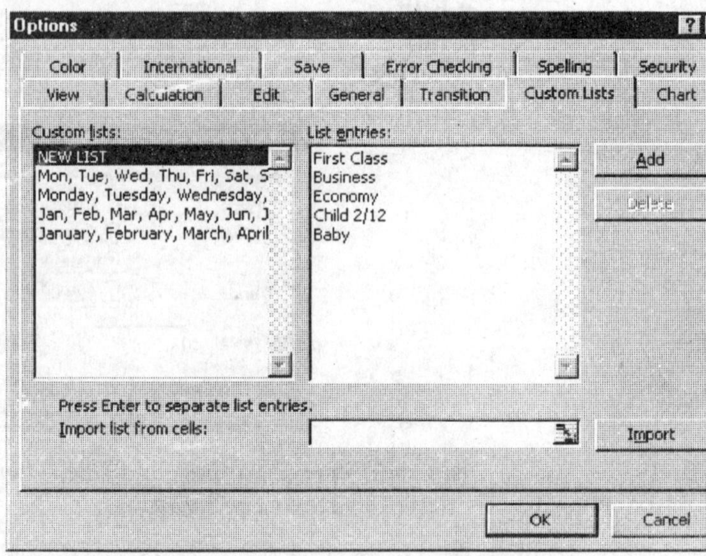

♦ Click the **Add** button.

The new series appears with the other existing lists. Each entry is separated from the previous one by a comma.

♦ Click **OK** to confirm.

Attaching comments to cells

A comment is a means of explaining or expanding on the value in a cell.

Creating a comment

♦ Activate the cell where you want to make a comment.

♦ **Insert Comment** ♦ [Shift] [F2]

♦ Enter the text in the comment box.

The comment is entered directly into a ScreenTip. Use [Enter] *to change lines.*

♦ Press [Esc] or click outside the box.

*A red triangle marks the top right corner of a cell that contains a comment. This indicator is only visible when the one of the comment indicator options is active in the (**Tools - Options - View** tab) dialog box.*

Displaying a comment

♦ Point to the cell that contains the red triangle.

♦ If the triangle is not visible, use the buttons from the **Reviewing** bar:

/ To scroll through the comments concerning the current worksheet.

 To show/hide all the comments.

❑ *To edit a comment, select the corresponding cell, then click* .

To delete a comment, select the cell concerned, then click .

Using speech playback

Excel 2002 provides you with certain tools which make it possible for your computer to "read aloud" the values or text you enter in cells. To use this function, your computer must have a sound card and speakers.

♦ To show the **Text To Speech** toolbar, use **View - Toolbars - Text To Speech** or right-click any toolbar and choose **Text To Speech** or use **Tools - Speech** and choose the **Show Text To Speech Toolbar** option.

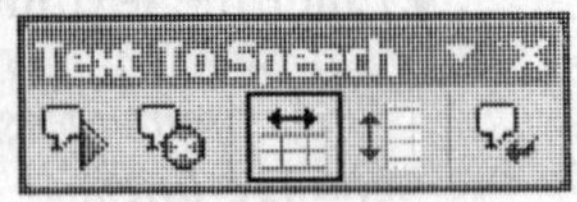

*The tools on the **Text To Speech** toolbar control the audio feedback features.*

♦ To hear the contents of cells that have already been entered on the worksheet, select those cells.

If you do not make a selection, Excel will start from the active cell and work through the cells below it or to the right of it, stopping when it comes across empty cells.

♦ Click the **Speak Cells** tool button.

Your computer starts to "speak"! A computer generated voice reads out whatever is displayed in the selected cells; if a cell contains a formula, the result is read, unless you are displaying formulas instead of results.

♦ To pause the playback, click the **Stop Speaking** tool button.

♦ Resume the playback by clicking the **Speak Cells** tool button again.

- You can change the order in which Excel reads cell ranges when you do not make a specific selection. Click the **By Rows** tool button for Excel to read all the cells to the right of the active cell then those on the next row or the **By Columns** tool button to read down from the active cell then from the next column on the right and so on.
- If you wish, you can hear the playback of each cell as you enter data into it. To do this, click the **Speak On Enter** tool button .

  You will hear the text "Cells will now be spoken on enter", confirming that the feature is activated.
- Enter your text or values in the cell and confirm your entry.

  After a brief pause, the value or text entered is spoken aloud.

  *When you have finished with the **Speak On Enter** feature, click the corresponding tool button again to turn it off, otherwise this feature will stay active even when you close the **Text To Speech** toolbar. When this feature is deactivated, you will hear the text "Turn off Speak On Enter".*
- To close the **Text To Speech** toolbar, click the button in its corner or use the **View - Toolbars** command and deactivate the corresponding option or use **Tools - Speech** and deactivate the **Show Text To Speech Toolbar** option.

❑ *You can choose a different voice and reading speed for your computer. To do this, go into the Windows **Control Panel (Start - Settings - Control Panel)** and double-click the **Speech** folder. Click the **Text To Speech** tab if necessary then choose a voice from the **Voice selection** drop-down list. To have the chosen voice read a sample text, click the **Preview Voice** button. To change the speed at which the cell contents are spoken, use the **Voice speed** cursor to speed up or slow down the voice. The **Audio Output** button allows you to change the audio output device, if required, and open the **Volume Control** dialog box.*

Modifying cell contents

♦ Double-click the cell concerned:

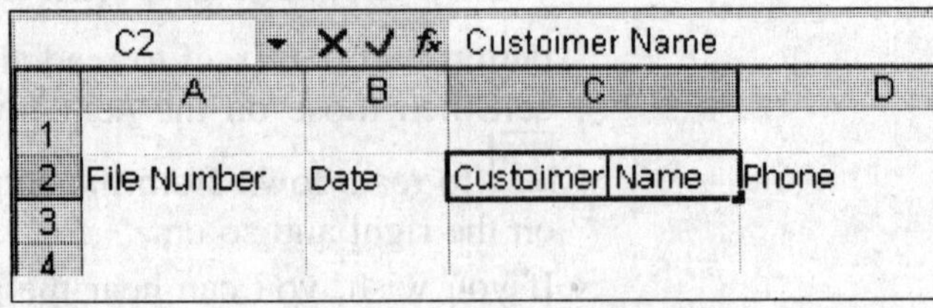

*An insertion point (flashing vertical bar) appears in the cell and **Edit** is displayed on the status bar.*

♦ Make the necessary changes.

*When **Insert** mode is active, the new characters are added to the existing ones. In **Overtype** mode, the new characters replace the existing ones.*

♦ Press [Ins] to change from **Insert** to **Overtype** and vice versa.

♦ When you have finished, enter.

❑ *You can also click the cell then edit its contents directly in the formula bar.*

Clearing cell contents

♦ Select the cells you wish to clear and press the [Del] key.

The cell contents are erased but not the formatting.

♦ To delete the contents and/or the formatting and/or any comments attached, use the **Edit - Clear** command.

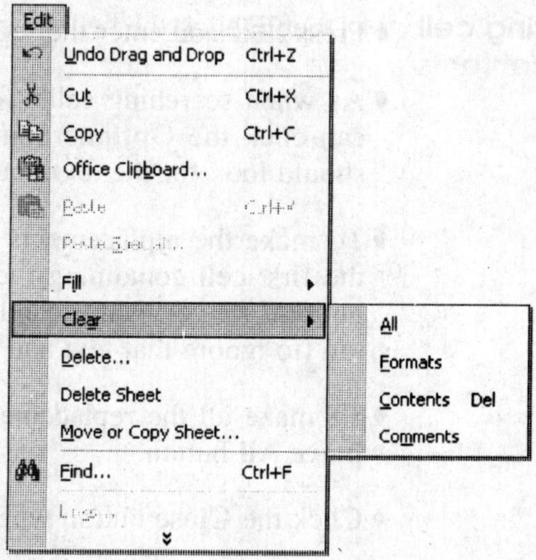

♦ Choose which elements you wish to delete then click **OK.**

❑ *You can also select the cells then drag with the fill handle back over that selection.*

Replacing cell contents and/or formats

It is possible to replace the text and/or format contained in several cells by another text and/or format. This technique also allows you to change text within formulas.

Replacing text

♦ If the replacement is to be carried out over the active worksheet or all the worksheets in the workbook, activate a single cell. To make the replacement in a portion of the active sheet, select the range of cells concerned.

♦ **Edit**
Replace ♦ Ctrl **H**

♦ In the **Find what** box, enter the text you wish to replace.

*You can enter letters, numbers, punctuation marks or wildcard characters: ? replaces one character; * replaces several.*

♦ Press [Tab] and enter the replacement in the **Replace with** box.

♦ As when searching cells, (cf. Finding a cell by its contents) you can click the **Options** button and specify how and where Excel should look for the text you are replacing.

♦ To make the replacements one by one, click **Find Next** to go to the first cell containing the required text then click the **Replace** button (if you want to replace that value) or the **Find Next** button (to ignore that text and continue searching).

♦ To make all the replacements with a single action, click the **Replace All** button.

♦ Click the **Close** button when you have finished.

Replacing formatting

♦ Activate a cell or select the specific range of cells involved.

♦ **Edit** ♦ [Ctrl] **H**
Replace

♦ If necessary, click the **Options** button to show all the search options.

♦ Delete any text that may be in the **Find what** or **Replace with** boxes.

♦ Click the first **Format** button and in the **Find Format** dialog box, select the required format options.

*The **Choose Format From Cell** button is used to select a cell and retrieve that cell's formatting automatically.*

♦ Click **OK**.

♦ Click the second **Format** button and in the **Find Format** dialog box, select the required format options and click **OK**.

♦ Make your replacements one by one using the **Find Next** and **Replace** buttons or use the **Replace All** button to make all the replacements with one action.

♦ Click the **Close** button.

❑ *You can replace text and formatting simultaneously: if you want to do this, enter the text in the **Find what** or **Replace with** boxes and choose the format options by clicking the **Format** buttons.*

Sorting data in a table

Sorting by one criterion

♦ Select the table you want to sort.

♦ Using  or  activate a cell in the column you want to sort by.

♦ Use:

 to sort in ascending order.

 to sort in descending order.

> *If there are no blank rows or columns in the table, you do not need to select it.*

Sorting by several criteria

♦ Select the table to be sorted.

♦ **Data**
Sort

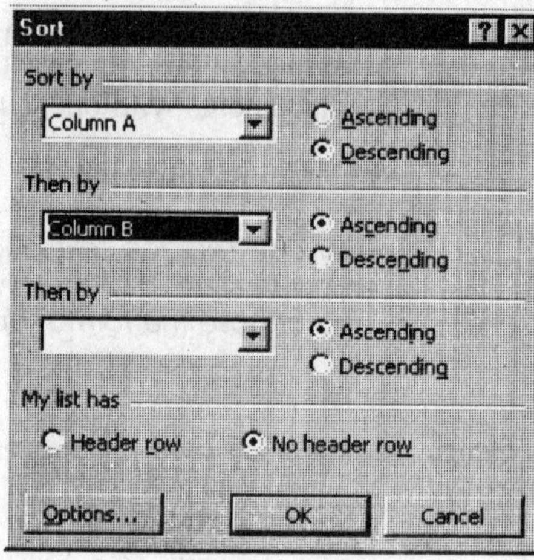

You can sort by up to three columns.

- Indicate the columns by which you want to sort. **In** a data list, select the names of the corresponding fields.
- For each column, specify whether to sort in **Ascending** or **Descending** order.
- To exclude the first row of the table from sorting, activate **Header row.**
- Click **OK.**

❑ *The **Options** button on the **Sort** dialog box can be used to:*

- *Make a **Case sensitive** sort, differentiating upper and lowercase letters,*
- *Change the **Orientation**, sorting in rows rather than columns.*
- *Select a **First key sort order** from the custom lists (so you can sort a table in a logical order, such as names of days, rather than in alphabetical order.*

Checking the spelling in a text

♦ To check the whole worksheet, activate any cell. To check part of the text, select it.

♦ **Tools**
Spelling ♦ F7

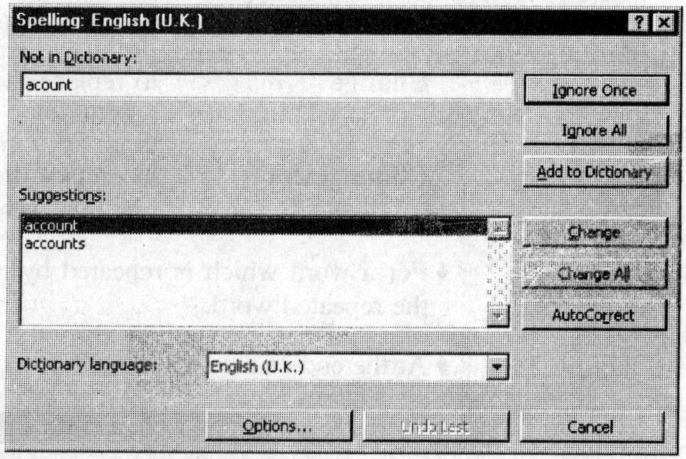

Excel reads the text, stopping at each unrecognised word. This may be:

– one which is absent from Excel's dictionary,

– one which contains an unusual combination of lower case and capital letters,

– one which is typed twice (for example: we know that that is true).

Spelling is checked against Excel's main dictionary, and against as many personal dictionaries as you wish (by default, the only existing one is CUSTOM.DIC).

♦ If the word is correctly spelt, click:

Ignore once	to leave the word unchanged and continue the check.
Ignore All	to leave a particular word unchanged each time it occurs in the text.

Add to Dictionary to add the word to the current dictionary.

♦ If the word contains a mistake, correct it by a double-click on one of the suggestions or enter the correct spelling in the **Not in Dictionary** box, then click:

Change to replace the incorrect word with the correct one.

Change All to replace the incorrect word with the correct one each time it occurs.

♦ For a word which is repeated by mistake, click **Delete** to delete the repeated word.

♦ At the end of the spelling check a dialog box appears:

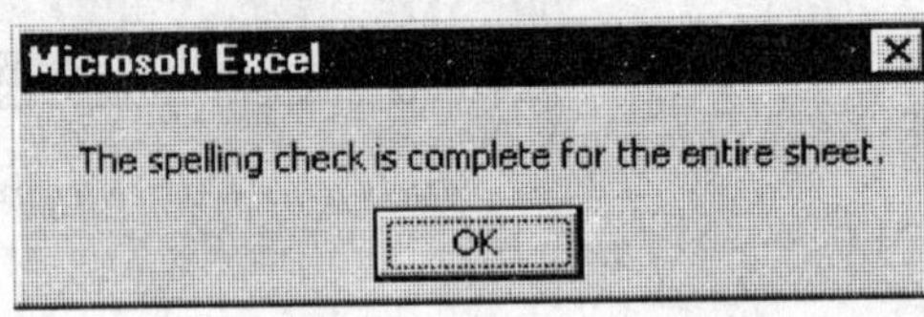

♦ Click **OK**.

Naming cells

A range of cells can be given a name, which makes it easier to select or insert in a formula.

First method

♦ Select the range of cells you want to name.

♦ **Insert**
Name
Define

♦ Ctrl F3

Excel proposes to take the contents of the cell above or to the left of the selection as the name of the range.

♦ If you prefer, enter a different name.

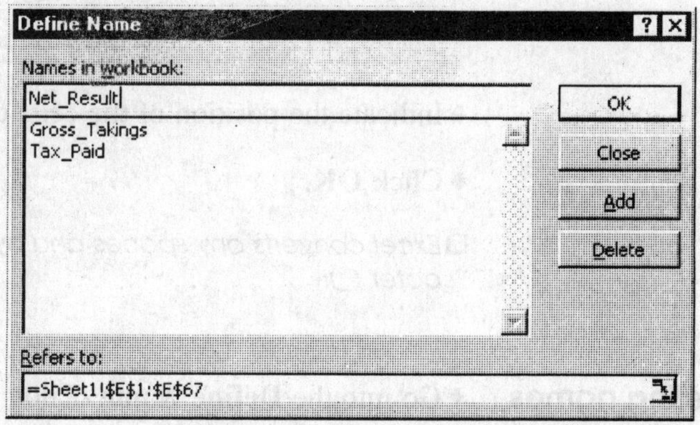

There must be no spaces or hyphens in these names! You can use the [button] *button to collapse the dialog box, making it easier to change the selection.*

♦ Click **Add**.

♦ Name any other ranges in the same way.

♦ Click **OK** or **Close**.

Second method

This method uses the existing column or row labels as the names of the selected ranges (but does not include those labels in the named range).

♦ **Insert**
Name
Create

♦ Ctrl Shift F3

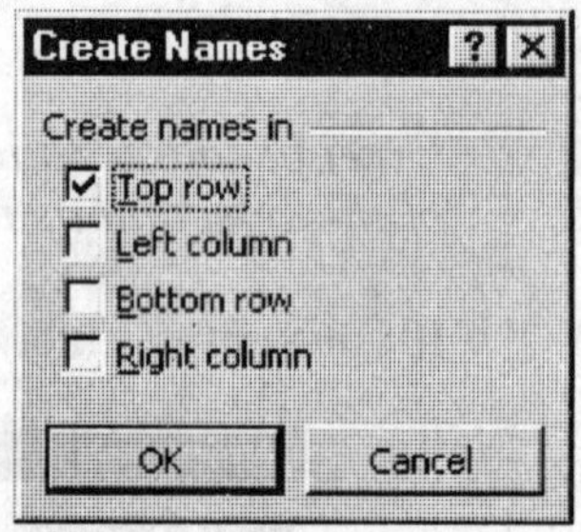

♦ Indicate the position of the cells containing the names.

♦ Click **OK**.

❑ *Excel converts any spaces and hyphens into the underscore character (_).*

Deleting names

♦ Go into the **Define Name** dialog box.

♦ Select the name to be deleted.

♦ Click the **Delete** button.

♦ Click **OK**.

Modifying named ranges

<u>Changing which cells are associated with the name</u>

♦ Select the new range of cells required.

♦ **Insert**
Name
Define

♦ Ctrl F3

♦ Enter the new name.

You must type in the name again and not simply select it from the list of names.

♦ Click the **Add** button.

❑ *You can also redefine the cells in a named range by selecting the range name in the **Define Name** dialog box, clicking the*  *button and selecting the new cells in the worksheet.*

<u>Changing the name of the range</u>

♦ **Insert**
Name
Define

♦ Ctrl F3

♦ In the list, select the name concerned.

♦ Enter the new name in the **Names in workbook** box.

♦ Click the **Add** button.

This action does not delete the previous name; if you wish, delete that from the list (cf. above).

♦ Click **OK**.

Selecting a range of cells by its name

♦ Click the ▾ button on the left of the formula bar.

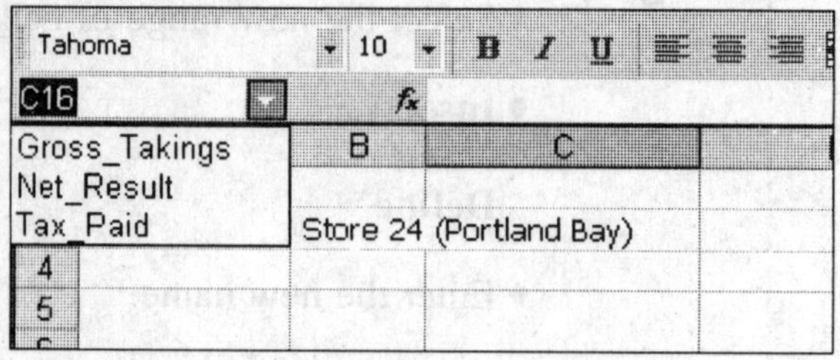

Excel opens a list of all the named ranges in the workbook.

♦ Click the name you require.

Displaying a list of names and associated references

This action will paste into the worksheet a list of all the workbook's named ranges (in one column) and the corresponding cell references (in the next column).

♦ Activate the cell from which the list of names should appear.

♦ **Insert**
Name
Paste

♦ Click the **Paste List** button.

.... *Personal notes* ....

Copying data into adjacent cells

This is probably the fastest way to copy values or formulas.

♦ Activate the cell you want to copy.

♦ Point to its fill handle.

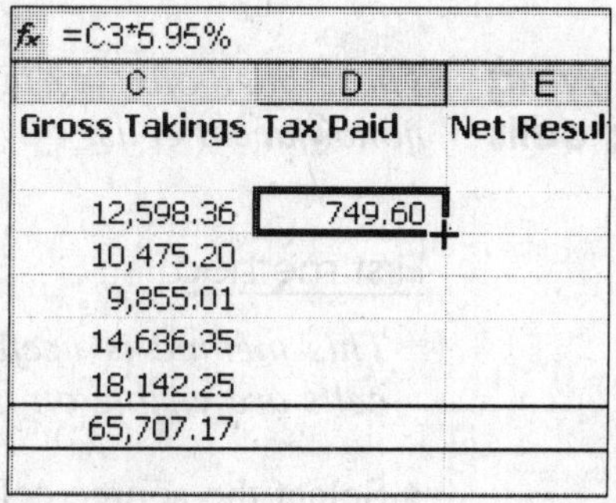

The fill handle is the small dark square in the right-hand corner of the cell. Notice the change in the mouse pointer's shape.

♦ Drag the fill handle to the last destination cell for the copy.

The cells over which you drag are enclosed inside a hatched border.

♦ When you reach the last cell, release the mouse button.

As soon as you finish copying, the ***Auto Fill Options*** *button* 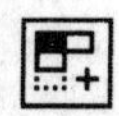 *appears to the bottom right of the copied range.*

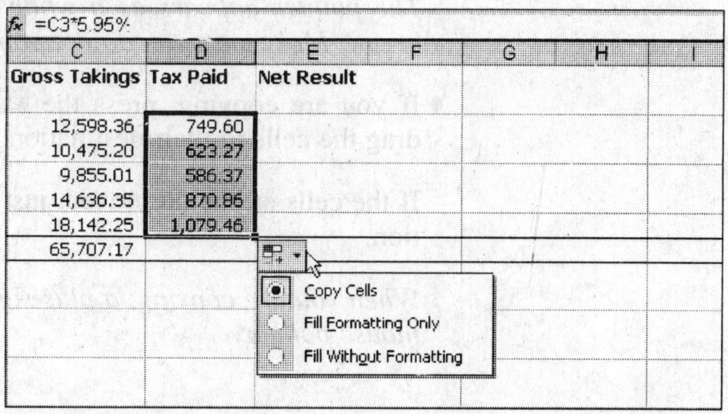

♦ Click the button to see the options you can use in relation to the copy; you can just **Copy Cells** as they are, **Fill Formatting Only** (copy just the format) or **Fill Without Formatting** (copy just the contents).

Copying and moving cells

These methods are intended for moving data or copying into nonadjacent cells.

First method

This method is useful when the source cells and the destination cells are visible on the screen at the same time.

♦ Select the source cells.

♦ Point to the edge of the selected range.

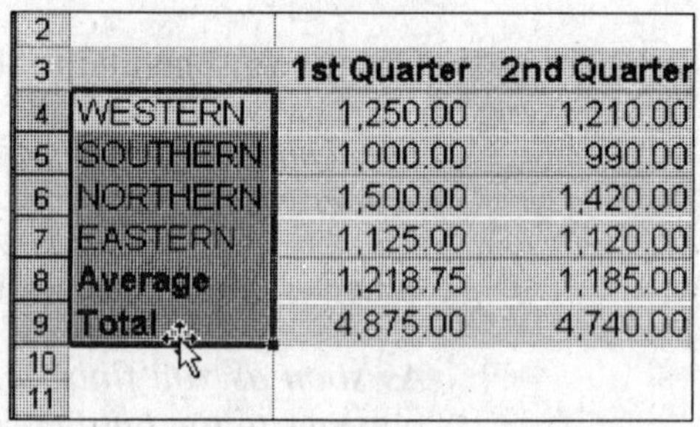

The pointer appears as a white arrow on top of a four-headed arrow. Make sure you do not point to the fill handle.

♦ If you are copying, press the Ctrl key and, without releasing it, drag the cells to their destination.

If the cells are being moved, just drag the cells to their new position.

When you are copying, a plus sign (+) appears to the right of the mouse pointer.

♦ Release first the mouse button, then the Ctrl key, if you have been using it.

The cell contents and their formatting are thus moved or copied.

Second method

♦ Select the source cells.

♦ If you are copying the cells, use:

Edit
Copy ♦ Ctrl C

♦ If you are moving the cells, use:

Edit
Cut ♦ Ctrl X

The selected cells are surrounded by a flashing border.

♦ Activate the first cell of the destination range.

Even when several cells are being copied or moved you should only activate one destination cell.

♦ **Edit**
Paste ♦ Ctrl V

When you paste copied data, the ***Paste*** *button appears to the bottom right of the destination range. If you wish, click this button for further options relating to what can be pasted.*

Copying cells into several sheets

♦ Select the cells you want to copy.

♦ Select the other worksheets involved, by holding down Ctrl and clicking their tabs.

♦ **Edit**
Fill
Across Worksheets

♦ As required, choose to copy **All** or just the **Formats** or just the **Contents**.

♦ Click **OK**.

❑ *You can also use the drag and drop method to copy cells to another sheet. Select the cells then hold down Ctrl and Alt: drag the cells to the tab of the required sheet then to the destination cells on that sheet.*

Copying/moving multiple items

♦ If the task pane is not displayed, show it with the **View - Task Pane** command. Click the ▾ button at the top of the pane and choose the **Clipboard** option, or use the **Edit - Office Clipboard** command.

*If the **Show Office Clipboard Automatically** option is active (find this by clicking the **Options** button at the bottom of the **Clipboard** task pane), the **Clipboard** task pane appears automatically as soon as you have made two consecutive move or copy actions or once you have used Ctrl **C** twice.*

♦ Select the cells concerned and transfer them into the clipboard using **Cut** or **Copy**. This can be done as many times as necessary.

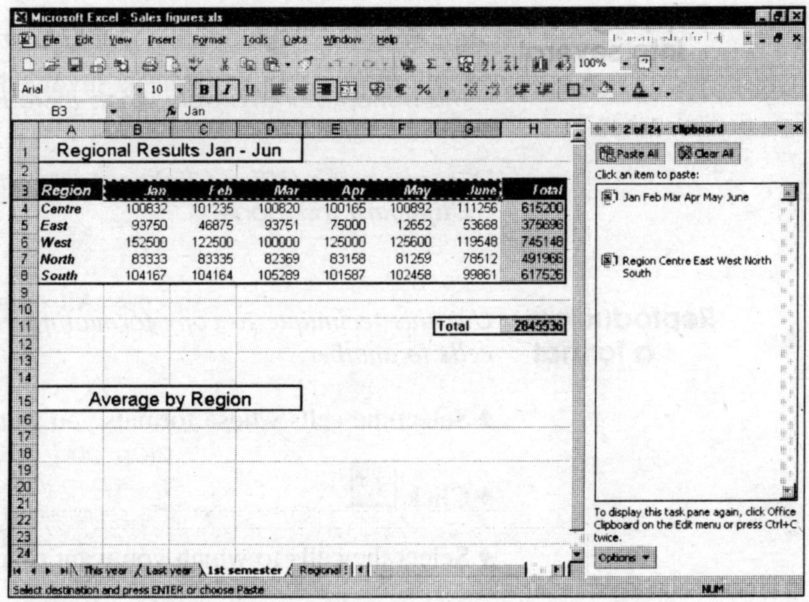

A preview of the cut and/or copied items appears in the ***Clipboard*** *task pane. Up to 24 items can be stored there.*

The ***Office Clipboard*** *contains all the items cut or copied from the various Office applications (Excel, Word, PowerPoint etc.).*

♦ Activate the first destination cell.

♦ To paste one of the items from the **Clipboard** task pane, click that item.

♦ Insert each item from the **Clipboard** task pane in this way, as many times as required.

When you point to an item, an arrow appears on its right. Click this arrow to see options allowing you to ***Paste*** *or* ***Delete*** *the item.*

♦ If necessary, close the **Clipboard** task pane by clicking its ☒ button.

- *The* Paste All *button on the **Clipboard** task pane pastes all the items within. They are pasted in a column, from top to bottom. This button is unavailable when there is a picture or object in the list.*

- *To empty the **Office Clipboard**, click the* Clear All *button on the **Clipboard** task pane.*

Reproducing a format

Use this technique to copy formatting elements from one range of cells to another.

♦ Select the cells whose formats you want to copy.

♦ Click .

♦ Select the cells to which you want to apply the format.

- *You can also copy formats by making a standard copy/paste operation then clicking the **Paste** button at the bottom of the copied cells and choosing the **Formatting only** option. The original cell values are not altered.*

> *If the formatting has to be reproduced several times, double-click the tool. Press* Esc *to cancel this function.*

Copying values, results and/ or formats

♦ Select the cells containing the results or formats you want to copy.

♦ Go into **Edit - Copy**.

♦ Activate the first cell of the destination cell range.

♦ Open the list attached to the tool button:

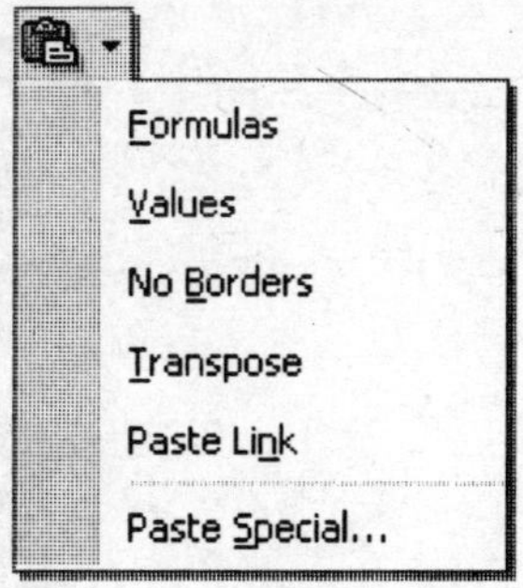

♦ Choose:

Formulas to copy the cell contents (formulas or values) without the associated formatting,

Values to copy just the results of formulas, again without formatting,

No Borders to copy the contents and the formats but not the borders

Paste Special to see further paste options.

These options can also be found using the ***Edit - Paste Special*** *command.*

Making simple calculations while you copy

This method is a way of copying data and at the same time making simple operations, such as additions or subtractions combining the copied data and the existing data in the target cells.

♦ Select the data you wish to copy and start the copying process (**Edit - Copy**).

♦ Activate the first destination cell (the target cells must contain some data).

♦ **Edit**
Paste Special

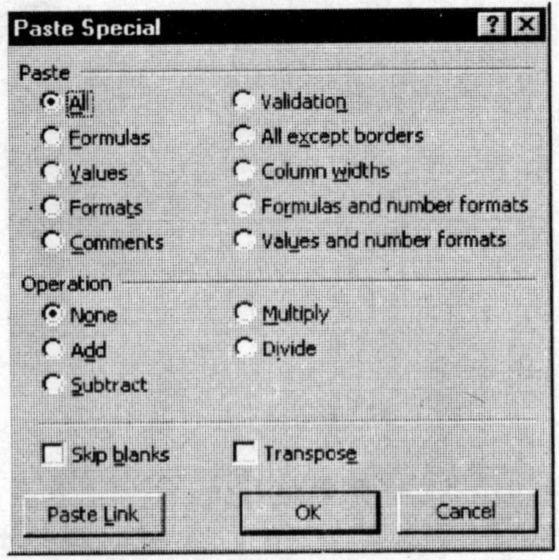

♦ In the **Paste** frame, choose which elements you wish to copy.

♦ Next, specify the **Operation** you wish to perform.

♦ If you want to omit any empty cells in the selection, tick the **Skip blanks** check box.

♦ Click **OK**.

Transposing data as you copy

You can transpose, or switch the rows and columns in a table when you copy it to another location.

♦ Select the data you wish to copy and start the copying process then activate the first destination cell.

♦ Expand the list on the  tool button and choose the **Transpose** option.

When the data is pasted, the rows become columns and vice versa.

Copying Excel data into Word and establishing a link

When a link is in place, any changes made to the data in the original Excel workbook are carried over into the file containing the exported data.

♦ Open the Excel workbook containing the data you want to copy.

♦ **Edit**
Copy ♦ Ctrl C

♦ Open the Word application and the document into which you want to paste the Excel data.

♦ Put the insertion where the data should be pasted then use the **Edit - Paste Special** command.

♦ Activate the **Paste link** option.

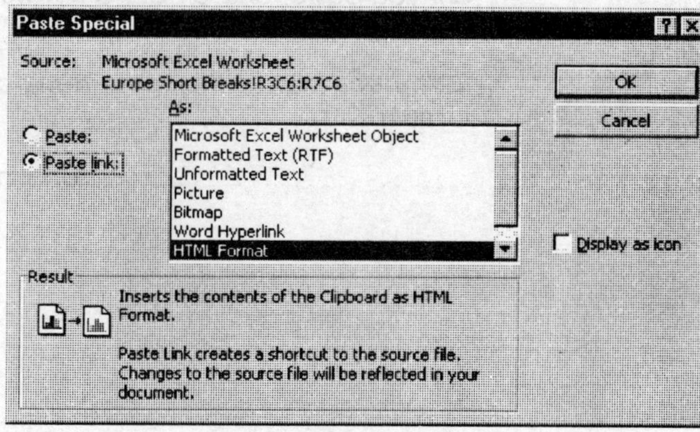

♦ From the **As** list, select the format in which you want to paste the data.

♦ Activate the **Display as icon** option if you want the linked data to be displayed in the form of an icon.

♦ Click **OK**.

Creating a link between cells during copying

- ♦ Select the data you wish to copy.
- ♦ Start the copying process (**Edit - Copy**).
- ♦ Activate the first target cell for the copied data.
- ♦ Expand the list on the  tool button and choose the **Paste Link** option.

The destination cells now contain formulas that can show the contents of each source cell. If you modify a source value, it is carried over immediately into the target cell.

❑ *Creating a link as you copy does not automatically retrieve the cell formatting.*

❑ *If you paste, and create a link with, an empty cell, Excel shows a zero value.*

❑ *You can obtain the same result by inserting an* ***=CELL*** *type formula.*

.... *Personal notes* ....

Entering a calculation formula

♦ Activate the cell which will display the result.

♦ Type =.

***Enter** appears on the status bar; you are in data entry mode.*

♦ Activate the first cell involved in the calculation.

*This cell is shown with a flashing border and its reference appears in the formula bar. The status bar now says **Point**.*

♦ Type in the mathematical operation to be carried out:

+	for addition
-	for subtraction
/	for division
*	for multiplication
%	for percentage
^	for exponentiation.

♦ Click each cell involved in the calculation formula, adding the relevant mathematical operators.

The cells used in the calculation keep there coloured borders as long as you are still creating the formula.

You can follow the development of the formula on the formula bar:

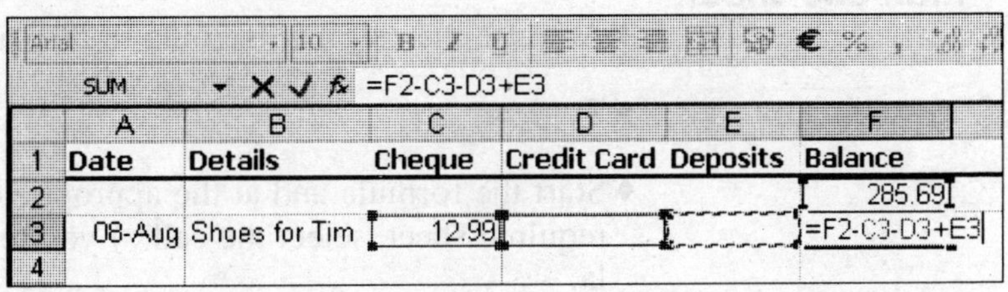

♦ When you have indicated the last cell in the formula, confirm with Enter or by clicking the ✓ button on the formula bar.

The result of the calculation appears in the active cell but the cell's true content is the formula, which is displayed in the formula bar whenever that cell is active.

❑ *If you know the cell references you can type them in rather than using the mouse or arrow keys to activate them.*

❑ *Calculation formulas can contain up to 1024 characters.*

❑ *Formulas in a table are recalculated automatically whenever you modify the values involved in that formula. If the recalculation process is making you lose time, you can stop automatic recalculation by activing one of these options,* ***Automatic except tables*** *or* ***Manual (Tools - Options - Calculation*** *tab). If you have deactivated automatic calculation, you can press* F9 *to recalculate the formulas manually.*

❑ *When you are editing a calculation formula, the names of the cells involved are displayed in different colours on the formula bar. In the worksheet, each cell or range of cells involved in the formula has a border of the same colour.*

> *Remember that you can use the fill handle in the bottom right corner of the active cell to copy formulas to adjacent cells.*

Calculating values from more than one sheet

You can enter a formula into one worksheet that refers to cells on a different worksheet.

♦ Activate the cell that is going to display the result.

♦ Type =

♦ Start the formula and at the appropriate place, click the tab of the required sheet, select the cell(s) you require and finish the formula.

♦ Confirm.

Cell B5 subtracts cell F4 of the "Last Year" sheet from cell F4 of the "This Year" sheet.

❑ *You can also calculate values from several different workbooks. When doing this, make sure all the workbooks are open. Use the **Window** menu to go to a cell in a worksheet in a different workbook.*

Adding up a group of cells

♦ Activate the cell which is going to display the result.

♦ Click Σ or press Alt =

Excel displays the SUM() function and guesses which cells you want to add up.

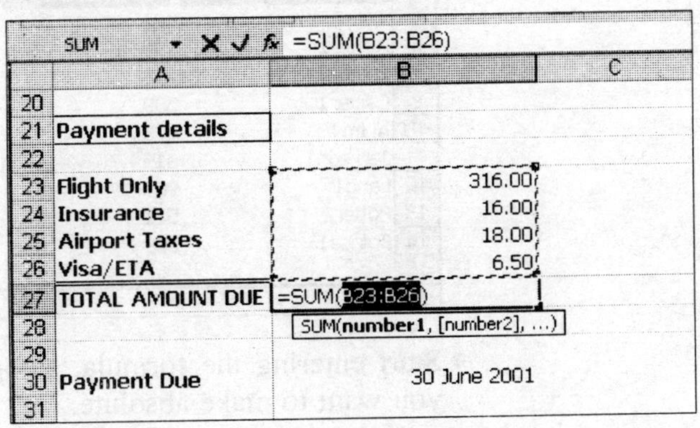

♦ If you are not satisfied with this selection, change it.

♦ Press Enter to confirm.

❑ *When you select a range of cells containing numerical values, Excel displays the sum of those values on the status bar, by default. If you right-click this result on the status bar, you can choose another function and display the average, the number of non-blank cells (count), the number of cells containing numbers, the highest value (max) or the lowest value (min) from the selected cells.*

Including an absolute cell reference in a formula

Making a cell reference absolute ensures that it does not evolve when the formula containing it is copied.
*In the example below, the formula in cell F6 (E6*F3) is about to be copied into the cells below it in column F. When the formula is copied into cell F7, it will adjusted to E6*F4; this will inevitably cause problems as F4 is blank! To produce a correct result the formula should read E6*F3. The reference to cell F3 must be made absolute before the formula is copied:*

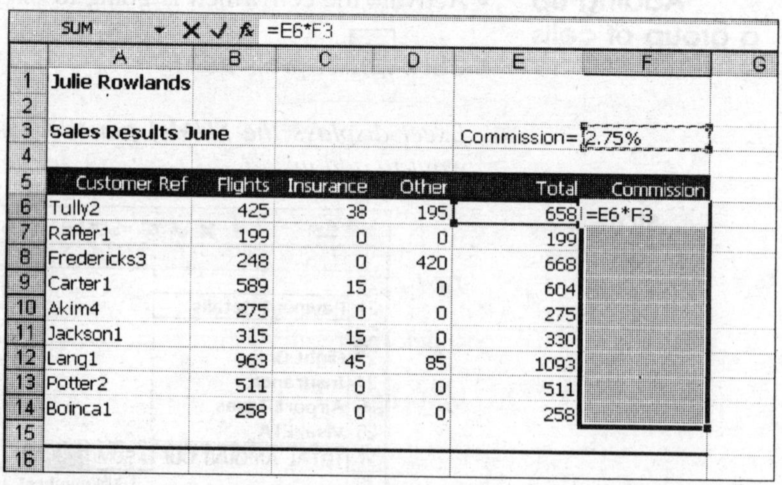

SUM =E6*F3

	A	B	C	D	E	F
1	Julie Rowlands					
2						
3	Sales Results June				Commission=	2.75%
4						
5	Customer Ref	Flights	Insurance	Other	Total	Commission
6	Tully2	425	38	195	658	=E6*F3
7	Rafter1	199	0	0	199	
8	Fredericks3	248	0	420	668	
9	Carter1	589	15	0	604	
10	Akim4	275	0	0	275	
11	Jackson1	315	15	0	330	
12	Lang1	963	45	85	1093	
13	Potter2	511	0	0	511	
14	Boinca1	258	0	0	258	
15						
16						

♦ Start entering the formula, stopping after the cell reference that you want to make absolute.

♦ Press F4.

The cell reference now contains $ signs before the column letter and before the row number.

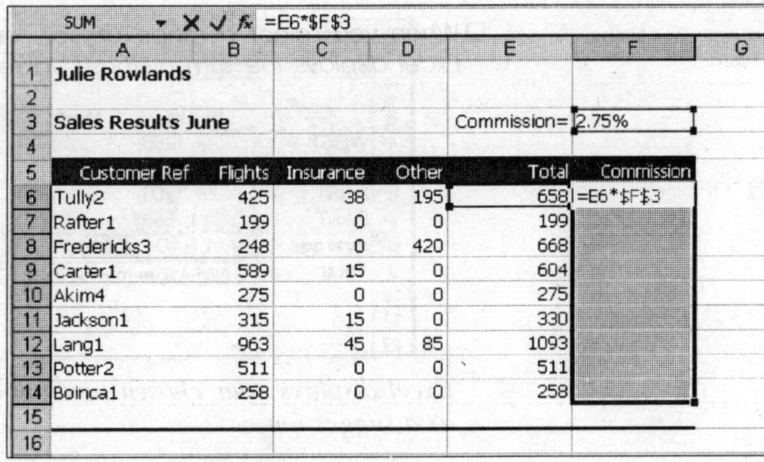

♦ Complete the formula if necessary, then enter.

> *When you press [F4] the cell reference becomes absolute, but press [F4] a second time and only the row reference remains absolute. Press [F4] a third time and only the column reference is absolute.*

Using simple statistical functions

♦ Click the cell where the result will be displayed.

♦ Open the list on the [Σ ▾] tool button by clicking the black arrow.

♦ Click the required function:

Average	to calculate the average of a set of cells.
Count	to count up within a set of cells the number of cells containing numerical values.
Max	to extract the highest value from a group of cells.
Min	to extract the lowest value from a group of cells.

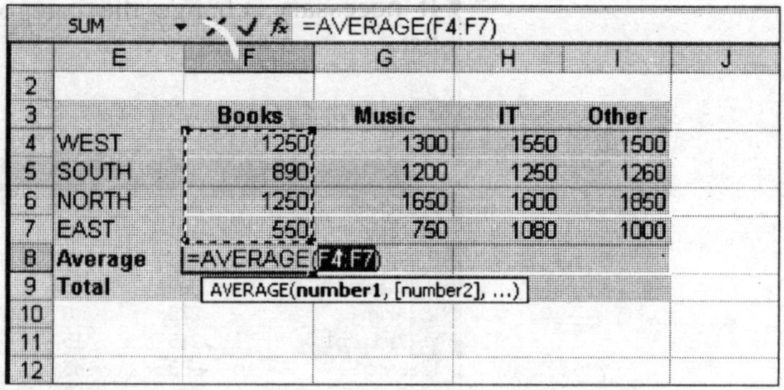

Excel displays your chosen function and selects a group of cells as a suggestion.

♦ If the suggested selection is incorrect, modify it.

♦ Confirm.

Inserting a function into a cell

♦ Click the cell where the result will be displayed.

♦ Click the *fx* button on the formula bar or use the **Insert - Function** command.

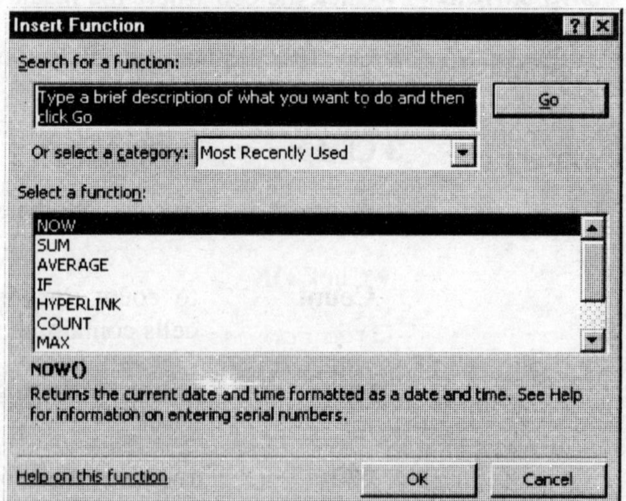

♦ If necessary, change the category in the **Or select a category** list.

*The **Most Recently Used** category shows the last functions you have used as well as the most frequently used ones.*

♦ Choose your required function from the list.

♦ Click **OK** at the bottom of the dialog box.

♦ To set each argument within the function:

– click the corresponding text box and click the button,

– on the worksheet, select the cell(s) corresponding to the argument,

– click to restore the dialog box.

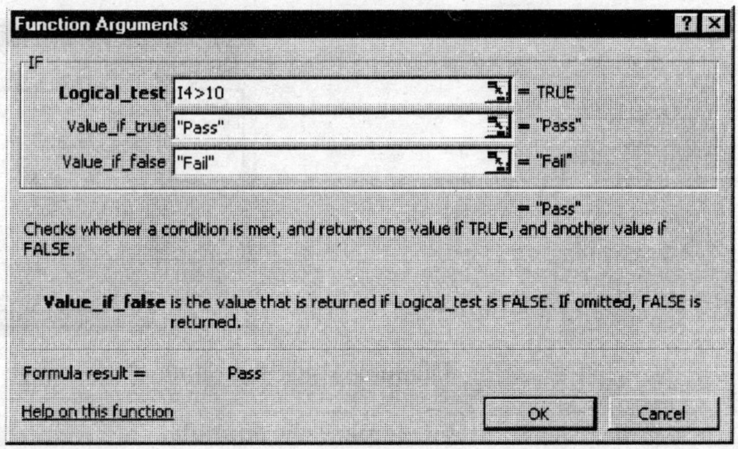

♦ Click **OK**.

❑ *You can also insert a function within a formula or within another function. To do this, start the formula and at the appropriate place click the button on the formula bar. This displays a list of the last functions used and the **More Functions** option which takes you to a full list of functions.*

❑ *To find a function easily, enter a brief description of the result you wish to obtain in the **Search for a function** text box on the **Insert Function** dialog box (**Insert - Function**) and click **OK** at the top of the dialog box. Excel will display a list of functions corresponding to your request.*

❑ *If you know the formula you want to use, you can enter it directly into the cell. If you do this, a ScreenTip appears, showing the different arguments you must set.*

Using named ranges in calculations

Using a name in a formula

♦ Start entering the formula then stop where the name is required.

♦ **Insert**
Name
Paste

♦ F3

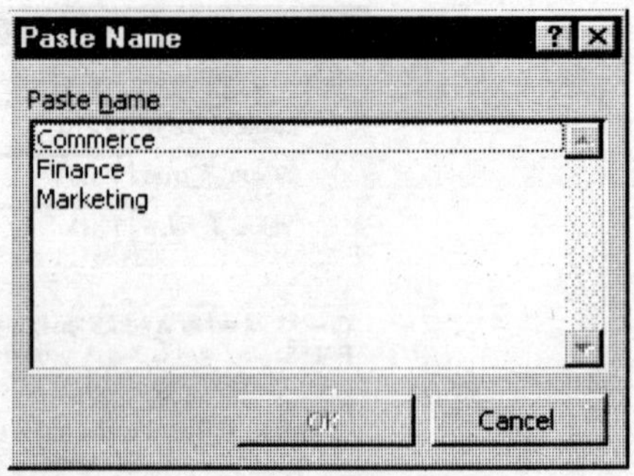

♦ Double-click the name of the range you want.

♦ Complete the formula.

❑ *You can also enter the name directly into the formula, instead of indicating the cell references.*

Replacing cell references with their name

In a formula, references to named ranges can be replaced by the corresponding names.

♦ Select the cells containing the formulas you want to modify.

♦ **Insert**
Name
Apply

♦ Click all the names concerned. If you select a name by mistake, click it again to deselect it.

♦ Click **OK**.

If you select names that are inappropriate for that formula (for example, cells containing text), Excel ignores those names.

Setting a condition in a formula

♦ Activate the cell where you want to display the result.

♦ Enter your condition, taking care to follow the syntax:
=IF(condition,action if TRUE,action if FALSE)

*You can insert the IF function and set each argument in the **Function Arguments** dialog box or enter the formula directly into the cell.*

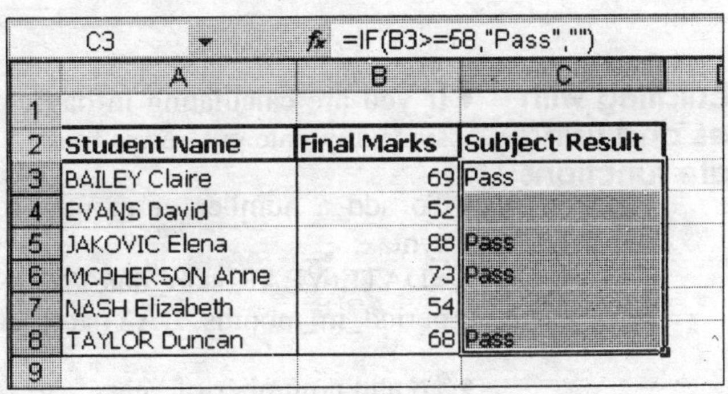

If the student's mark in cell B3 equals or is higher than 58, the text "Pass" is displayed in the cell; if the mark is lower, no text is displayed.

❑ *A variety of actions can be performed in a conditional expression:*

Display a number	*enter the number,*
Display a text	*enter the text between quotation marks,*
Display the result of a calculation	*enter the calculation formula,*
Display the contents of a cell	*enter to the cell,*
No display	*type "".*

❑ *For conditions, several operators are available:*

>	*greater than*
<	*less than*
<>	*different from*
>=	*greater than or equal to*
<=	*less than or equal to.*

❑ *You can set multiple conditions, linking them with the operators AND and/or OR:*
=IF(AND(cond1,cond2, ... ,condn),action to be carried out if all the conditions are satisfied,action to be carried out if any condition is not satisfied)
=IF(OR(cond1,cond2, ...,condn),action to be carried out if at least one condition is satisfied, action to be carried out if no condition is satisfied)

Calculating with dates and using date functions

♦ If you are calculating in days, proceed as for other calculations, since any date entered is treated as a number of days.

♦ To add a number of months to a start date, use the following syntax:
=DATE(YEAR(start_date),MONTH(start_date)+
period_in_months, DAY(start_date))

♦ To add a number of years, use:
=DATE(YEAR(start_date)+period_in_years,
MONTH(start_date),DAY(start_date))

For example to calculate the date two months from now, use:
=DATE(YEAR(NOW()),MONTH(NOW())+2,DAY(NOW()))

❑ *If the results of your calculations are four years ahead of what they ought to be, deactivate the **1904 date system** option in **Tools - Options - Calculation** tab.*

Using lookup functions

Functions of this type "look up" information in a table (often a large table) by locating one value and returning other values associated with the first piece of information, much as you could use a query to find information in database records.

The structure of the source table

♦ A table is made up of a column (or row) containing the compare values and other columns (rows) listing information associated with these values.

♦ The column (row) containing the compare values should be in the first position.

Using the VLOOKUP function

As a rule, data in a table are organised in columns, which is why you generally use the VLOOKUP (V for vertical) function. If the data are organised in rows, you would use the HLOOKUP function (H for horizontal).

♦ In the cell where you want to display certain information from the table, use the following function:
VLOOKUP (lookup_value,table_array,col_index_num,range_lookup)

Lookup_value refers to the compare value, a value that can be entered into the cell or directly in the formula.

Table_array is the table of values.

Col_index_num is the number of the column containing the value you are seeking (numbering begins at the first column in the table).

Range_lookup if entered as FALSE, this looks for an exact match or returns an error.

	A	B	C	D
1	**ISBN**	**Title**	**Author**	**Retail Price**
2	0014252052	Wild Swans	Chang, Jung	12.99
3	0140251774	Life of Jane Austen	Tomalin, Claire	7.99
4	0140256982	Mozart - The life of a Genius	Smith, Harold	15.99
5	0012458756	Pride and Prejudice	Austen, Jane	2.99
6	0012458758	Persuasion	Austen, Jane	2.99
7	0012458963	Scarlet Letter	Hawthorne, Nathaniel	2.99
8	0140488990	Tess of the d'Urbervilles	Hardy, Thomas	2.99
9	0152622842	Wuthering Heights	Bronte, Emily	2.99
10	0258625820	Dracula	Stoker, Bram	3.99

For this example, cells A2 to D10 have been named "booklist".

K3 fx =IF(J3="","",VLOOKUP(J3,booklist,2,FALSE))

	J	K	L	M	N
1					
2	**ISBN**	**Title**	**Price**	**Quantity**	**Total**
3	0012458758	Persuasion			
4	0152622842	Wuthering Heights			
5	0014252052	Wild Swans			
6					
7					

The function shown above looks in the second column of the "booklist" range to find the title that corresponds to the ISBN entered.

Making Euro currency conversions

♦ **Tools**
Euro Conversion

♦ If the **Euro Conversion** command is unavailable, you should install the corresponding add-in, by choosing **Tools - Add-Ins** and activating the **Euro Currency Tools** option in the **Add-Ins available** list. If this add-in does not appear in the list, click the **Browse** button to look for it and install it. If you see a message informing you that the necessary component is not installed, click **Yes** to confirm the installation (you may need to insert the Excel 2002 or Office XP CD-ROM).

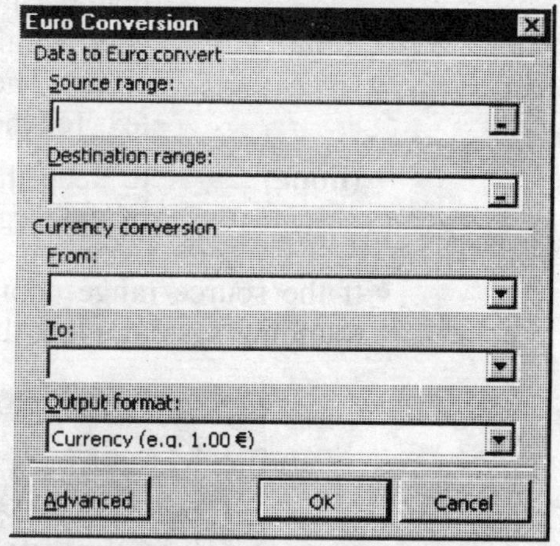

♦ Click the button to the right of the **Source range** box.

♦ Select the cell or (consecutive) cells containing the values you wish to convert and click to restore the dialog box.

♦ Click the button to the right of the **Destination range** box.

♦ Select the cell in which you wish to paste the converted values and click .

♦ In the **From** list, choose the currency from which you are converting.

♦ In the **To** list, choose the target currency for the conversion.

♦ In the **Output format** list, select the format you want the converted values to use:

Currency to apply a currency format corresponding to the currency chosen in the **To** list and reproduce the format of the source cells (borders, font etc.).

ISO to display the corresponding ISO code for the currency chosen in the **To** list and reproduce the format of the source cells. An example of an ISO code would be FRF for French francs or EUR for euros. The list of ISO codes appears in the help text for the EuroConvert function.

(none) to keep the current number format and formatting of the target cells.

♦ If the source range contains formulas or you wish to verify the rounding system, click the **Advanced** button.

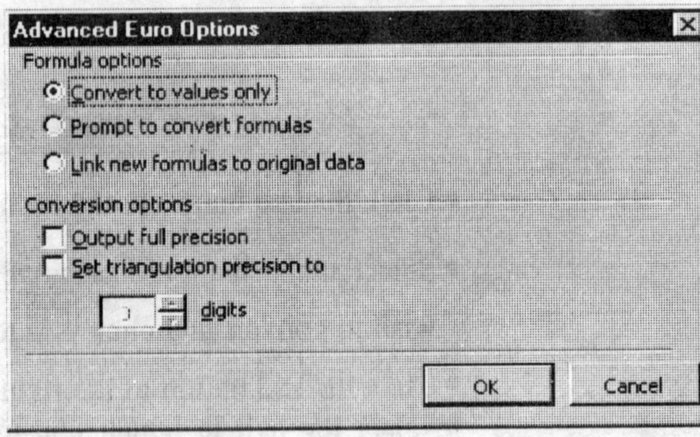

♦ From the **Formula options**, choose exactly what you want to do:

Convert to values only Excel shows the result of any formulas converted into euros (default option)

Prompt to convert formulas for each formula, Excel will offer you several options before converting.

Link new formulas to original data Excel uses the EuroConvert function, linking the result to the source data.

- ♦ If you do not want to use the European Union's currency rounding rules and control the rounding system yourself, choose from the options in the **Conversion options** frame:
  - tick the **Output full precision** option for Excel to include all the significant figures in the converted values without rounding.
  - tick the **Set triangulation precision to** option and indicate the number of **digits** to use when calculating the rounding. This option may be useful if you are converting two Euro zone currencies (from Irish pounds to French francs, for example), with the calculation being based on an intermediate conversion into euros.
- ♦ Click **OK** once, then click **OK** again.
- ♦ If you asked Excel to **Prompt to convert formulas** in the **Advanced Euro Options** dialog box, this dialog box will appear whenever Excel tries to convert a cell containing a formula:

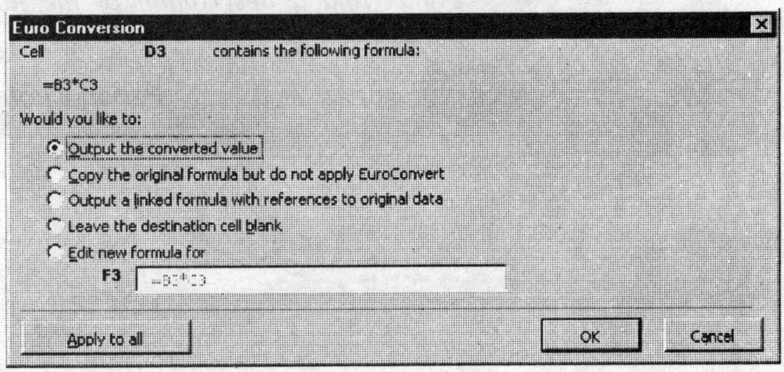

- ♦ In this case, choose how the conversion should be carried out then click **OK** to go onto the next formula or click **Apply to all** to use these settings for all formulas.

Finding a function

♦ **Help** ♦ F1
Microsoft Excel Help

♦ If the Office Assistant appears, click its **Options** button, deactivate the **Use the Office Assistant** check box, click **OK** then use **Help - Microsoft Excel Help** again.

♦ Activate the **Contents** tab.

♦ Expand the **Microsoft Excel Help** category, if necessary, by clicking the [+] sign.

♦ If necessary, expand the **Function Reference** category by clicking [+].

All the Excel functions are listed here, thematically.

♦ Expand one of the categories of functions.

When you select a function in the left pane of the window, the syntax and a description of the function appears in the right pane.

.... Personal notes ....

Adding statistics to a table

By inserting automatic subtotals, you can obtain rows of statistics. This is an easy way to summarise the information in a table.

♦ Sort the table by the column containing the entries you want to group together, as a first step to producing a subtotal for each group.

♦ Select the table.

♦ **Data**
Subtotals

♦ In the **At each change in** list, select the column used for grouping.

♦ Next choose the type of statistic you require from the **Use function** list.

♦ Finally mark the columns containing the values involved in the calculation.

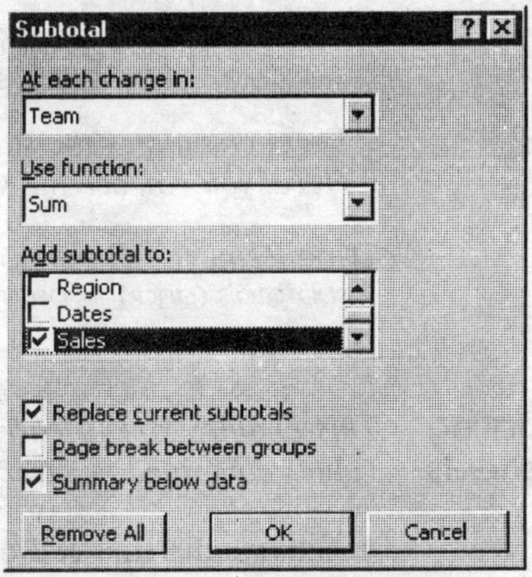

♦ Leave the **Replace current subtotals** option active if you wish to replace any existing subtotals by those you are now creating.

♦ Activate the **Page break between groups** option to insert a page break automatically between each group of subtotals.

♦ Leave the **Summary below data** option active to place totals and subtotals below the detailed data. If this option is active, the subtotals will appear alone above the details.

♦ Click **OK**.

	A	B	C	D
1	Team	Region	Dates	Sales
2	Cierzniak	West	10-Jan	99.86
3	Cierzniak	West	17-Jan	93.76
4	Cierzniak	Centre	24-Jan	50.00
5	Cierzniak	West	24-Jan	50.00
6	Cierzniak	East	31-Jan	18.75
7	Cierzniak	West	31-Jan	104.16
8	Cierzniak	West	07-Feb	100.00
9	Cierzniak	Centre	07-Feb	35.29
10	Cierzniak	West	14-Feb	108.33
11	**Cierzniak Total**			660.15
12	Dillon	North	10-Jan	152.50
13	Dillon	North	17-Jan	122.53
14	Dillon	North	24-Jan	100.00
15	Dillon	East	24-Jan	46.87
16	Dillon	East	31-Jan	18.75
17	Dillon	North	31-Jan	125.00
18	Dillon	North	07-Feb	125.00
19	Dillon	North	14-Feb	100.00
20	Dillon	Centre	14-Feb	33.83
21	**Dillon Total**			824.48
22	Hardy	East	10-Jan	93.75

Excel calculates the statistics required and constructs an outline. Here, you can see the sum of the sales for each team.

❑ *The **Remove All** button on the **Subtotal** dialog box deletes all the subtotals (and the outline structure) from the selected table.*

Consolidating worksheets

This enables you to carry out an analysis (for example, a sum) of values contained in several tables, possibly on different sheets.

♦ Activate the first cell of the range where you want to display the results.

♦ **Data**
Consolidate

♦ From the **Function** list, choose the calculation you want to perform.

♦ Go into the **Reference** box.

♦ For each sheet to be consolidated:

– click the  button to minimise the dialog box.

– activate the worksheet and select the cells concerned.

– click the  button to restore the dialog box.

– click the **Add** button.

♦ If you have included data labels in your selection, indicate where they are located by checking one of the boxes under **Use labels in**.

♦ If you wish to create a permanent link between the source sheets and the destination sheet, activate the **Create links to source data** check box.

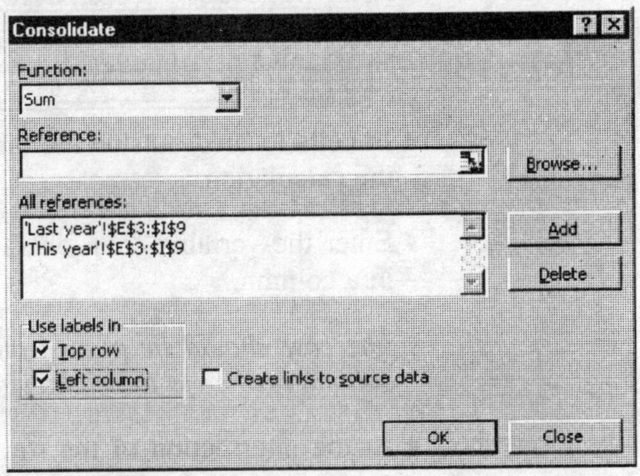

This consolidation will add the values from cells E3 to I9 on the Last year and This year worksheets.

♦ Click **OK**.

When you request a link, Excel produces an outline of the table as well.

Creating a two-input table

The table below shows how the amount paid back monthly on a loan varies according to the number of instalments and the sum borrowed. The interest rate is fixed at 11%. The whole table is based on the formula in cell A6.

A6 ▾ fx =ABS(PMT(B2/12,B3,B1))

	A	B	C	D	E	F
1	Capital	5,000.00				
2	Interest rate	11%				
3	Instalments	12				
4						
5						
6	441.91	12	18	24	30	36
7	5,000.00	441.91	302.59	233.04	191.39	163.69
8	10,000.00	883.82	605.19	466.08	382.78	327.39
9	15,000.00	1,325.72	907.78	699.12	574.17	491.08
10	20,000.00	1,767.63	1,210.37	932.16	765.56	654.77
11	25,000.00	2,209.54	1,512.96	1,165.20	956.95	818.47
12	30,000.00	2,651.45	1,815.56	1,398.24	1,148.34	982.16
13	35,000.00	3,093.36	2,118.15	1,631.27	1,339.73	1,145.86
14	40,000.00	3,535.27	2,420.74	1,864.31	1,531.12	1,309.55
15	45,000.00	3,977.17	2,723.33	2,097.35	1,722.51	1,473.24
16	50,000.00	4,419.08	3,025.93	2,330.39	1,913.90	1,636.94

♦ In cells located outside the table, enter the initial input values for the calculation.

♦ Enter the variable data, one series in a row, and the other series in a column.

The row should be placed one row above the column, and one column further to the right.

♦ At the intersection of the row and the column enter the calculation formula, referring to the input cells outside the table.

♦ Select the range of cells including the formula and all the result cells.

♦ **Data**
Table

♦ In the **Row input cell** box, indicate which input cells corresponds to the variable data in the row.

♦ In the **Column input cell** box, indicate which input cell formula corresponds to the column data.

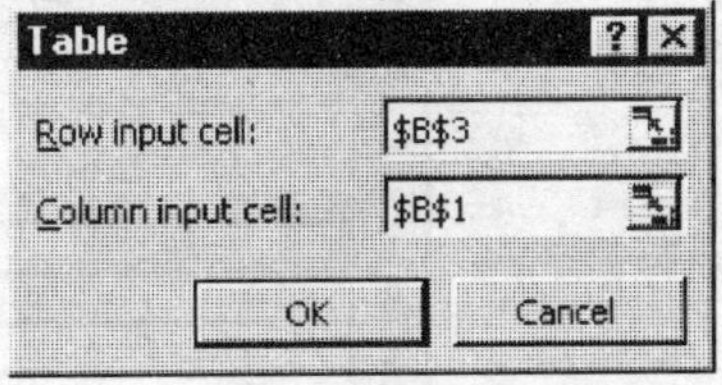

♦ Click **OK**.

Calculating with array formulas

Instead of using one formula repeated several times, you can sometimes use an array formula to make the same calculation over a range of cells. In fact some functions can only be applied as array formulas. An array formula also takes up less memory space than a group of ordinary formulas. In the example below, the second table shows the difference between a national average and the figures shown in the top table. As the same calculation is required for each of these figures, the second table was created with an array formula.

♦ To create an array formula, proceed as for an ordinary calculation, but instead of working on individual cells, work on a selected range of cells and enter using [Ctrl] [Shift] [Enter], instead of [Enter] or [Ctrl] [Enter].

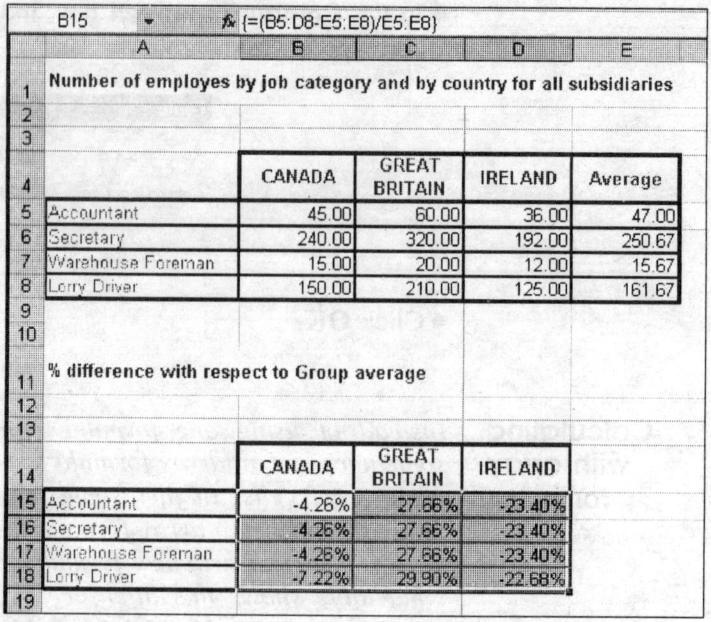

B15 | {=(B5:D8-E5:E8)/E5:E8}

	A	B	C	D	E
1	Number of employes by job category and by country for all subsidiaries				
2					
3					
4		CANADA	GREAT BRITAIN	IRELAND	Average
5	Accountant	45.00	60.00	36.00	47.00
6	Secretary	240.00	320.00	192.00	250.67
7	Warehouse Foreman	15.00	20.00	12.00	15.67
8	Lorry Driver	150.00	210.00	125.00	161.67
9					
10					
11	% difference with respect to Group average				
12					
13					
14		CANADA	GREAT BRITAIN	IRELAND	
15	Accountant	-4.26%	27.66%	-23.40%	
16	Secretary	-4.26%	27.66%	-23.40%	
17	Warehouse Foreman	-4.26%	27.66%	-23.40%	
18	Lorry Driver	-7.22%	29.90%	-22.68%	
19					

You can recognise an array formula by the braces surrounding it.

Setting a goal value

This is a technique for working out the value that a given cell must contain if the result of a calculation is to correspond to a goal value.

♦ Activate the cell you wish to set to a certain value and ensure that it contains a calculation formula.

♦ If possible, show the cell containing the variable value in the same workspace.

♦ **Tools**
Goal Seek

♦ Set the goal value in the **To value** box and indicate the variable cell in **By changing cell**.

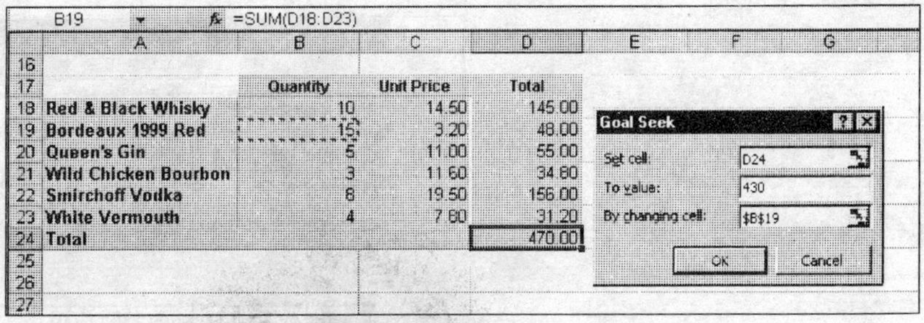

The spending budget is 430. The buyer has decided to economise on wine. How many bottles can he still purchase?

♦ Click **OK**.

As soon as Excel finds a solution, it displays its results on the worksheet.

♦ To accept the result suggested by Excel, click **OK**. The new values are incorporated into the sheet. To return to the original values, click **Cancel**.

Making scenarios

A scenario enables you to solve a problem by considering several hypotheses.

Creating scenarios

♦ **Tools**
Scenarios

♦ For each scenario to create:

– Click **Add**.

– Enter the **Scenario name**.

– Delete whatever appears in the **Changing cells** box and hold down Ctrl while selecting from the sheet the cells with the values to vary in this scenario.

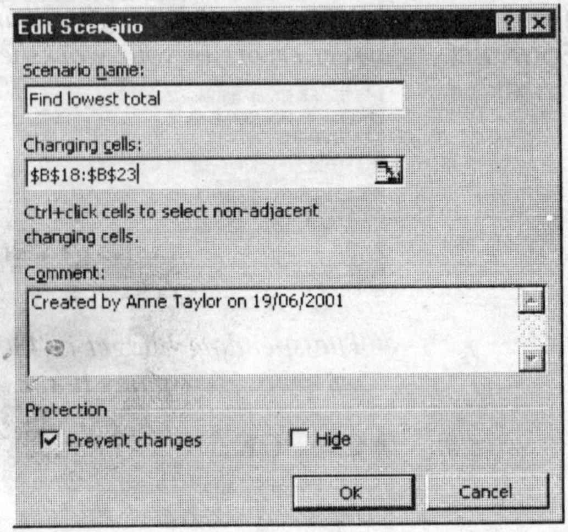

– Click **OK**.

– Enter the values for each changing cell and click **OK**.

Using a scenario

♦ If you only want to run one scenario select it then click **Show**. The result replaces the current values on your worksheet (this is why it is a good idea to start by creating a scenario containing the current values). If you want a summary report of all the scenarios, click **Summary**.

♦ If necessary, select the cells whose results interest you.

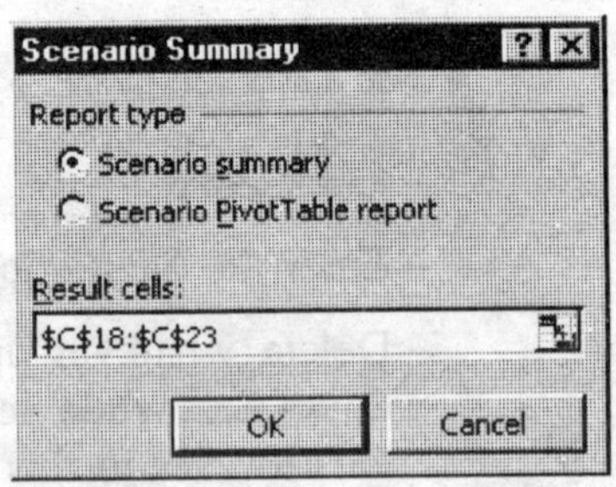

♦ Click **OK**.

The summary is presented as an outline on a separate worksheet.

Showing/hiding the Formula Auditing toolbar

*The **Formula Auditing** toolbar contains tools to help you find and correct errors in your worksheets.*

♦ **Tools**
Formula Auditing
Show Formula Auditing Toolbar

*This command shows or hides the **Formula Auditing** toolbar. A tick next to the toolbar name indicates that it is currently on display.*

❑ *You can also hide the **Formula Auditing** toolbar by clicking its [X] button. This button is only available when the toolbar is presented in its own window (as a floating toolbar).*

Displaying formulas instead of results

♦ **Tools**
Formula Auditing
Formula Auditing Mode

♦ Ctrl '

♦ Use the same command or shortcut key to display results once again.

Analysing errors in formulas

Excel can check a certain number of errors made on the worksheet, such as the appearance of an error value (for example, "#NAME?" or "#VALUE!"), numbers stored as text and so on.

Analysing errors in one formula

♦ In the **Options** dialog box (**Tools - Options - Error Checking** tab), check that the **Enable background error checking** option is active and if necessary, change the type of errors that Excel should find by activating or deactivating the various **Rules**.

♦ Activate the cell containing the error, indicated by a coloured triangle (green by default) in the upper left corner of the cell.

♦ Point to the icon at the left of the active cell: a description of the error you have made appears in a ScreenTip.

♦ Click the button to open its drop-down list.

A list of options appears, based on the type of error Excel has found (the first option reminds you what type of error has been made).

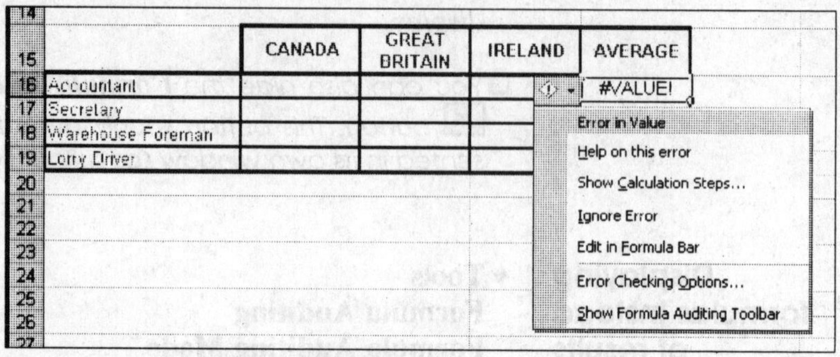

♦ Click the option of your choice:

Help on this error	displays the help window.
Show Calculation Steps	Shows the **Evaluate Formula** dialog box (cf. the next section).
Ignore Error	Deactivates the error indicator: both the coloured triangle and the tag disappear.
Edit in Formula Bar	Places the insertion point in the formula bar so you can modify the formula.
Error Checking Options	Shows the **Options** dialog box so you can choose which **Rules** Excel uses for **Error Checking**.
Show Formula Auditing Toolbar	displays the **Formula Auditing** toolbar.

Depending on the type of error, other options may appear.

❑ *If none of these options interest you, activate another cell to close this options menu.*

Analysing the errors in all formulas

♦ In the **Options** dialog box (**Tools - Options - Error Checking** tab), check that the **Enable background error checking** option is active and if necessary, change the type of errors that Excel should find by activating or deactivating the various **Rules**.

♦ Activate the worksheet you wish to check for errors.

♦ **Tools**
Error Checking
or
click the  tool button on the **Formula Auditing** toolbar.

*Excel selects the first cell containing a mistake and in the **Error Checking** dialog box, shows the formula and the error in detail.*

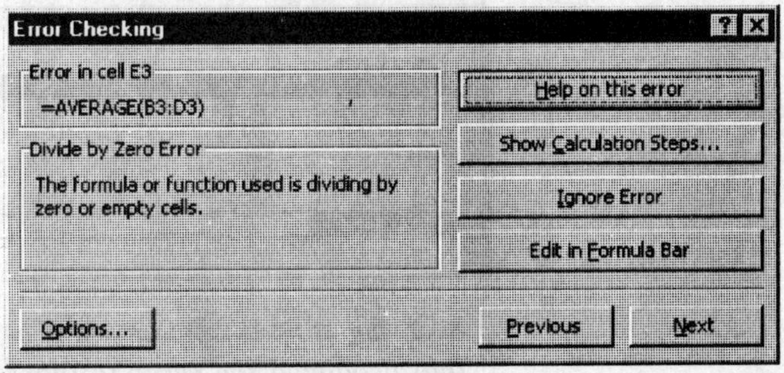

♦ You can choose to get **Help on this error**, to **Show Calculation Steps**, to **Ignore Error** or to **Edit in Formula Bar** (these options are explained under the previous heading) by clicking the appropriate button.

*The buttons on the **Error Checking** dialog box may differ depending on the type of error.*

♦ Depending on the option you choose, the **Restart** button may appear in the **Error Checking** dialog box which enables you to continue checking the worksheet.

♦ If you wish to go on to the next or previous error without working on the current one, click the **Next** or **Previous** button.

❑ *The **Reset Ignored Errors** button (**Tools - Options - Error Checking** tab) reactivates error indicators in cells where you have chosen the **Ignore Error** option.*

Finding the cells that are causing an error

When a formula result shows an error value in a cell, such as #NAME?, #N/A or #DIV/0!, you can trace all the cells that are involved in that formula.

♦ Activate the cell containing the error.

♦ Click the tool button on the **Formula Auditing** toolbar.

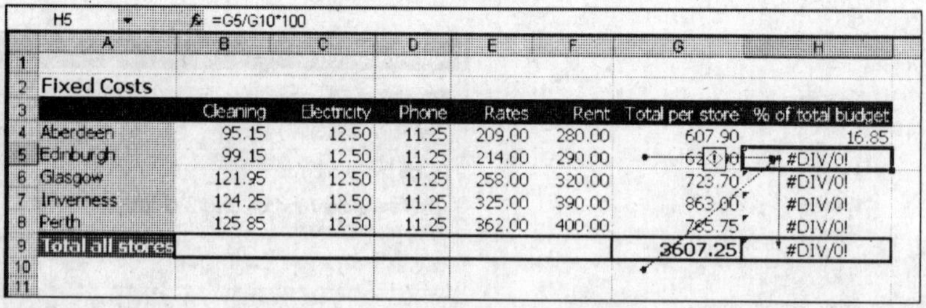

H5 =G5/G10*100

	A	B	C	D	E	F	G	H
1								
2	Fixed Costs							
3		Cleaning	Electricity	Phone	Rates	Rent	Total per store	% of total budget
4	Aberdeen	95.15	12.50	11.25	209.00	280.00	607.90	16.85
5	Edinburgh	99.15	12.50	11.25	214.00	290.00	6[illegible]0	#DIV/0!
6	Glasgow	121.95	12.50	11.25	258.00	320.00	723.70	#DIV/0!
7	Inverness	124.25	12.50	11.25	325.00	390.00	863.00	#DIV/0!
8	Perth	125 85	12.50	11.25	362.00	400.00	785.75	#DIV/0!
9	Total all stores						3607.25	#DIV/0!
10								
11								

Auditing arrows appear on the screen. Red arrows link the cell that produced the error to those to which it refers while the blue arrows show the precedents of the cell that caused the error initially.

❑ *To clear the auditing arrows, click the tool button on the **Formula Auditing** toolbar.*

Evaluating formulas

This technique can be used to see the result of each part of a nested formula.

♦ Select the cell you wish to evaluate.

♦ **Tools**
Formula Auditing
Evaluate Formula
or click the  tool button on the **Formula Auditing** toolbar.

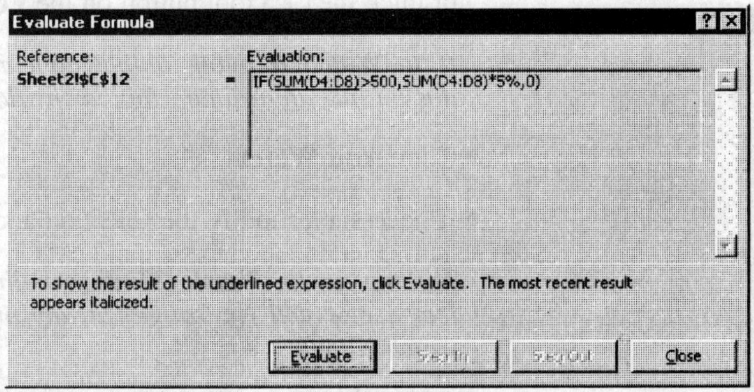

♦ Click **Evaluate** to see the result of the expression underlined in the **Evaluation** box. The result appears within the formula in italics.

♦ Click **Evaluate** again to see the result of the next underlined section and so on.

♦ When you have evaluated the whole formula, click the **Close** button to end the evaluation or the **Restart** button (that replaces the **Evaluate** button) to perform the evaluation again.

❑ *If the formula you are evaluating contains a reference to another formula, the **Step In** button shows the detail of that formula, when it is underlined, in a new part of the evaluation box. The **Step Out** button returns to the initial formula.*

Using the Watch Window toolbar

The Watch Window toolbar allows you to see cell contents and details of formulas, without those cells being necessarily on the screen.

♦ Select the cells you wish to examine.

♦ **Tools**
Formula Auditing
Show Watch Window
or click the tool button on the **Formula Auditing** toolbar.

*If the **Watch Window** toolbar appears on the worksheet, you can dock it like an ordinary toolbar by double-clicking its title bar.*

♦ Click **Add Watch**.

♦ If necessary, modify the selection and click the **Add** button.

*As long as the **Watch Window** toolbar is displayed, you can select a new cell (or range) at any time and add it to the list of watched items.*

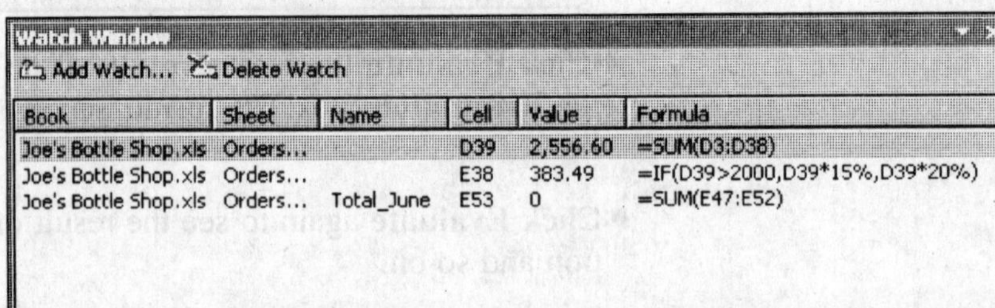

♦ When you no longer need the **Watch Window** toolbar, close it by clicking its button.

❑ *You can change the column widths on the **Watch Window** toolbar by dragging the vertical line between the column headers.*

❑ *To go rapidly to a cell listed in the **Watch Window** toolbar, double-click that cell's row in the list.*

❑ *To select all the cells containing formulas in order to add them to the **Watch Window** toolbar, use the **Edit - Go To** command, click the **Special** button and choose **Formulas**.*

Tracing the relationships between formulas and cells

Showing precedent cells

These are the cells which are linked to the calculation formula: they can be picked out with auditing arrows.

♦ Activate the cell containing the formula.

♦ **Tools**
Formula Auditing
Trace Precedents

or click the tool button on the **Formula Auditing** toolbar.

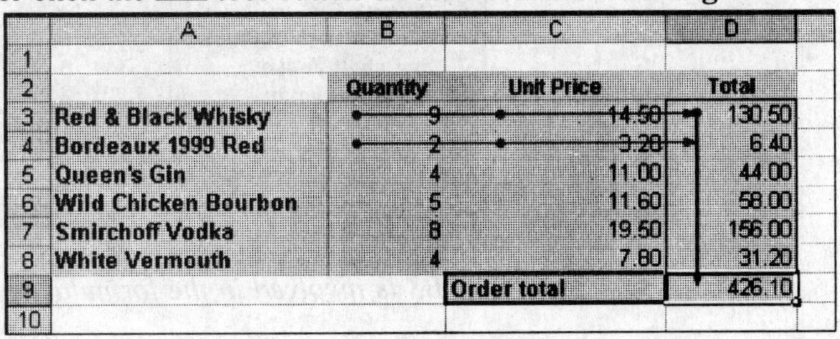

	A	B	C	D
1				
2		Quantity	Unit Price	Total
3	Red & Black Whisky	9	14.50	130.50
4	Bordeaux 1999 Red	2	3.20	6.40
5	Queen's Gin	4	11.00	44.00
6	Wild Chicken Bourbon	5	11.60	58.00
7	Smirchoff Vodka	8	19.50	156.00
8	White Vermouth	4	7.80	31.20
9			Order total	426.10
10				

In the example above, the command was repeated several times to show the precedents of cells D3, D4 and D9.

❑ *To clear the auditing arrows, use the **Tools - Formula Auditing - Remove All Arrows** command or the tool button.*

Showing dependent cells

Dependent cells are those that contain formulas that refer to a selected cell. Like precedents, they can be highlighted with arrows.

♦ Activate the cell concerned.

♦ **Tools**
Formula Auditing
Trace Dependents
or click the tool button on the **Formula Auditing** toolbar.

	A	B	C	D
1				
2		Quantity	Unit Price	Total
3	Red & Black Whisky	9	14.50	130.50
4	Bordeaux 1999 Red	2	3.20	6.40
5	Queen's Gin	4	11.00	44.00
6	Wild Chicken Bourbon	5	11.60	58.00
7	Smirchoff Vodka	8	19.50	156.00
8	White Vermouth	4	7.80	31.20
9			Order total	426.10
10				
11				
12			Total items ordered	32
13				

Cell B3 is involved in the formulas in cells D3 and D12.

❑ *To clear the auditing arrows, use the* ***Tools - Formula Auditing - Remove All Arrows*** *command or the* *tool button.*

Inserting rows/columns

♦ Select the entire row (or the entire column) after which you wish to insert the new row/column. You can select a row or column by clicking its header.

♦ Right-click the selection and choose **Insert**.

♦ Select the row or column before which you wish to insert the new row/column.

♦ **Insert**
Rows or **Columns**

❑ *When you insert a row or column, the inserted item adopts the formatting of the row or column previously located there. You can modify this by clicking the Insert Options button that appears next to the inserted item. In the menu that appears, choose to* ***Format Same As Above*** *or* ***Format Same As Below*** *(for a row), to* ***Format Same As Right*** *or* ***Format Same As Left*** *(for a column) or to* ***Clear Formatting*** *altogether.*

❑ *You can also insert a row or column by selecting a row or column (click its header) and pressing* Ctrl *+.*

Deleting rows/columns

♦ Select the rows (or columns) you wish to delete, by clicking their headers.

♦ Use **Edit - Delete** or right-click the selected row/column and choose **Delete**.

Modifying the width of a column/height of a row

♦ Select each column to be resized to the same width (or each row to be given the same new height); if only one column or row is concerned, do not select it.

♦ Point to the vertical line on the right of one of the selected columns (or to the horizontal line under the row number):

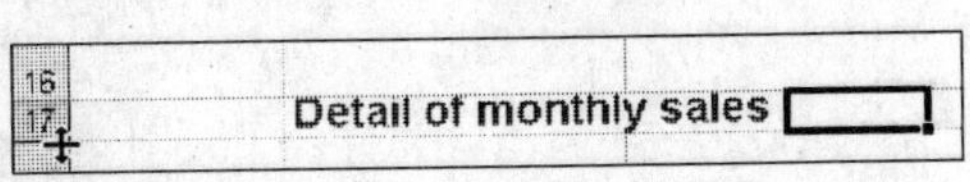

Notice the new appearance of the mouse pointer.

♦ Drag to the size required.

The new width (or height) is represented by a dotted line on the sheet and its value is displayed in a ScreenTip.

♦ Release when the correct width (or height) is obtained.

❑ *The width of a column is expressed as a number of characters (and in pixels). The height of a row appears as a number of points (and in pixels).*

> *To save memory, use this method to create space in your sheets rather than inserting more rows and columns.*

Adapting the width of a column/ height of a row to its contents

You can adjust column widths to fit the longest value in the column, and row heights to the tallest value in the row.

♦ For column width, double-click the vertical line to the right of the column letter.
For row height, double-click the horizontal line below the row number.

Inserting blank cells

Cells are inserted below the active cell or to its left.

♦ Select as many cells as you are going to insert.

♦ **Insert - Cells** or right-click the selection and choose **Insert**.

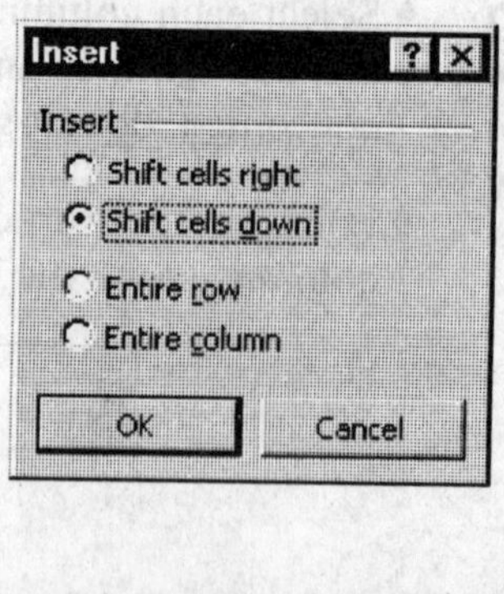

♦ Activate either the first or the second option to indicate what you want to do with the cells already in place.

♦ Click **OK**.

Deleting cells

♦ Select the cells you wish to delete.

♦ **Edit**
Delete
or right-click the selection and choose **Delete**.

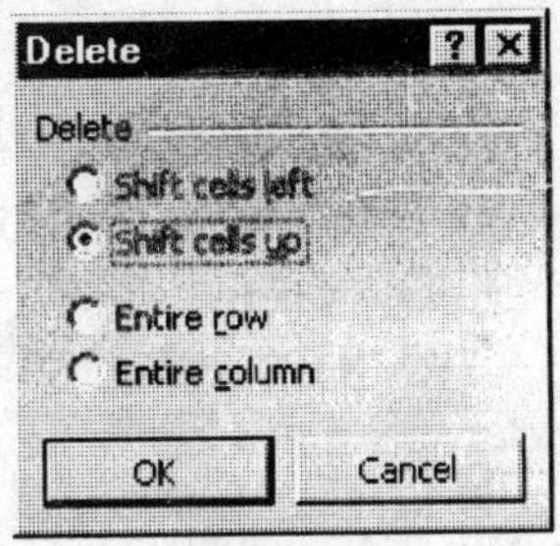

♦ Activate the first or second option to indicate how to shift the existing cells once the selected cells are deleted.

♦ Click **OK**.

Moving cells/rows/columns then inserting them

This action moves cells (rows/columns) and inserts them between existing cells.

♦ Select the cells, rows or columns to be moved.

♦ Point to one edge of the selected range.

♦ Holding the **Shift** key down, drag the selection into position.

♦ Release the mouse when the insertion point (displayed as a thick grey line) is correctly placed.

❑ *Holding down* Ctrl *as well as* ⇧Shift *when you drag a selection, moves a copy of the cells, rows or columns instead of the original item.*

.... *Personal notes* ....

Applying an automatic format to a table

♦ Select the table to be formatted.

♦ **Format**
AutoFormat

♦ Choose the most suitable format from the **Table format** list.

♦ If necessary, click the **Options** button to customise the AutoFormat, deactivating the elements you do not wish to apply.

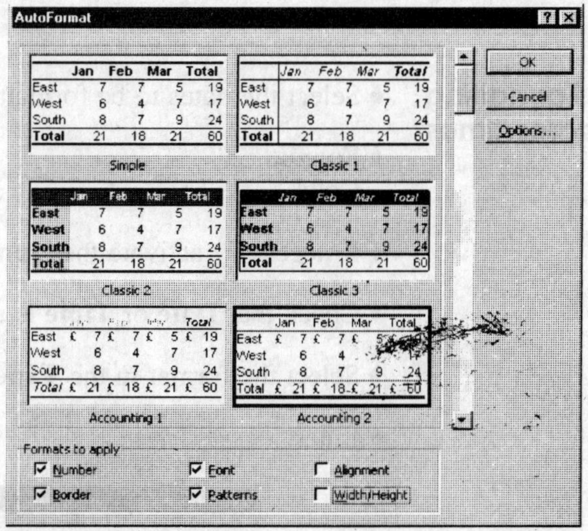

♦ Click **OK**.

Formatting numerical values

♦ Select the values concerned.

♦ Choose one of the number formats from the **Formatting** toolbar. The examples below are based on a figure of 10000:

$ / $	Currency	($10,000.00/£10,000.00 etc)
€	Euro	(€ 10,000.00)
%	Percent Style	(1000000%)
,	Comma Style	(10,000.00)

♦ If necessary, click the tool button to show one more decimal place or to show one less.

❑ *The currency type used by the **Currency** style depends upon your computer's regional settings.*

❑ *Number symbols (#) may appear if a cell's width is insufficient once the format has been applied. The full contents of the cell will appears in a screen tip if you point to the symbols.*

Formatting dates/times

♦ Select the dates to be formatted.

♦ **Format**
Cells ♦ Ctrl 1

♦ If necessary activate the **Number** tab.

♦ Check that **Date** or **Time** is active in the **Category** list box.

♦ Select the format in the **Type** list.

♦ Enter.

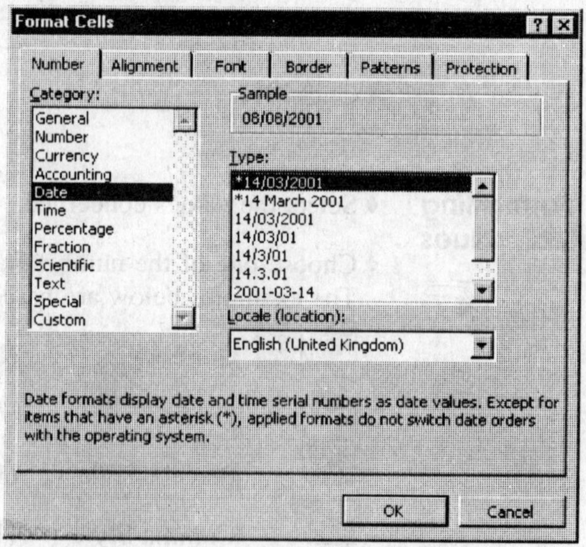

Creating a custom format

- Select the cells to which you wish to apply the format.
- **Format**
  Cells
  Number tab
  ♦ Ctrl 1
- If your format resembles an existing one, select the category concerned then the format required.
- Activate **Custom** in the **Category** list then enter or modify the custom format in the **Type** box:

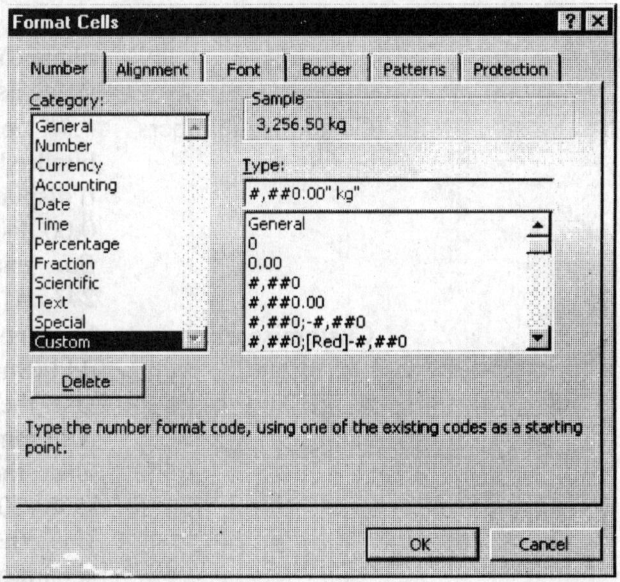

- A custom format can, contain up to four sections, separated by semi-colons which define, respectively, the format of positive numbers, negative numbers, null values and the format of text. For example: 0.00" kg";[red]-0.00" kg";0;[blue] This example shows positive values with two decimal places followed by the text "kg", negative values in red, preceded by a minus sign and followed by the text "kg", null values as zero and any text in the colour blue. Leaving a section empty applies no special format to that type of value.

- If you define only one section, it is used for all number types. For example: #, ##" net" With this format, whatever the value (positive, negative or null), the hundreds and thousands are separated by a comma and the value is followed by the text "net".
- You can use these guidelines to help you create your own formats:

If you wish to:	Keep these rules in mind:
Add text to a custom format	Any text added to a format including spaces, must be entered between quotation marks. Do not leave spaces before the quotation marks, as Excel interprets a space as a request to divide by 1000!
Customise numbers	#.## puts a separator betweens the hundreds and thousands 0 displays integers without decimals 0.00 displays two decimal places For example *#,##0.00"grams"* displays *2415* as *2,415.00 grams*.
Customise dates	Use these codes for days: d (1) dd (01) ddd (Sun) dddd (Sunday). Use these codes for months: m (1) mm (01) mmm (Jan) mmmm (January). Use these codes for years: yy (01) yyyy(2001). Use the character of your choice as separator. For example *ddd dd mmm yyyy* displays *02/02/01* as *Friday 02 Feb 2001*.
Customise text	Use the @ symbol to indicate text you enter or existing text in the cell. For example *@" Distribution Centre"* displays *Ilford Distribution Centre* if you just enter *Ilford*.

- When your format is complete, click **OK** or press Enter to apply it.

Creating conditional formats

You can define conditional formats, which are applied only to cells that meet your specified conditions (for example, they contain certain values or formulas).

♦ Select the cells concerned.

♦ **Format**
Conditional Formatting

♦ In the **Condition 1** list, select:

Cell Value Is	if the condition refers to a value contained in the selected cells (a constant, or the result of a formula).
Formula Is	if the condition refers to a formula.

♦ In the first case, continue by selecting an operator of comparison and a value. In the second case, give the formula (one which will return TRUE or FALSE).
If the condition refers to a formula, enter an equals sign (=) in front of the formula.

♦ Click the **Format** button.

♦ Use the options under the **Font**, **Border** and **Patterns** tabs to define the format which will be applied to the cells if the condition is met.

♦ Click **OK**.

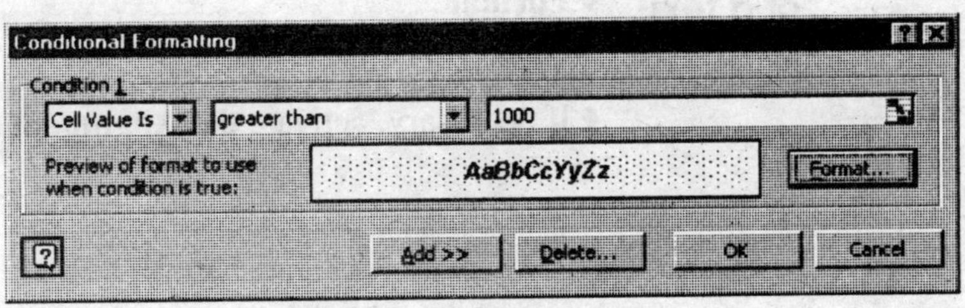

Here, the specified formatting will only be applied to cells containing a value greater than 1000.

♦ To define the format which will be applied if the condition is not met (or to define different formats connected to other conditions), click the **Add** button and continue as before.

♦ Click **OK** when you have defined all the required conditions and formats.

The formatting applied to the cells will vary automatically according to the cell content.

Hiding the contents of a cell

♦ Select the cell(s).

♦ **Format**
Cells
Number tab

♦ If necessary, activate **Custom** in the **Category** list.

♦ Delete everything in the **Type** box. Type in ;;; (three semi-colons).

♦ Enter.

❑ *To display the contents of the cells, apply any other format to them.*

Modifying the orientation of a text

♦ Select the cells concerned.

♦ **Format**
Cells

♦ Ctrl 1

♦ If necessary, activate the **Alignment** tab.

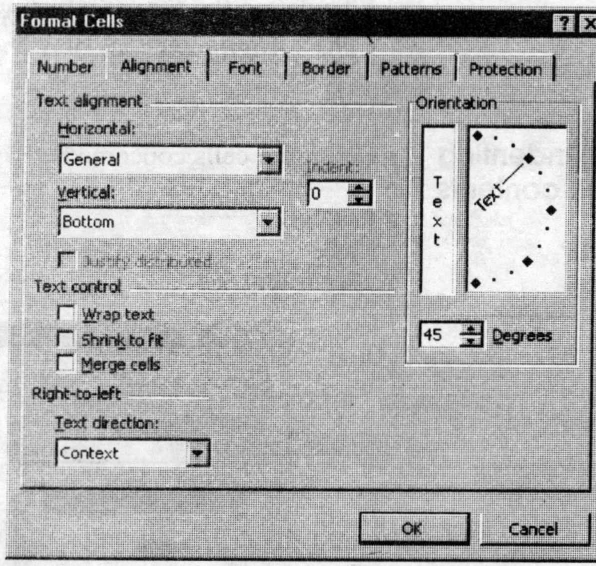

♦ In the **Orientation** frame, point to the word **Text** in the right hand box and drag it to the angle you require. You could also enter a value for the angle in the **Degrees** box.

♦ Click **OK**.

> To position characters one underneath the other, click the left hand box, in the ***Orientation*** frame, where the word ***Text*** is written vertically.

Aligning cell contents horizontally

The horizontal alignment of a cell is calculated with reference to the width of the column which contains it.

♦ Select the cells concerned.

♦ Click one of these three tool buttons:

left alignment

centered

right alignment

❑ *To justify the text in a cell, open the **Horizontal** list (**Format - Cells - Alignment** tab) and choose **Justify**.*

Indenting cell contents

♦ Select the cells concerned.

♦ **Format**
Cells
Alignment tab

♦ Ctrl 1

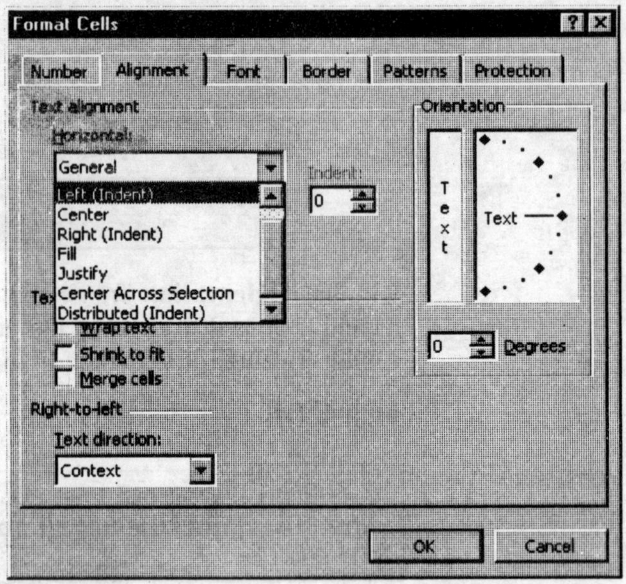

♦ According to the indent required, select from the **Horizontal** list a **Left (Indent)**, a **Right (Indent)** or a **Distributed (Indent)** (which makes a left and a right indent).

♦ Give the indent size in the **Indent** box.

♦ Click **OK**.

You can use the  *and*  *tool buttons to increase or decrease the left indent, respectively.*

Aligning cell contents vertically

The vertical alignment of a cell is defined with reference to the height of the row.

♦ Select the cells concerned.

♦ **Format**
Cells
Alignment tab

♦ Ctrl 1

♦ Select an alignment from the **Vertical** list.

♦ Click **OK.**

Adjusting row height to text

The row height is adjusted automatically to display the cell's contents without changing the column width.

♦ Activate the cell required or select the cells concerned.

♦ **Format**
Cells
Alignment tab

♦ Ctrl 1

♦ Activate the **Wrap text** option.

♦ Click **OK.**

Centering cell contents across several columns

This method can be used to centre a title over the width of the whole table.

♦ Select the cells across which the text should be centered.

The first cell in the range must contain the text.

♦ Click the tool button.

❑ *This command merges the cells involved.*

❑ *To undo this presentation (which will separate the merged cells and place the text in the cell on the far left of the merged group) select the cell containing the text and click the tool button again.*

Modifying the font and/or font size

♦ Select the cells or characters concerned.

♦ Select the **Font** and the **Font Size** from the corresponding list boxes on the **Formatting** toolbar.

Font Names preceded by TT indicate TrueType fonts managed by Windows.

❑ *You can also use the options on the* ***Font*** *page of the* ***Format Cells*** *dialog box (****Format - Cells****).*

> *To set a default font and font size for all new folders, use* ***Tools - Options - General*** *tab (****Standard font*** *and* ***Size*** *options). These changes will only take effect the next time you start Excel.*

Adjusting the size of characters automatically

If this option is active, Excel reduces the size of the characters automatically when the cell is not wide enough to display them all.

♦ Select the cells concerned.

♦ **Format**
Cells
Alignment tab

♦ Ctrl 1

♦ Activate the **Shrink to fit** option.

♦ Click **OK**.

❑ *Characters which have been reduced in size return to their original size if you widen the column.*

Changing the colour of the characters

♦ Select the cells or characters concerned.

♦ Open the list by clicking the down arrow.

♦ Click the colour required.

❑ *You can also select a colour from the* ***Color*** *list in the* ***Format Cells*** *dialog box (****Format - Cells - Font*** *tab).*

> *The button displays the last colour chosen. To apply the same colour to another text, just click this tool button again without opening the list.*

Formatting characters

Character formats include bold type, italics and underlining.

♦ Select the cells or characters concerned.

♦ Activate the attributes to apply:

B	or Ctrl **B**	for **bold** characters
I	or Ctrl **I**	for *italic* characters
U	or Ctrl **U**	for underlined characters.

❑ *If you repeat the same command for the same text, you cancel the corresponding attribute.*

❑ *You can apply more than one attribute to the same text.*

♦ Select the cells or characters concerned.

♦ **Format** ♦ Ctrl 1
Cells
Font tab

♦ Activate all the formats to be applied to the text.

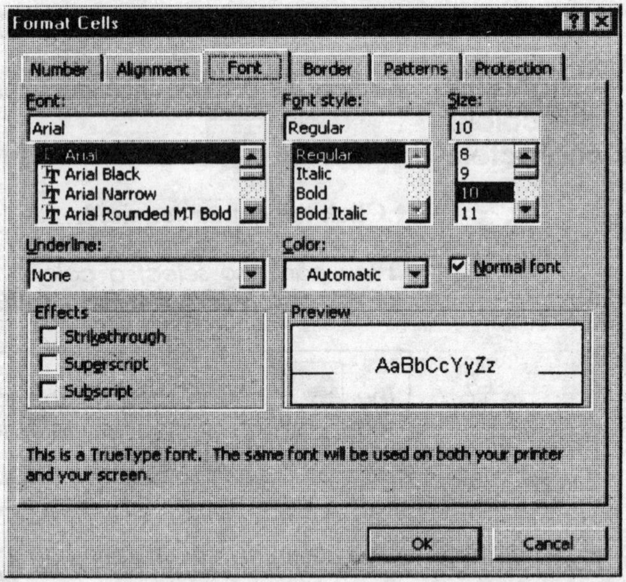

*The options in the **Effects** frame allow you to put a line through selected characters or place them in subscript or superscript. The **Underline** drop-down list gives you several underlining variations.*

♦ Click **OK**.

Using cell borders

Applying borders

♦ Select the cells concerned.

♦ Open the list by clicking the black arrow.

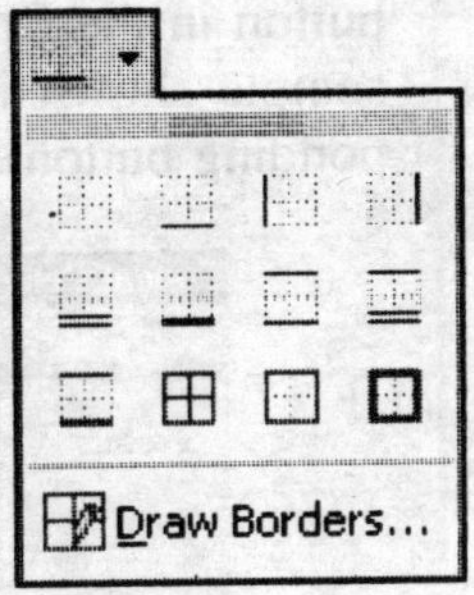

♦ Click the border you want to apply.

The tool button now displays the type of border you have chosen.

♦ Deselect the cells to view the finished result.

❑ *If you need coloured borders or dotted lines, you should use the second method, described below.*

❑ *To delete all borders, use the type of border.*

> *To apply the same border to another range of selected cells, simply click the button without opening the list.*

♦ Select the cells concerned.

♦ **Format** ♦ Ctrl 1
Cells
Border tab

♦ To place a border around the edge of the selected range, choose a **Style** and a **Color** for the border lines then click the **Outline** button. To apply the border to each individual cell in the selection, but not around the outside edges, choose the **Style** and **Color** then click the **Inside** button.

- To place a border along one or more specific edges of the selected range, choose a **Style** and **Color** then click the corresponding button in the **Border** section. You can even click an edge on the sample shown in the **Border** preview (this activates the corresponding button).

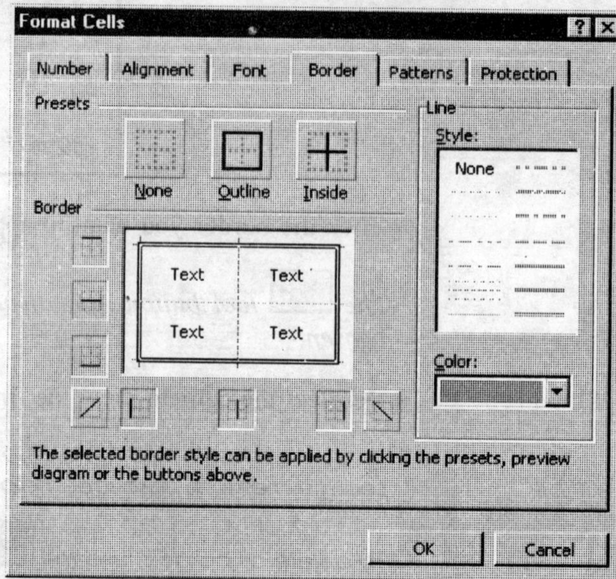

The  *and*  *buttons draw diagonal lines across individual cells.*

- Confirm with **OK**.

- Click outside the selection to view the final result.

Drawing borders

- Open the 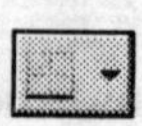 list by clicking the black arrow.
- Click the **Draw Borders** option.

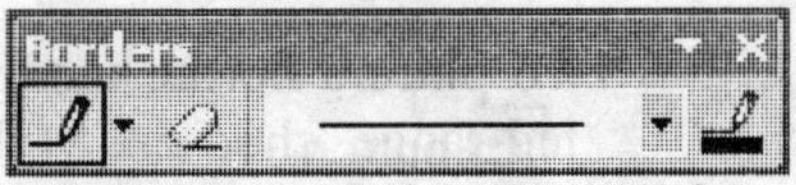

The ***Borders*** *toolbar appears and the pointer takes the shape of a pencil.*

♦ The default drawing mode is **Draw Border** which draws an outline around the selected area. If you wish to draw inside grid-lines instead, open the list on the tool button and choose the **Draw Border Grid** option.

When you choose ***Draw Border Grid*** *mode, the pencil pointer is accompanied by a small grid.*

♦ If required, open the list and choose a line style.

♦ Click if you want to select another colour.

♦ To draw a border along one edge of a range of cells, drag along that edge.

♦ To draw a border around the outside of a range or a grid within a range, drag from the starting cell up to the last cell required.

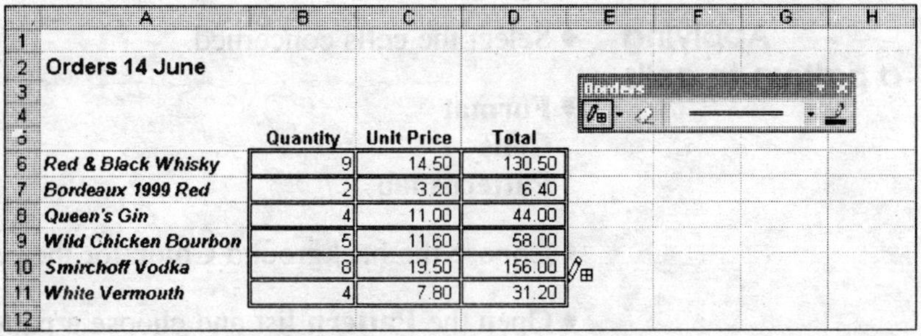

♦ To remove one or more borders, click the tool button (the pointer becomes an eraser) and drag along the borders you wish to erase.

♦ To deactivate the border drawing mode, press Esc or click the tool button again.

♦ If you no longer need it, close the **Borders** toolbar by clicking its [X] button.

*While you are using **Draw Border** mode, you can temporarily switch to **Draw Border Grid** mode by holding down the [Ctrl] key. Holding down the [Shift] key switches to erasing mode, with the pointer becoming an eraser temporarily.*

Applying colour to cells

♦ Select the cells concerned.

♦ Open the [Fill Color] list by clicking the down arrow.

♦ Choose the colour.

The [Fill Color] tool button displays the last colour chosen. You can apply the same colour to another selection simply by clicking this tool button (without opening the list).

❑ *You can also select a colour from the **Color** swatches in the **Format Cells** dialog box, under the **Patterns** tab.*

Applying a pattern to cells

♦ Select the cells concerned.

♦ **Format**
Cells
Patterns tab

♦ [Ctrl] 1

♦ Choose the background **Color** for the cells.

♦ Open the **Pattern** list and choose a pattern and its colour.

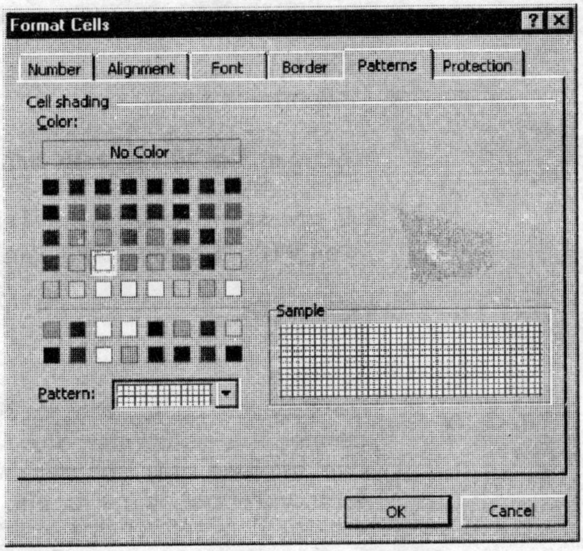

♦ Click **OK**.

Merging cells

Cells which have been merged become one cell:

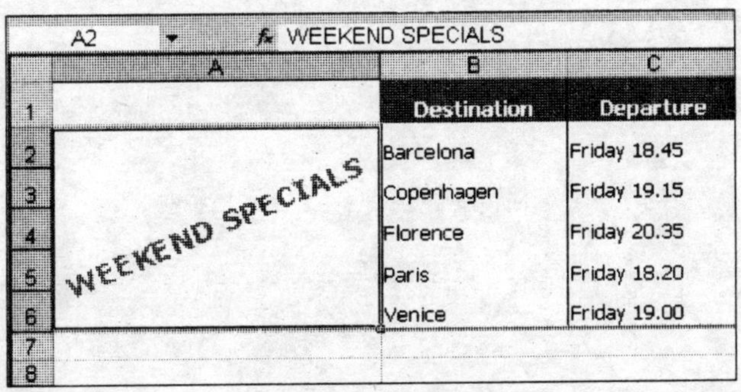

The text WEEKEND SPECIALS in the content of cell A2 but appears across the merged cells A2, A3, A4, A5 and A6.

♦ Select the cells concerned.

Only the data in the first cell of the selection (at the top left of the range of cells) will appear in the merged cells.

♦ **Format**
Cells
Alignment tab

♦ Ctrl 1

♦ Activate the **Merge cells** option.

♦ If necessary, specify the **Text alignment** and **Orientation** that you wish to apply to the data in the merged cells.

♦ Click **OK**.

The tool button merges selected cells (usually in a row) and centres the data horizontally in the merged cells. If more than one of these cells contains data, Excel will only retain the contents of the cell on the far left.

. . . . *Personal notes* . . . .

Creating a style

A style is a way of saving a collection of attributes that you can then apply to other cells more quickly.

♦ Activate the cell whose formatting is to be saved as a style.

♦ **Format**
Style ♦ Alt '

♦ Name the new style.

A description of the style is displayed in the ***Style Includes*** *frame.*

♦ Deactivate any attributes you do not require.

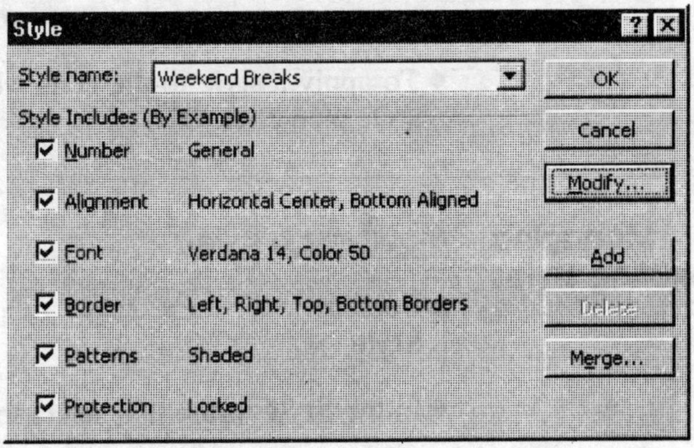

♦ Use the **Modify** button if you want to change any aspects of the style before saving it.

♦ Click **OK** to confirm.

Styles are defined only for the active workbook.

Applying a style

♦ Select the cells to be formatted.

♦ **Format**
Style ♦ Alt '

♦ Select the style you want to use in the **Style name** list.

♦ Click **OK**.

Using styles from another document

♦ Open the workbook containing the styles, then the workbook where you are going to apply them, and stay in that one.

♦ **Format**
Style

♦ Click the **Merge** button.

♦ Excel lists the workbooks which are currently open: double-click the one containing the styles you are going to use.

♦ To apply a style to the cells which you have selected, choose the style then click **OK**.

Managing existing styles

Modifying a style

♦ **Format**
Style ♦ Alt '

♦ In the **Style name** list, select the style you want to modify.

♦ Click the **Modify** button.

♦ Make the necessary changes then click **OK**.

♦ Click **OK** again.

All the cells to which the style has been applied are modified instantly.

Deleting a style

♦ **Format**
Style ♦ Alt '

♦ Select the style from the **Style name** list, then click the **Delete** button.

♦ Click **OK**.

All the cells where the style was applied lose the style attributes and take on standard formatting.

❑ Be careful, deleting a style cannot be undone.

Creating a template

*A **template** is a document containing formatting and/or data which you can save and use to create new workbooks.*

♦ Set up the template workbook, adding any elements you want workbooks created from this template to have. If required, activate worksheet or cell protection.

♦ **File**
Save As

♦ Open the **Save as type** list and click **Template**.

*Excel proposes the default folder for storing templates, called **Templates**.*

♦ Give the new template a name.

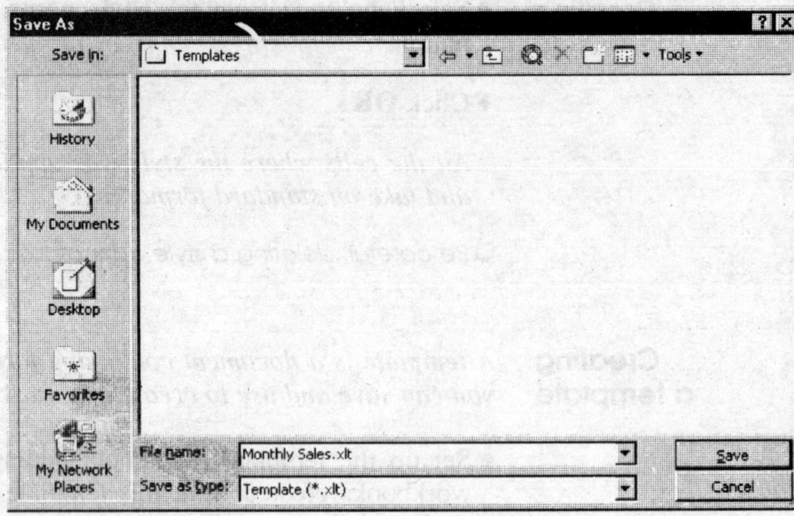

♦ If necessary, select another folder or a subfolder of **Templates**.

♦ Click the **Save** button.

❑ *Template files have an .XLT extension (but depending on your Windows settings, this extension may not be visible).*

❑ *To modify a template, proceed as for any other workbook, taking care to select **Templates** in the **Files of type** list in the **Open** dialog box. As a general rule, templates are saved in **C:\Windows\Application Data\Microsoft\Templates**.*

.... *Personal notes* ....

Creating an outline

An outline is a way of viewing or printing the main results of a table, without looking at unnecessary detail.

Automatically

If you have built your table with formulas (sums, averages and so on) you can create an automatic outline.

♦ Select the table concerned.

♦ **Data**
Group and Outline
Auto Outline

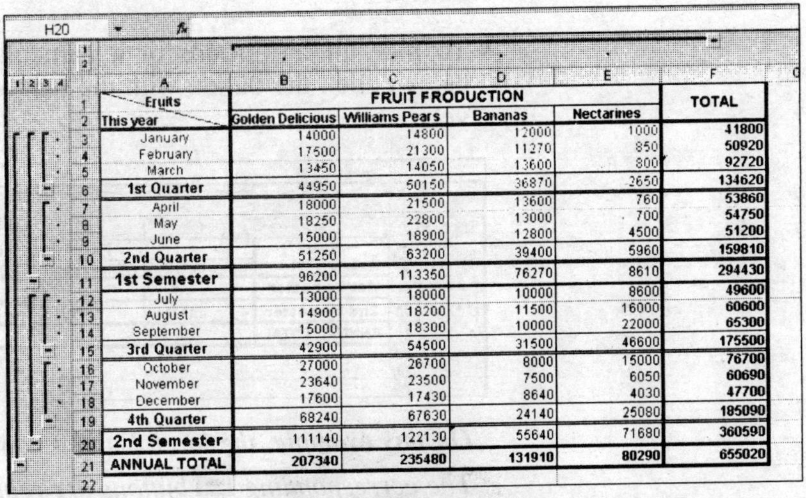

	Fruits / This year	Golden Delicious	Williams Pears	Bananas	Nectarines	TOTAL
		FRUIT FRODUCTION				
3	January	14000	14800	12000	1000	41800
4	February	17500	21300	11270	850	50920
5	March	13450	14050	13600	800	92720
6	1st Quarter	44950	50150	36870	2650	134620
7	April	18000	21500	13600	760	53860
8	May	18250	22800	13000	700	54750
9	June	15000	18900	12800	4500	51200
10	2nd Quarter	51250	63200	39400	5960	159810
11	1st Semester	96200	113350	76270	8610	294430
12	July	13000	18000	10000	8600	49600
13	August	14900	18200	11500	16000	60600
14	September	15000	18300	10000	22000	65300
15	3rd Quarter	42900	54500	31500	46600	175500
16	October	27000	26700	8000	15000	76700
17	November	23640	23500	7500	6050	60690
18	December	17600	17430	8640	4030	47700
19	4th Quarter	68240	67630	24140	25080	185090
20	2nd Semester	111140	122130	55640	71680	360590
21	ANNUAL TOTAL	207340	235480	131910	80290	655020

Buttons for managing the various levels of the outline appear to the left of and/or above the worksheet. The outline above is composed of several levels: level 1 shows the most important elements, the grand totals, level 2 shows semester totals, level 3 quarterly totals and so on. All the levels have been expanded in this outline.

Manually

♦ Select the rows (or columns) that should be included in the same level.

♦ **Data**
Group and Outline
Group

♦ To insert a column or row into the level above, select the column or row then choose **Data - Group and Outline - Group**.

♦ To remove a column or row from a group, select it then choose **Data - Group and Outline - Ungroup**.

Using an outline

♦ To hide lower-level rows or columns, click the appropriate button.

♦ To hide all the groups of a particular level and all the levels below, click the button with the number corresponding to the level.

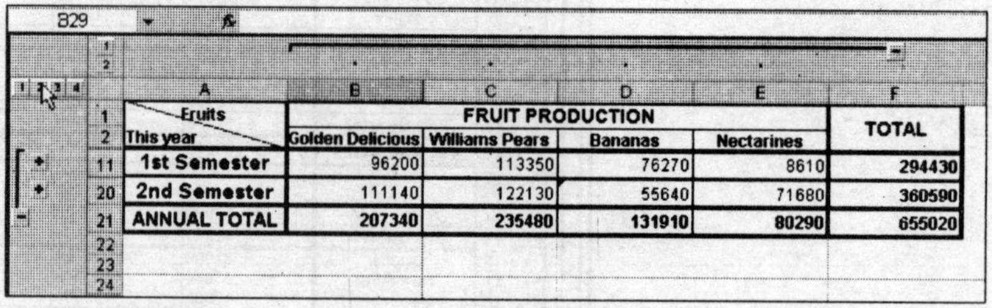

Fruits / This year	FRUIT PRODUCTION Golden Delicious	Williams Pears	Bananas	Nectarines	TOTAL
1st Semester	96200	113350	76270	8610	294430
2nd Semester	111140	122130	55640	71680	360590
ANNUAL TOTAL	207340	235480	131910	80290	655020

On this example, the level 3 and 4 rows are no longer displayed. The corresponding buttons are replaced by buttons.

♦ To make the hidden rows/columns visible again, click their buttons, or click the button with the number corresponding to the next level (for example click the **3** button to restore level **2**).

Removing an outline

♦ Activate the worksheet containing the outline.

♦ **Data**
Group and Outline
Clear Outline

Printing a sheet

♦ Activate the sheet you want to print.

♦ Click the  tool button.

Excel gives you a brief opportunity to ***Cancel*** *the print job; the data is then transmitted to Windows' Print Manager and the pages are printed.*

Setting the print options

♦ **File**
Print

♦ Ctrl P

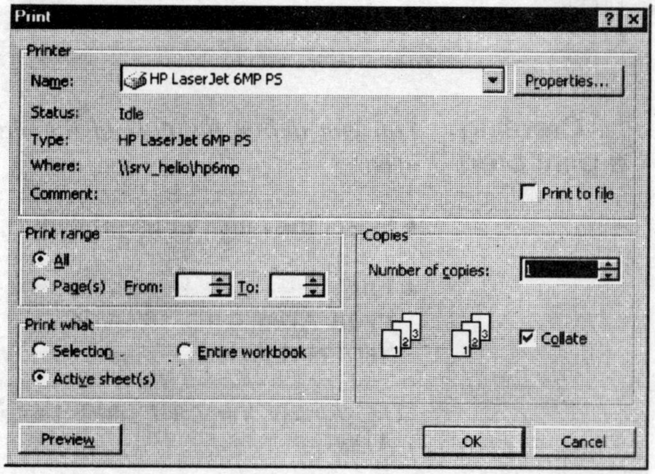

♦ The **Active sheet(s)** option, which is active by default in the **Print what** frame, prints the data from the active worksheet or any other sheets that happen to be selected.

♦ To print the range of cells selected in the active worksheet, choose the **Selection** option in the **Print what** frame.

♦ To print all the worksheets of the active workbook, select the **Entire workbook** option.

♦ To print a group of pages, click the **From** box and enter the number of the first page to print, then enter the number of the last page in the **To** box.

♦ If you wish to make several copies of your work, enter the **Number of copies** required in the **Copies** frame.

*If you are printing several copies of a multiple page document, the **Collate** option prints one complete copy of the document after another.*

❑ *You can also access the **Print** dialog box by clicking the **Print** button when you are in the **Print Preview** window.*

❑ *If what you are printing is several pages wide or high, you can choose how to print these pages by using the **Down, then over** or **Over, then down** options in the **Page order** frame in **File - Page Setup - Sheet** tab.*

Creating a print area

You can define the part of the sheet you want to print, as a print area.

♦ Select the range to be printed.

♦ **File**
Print Area
Set Print Area

❑ *To cancel the print area, use **File - Print Area - Clear Print Area**.*

Managing page breaks

Inserting a page break.

♦ Activate the cell which is going to be the first of your new page.

The page break will be inserted above and to the left of the active cell.

♦ **Insert**
Page Break

Almost instantly, a dotted line appears representing the page break.

> *To delete this type of page break, activate a cell in the next row or column and use* ***Insert - Remove Page Break****.*

Managing existing page breaks

♦ **View**
Page Break Preview

This option is also available in Print Preview: click the ***Page Break Preview*** *button.*

♦ A dialog box may appear, informing you that you can drag page breaks to move them. If you do not want this dialog box to appear every time you use the **Page Break Preview** option, activate **Do not show this dialog box again**, then click **OK**.

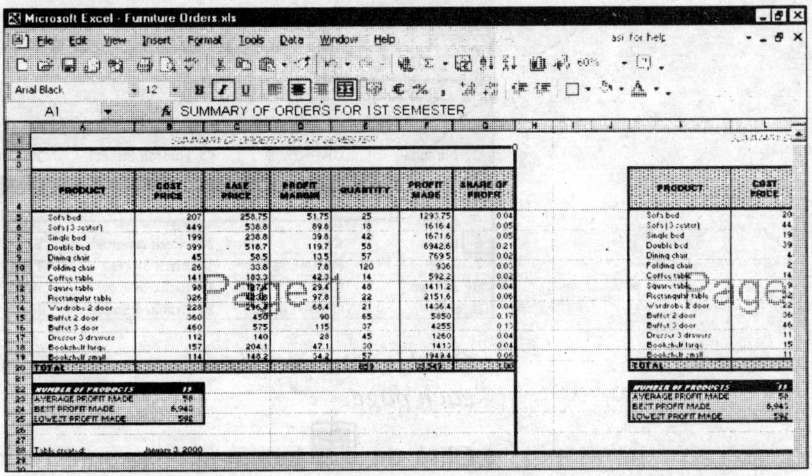

In this view, page breaks are represented by blue lines, solid lines for manual page breaks and dotted lines for automatic breaks. These lines do not stop you working normally in the sheet (you can enter and edit data, change the presentation and so on).

♦ To move a page break, drag the blue line representing it.

♦ To return to the usual view of the page, use the command **View - Normal**.

Repeating titles on each page

You can repeat certain rows and/or columns, often those containing titles, on each printed page.

♦ **File**
Page Setup
Sheet tab

♦ Activate the **Rows to repeat at top** and/or **Columns to repeat at left** option(s).

♦ Click the button to minimise the dialog box then, in the worksheet, select at least one cell from the row(s) or column(s) which you want to repeat. The pointer becomes a black arrow.

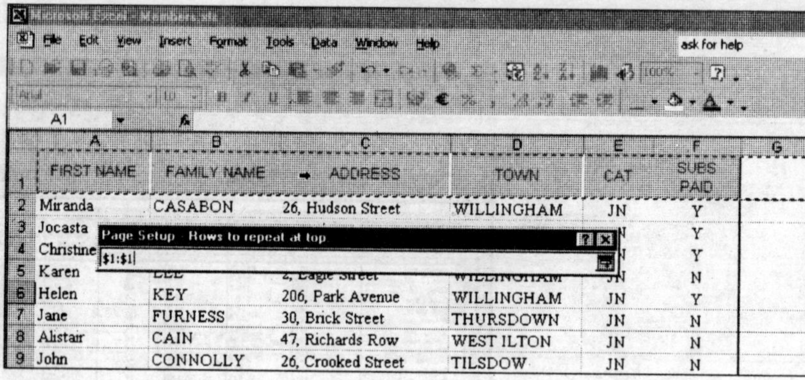

On this example, the row containing the titles will be printed on each page.

♦ Click the button to restore the dialog box.

♦ Click **OK.**

Previewing a sheet before printing

♦ **File**
Print Preview

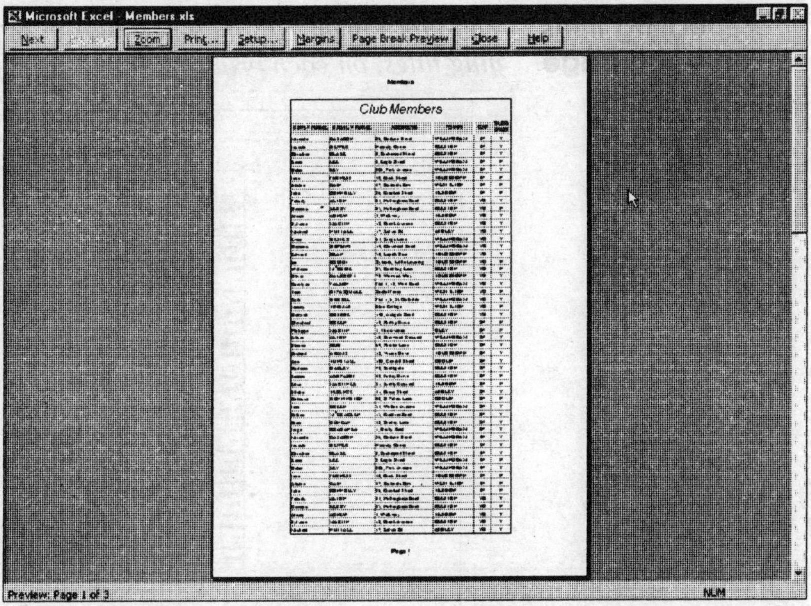

This produces a scaled-down view of the sheet as it will look when printed. On the status bar Excel displays the current page number and the total number of sheets to be printed.

- To zoom in on a preview, place the mouse pointer on the item to be magnified and click.

Before you click, the mouse pointer appears as a magnifying glass; afterwards it becomes an arrow.

- To return to the scaled-down preview, click the page again.
- To display another page use the **Next** and **Previous** buttons.

In the scaled-down preview, you can also use the vertical scroll bars to change page.

- To modify margins and column widths, click the **Margins** button.

Handles appear at various points in the window:

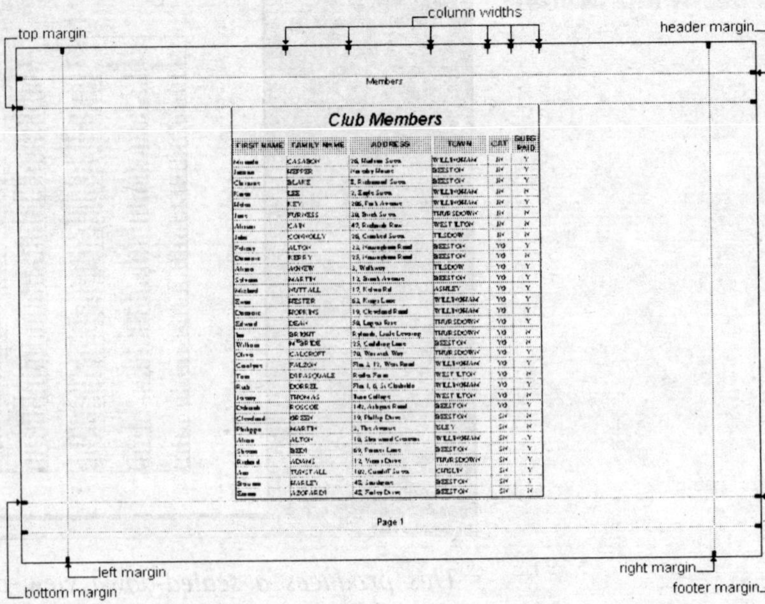

♦ Drag the appropriate handle.

♦ To start printing, click the **Print** button.

♦ Check that the printing options are correct, then enter.

♦ To leave the preview window, click the **Close** button or press Esc.

❑ *The **Page Break Preview** button makes the page breaks visible, so that you can reposition them.*

Modifying page setup options

Going into the page setup options

♦ If you are in **Print Preview**, click the **Setup** button. If you are working in the document, use:
File
Page Setup

Modifying the page orientation

♦ Go into the page setup options.

♦ If necessary, activate the **Page** tab.

♦ Choose the appropriate **Orientation**.

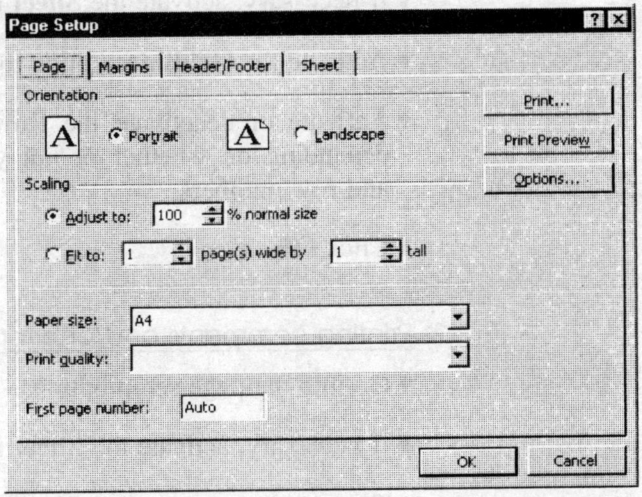

***Portrait** is also known as "Vertical" or "French" style. **Landscape** is also known as "Horizontal" or "Italian" style.*

♦ Enter.

Changing the scale of printed pages

♦ Display the page setup options.

♦ If necessary, activate the **Page** tab.

♦ In the **Adjust to** text box under **Scaling**, give the percentage of the normal scale to apply.

♦ Enter.

> *If the **Fit to** option is active under the **Page** tab in the **Page Setup** dialog box, Excel automatically adjusts the scale of printing so that the document fits the number of pages you specify.*

Printing gridlines

♦ Go into the page setup options.

♦ If necessary, activate the **Sheet** tab.

♦ Activate the **Gridlines** option to print the sheet grid.

♦ Activate or deactivate the **Row and column headings** option, depending on whether or not you want to print column letters and row numbers.

♦ Click **OK**.

Printing comments and/or error values

♦ Go into the page setup options.

♦ If necessary, activate the **Sheet** tab.

♦ To print comments as a list, with their text and the cell references, on a separate page, activate **At end of sheet** in the **Comments** text box. To print comments as they appear on the worksheet, activate the **As displayed on sheet** option (first show them on the sheet with the **View - Comments** command).

♦ To determine how error values are printed, use the options in the **Cell errors as** box: **displayed** shows them as they appear on the screen; **<blank>** shows an empty cell; **--** shows two dashes instead of the error value and **#N/A** show this symbol regardless of the cell's real error value.

Defining margins and position on the page

♦ Go into the page setup options.

♦ If necessary, activate the **Margins** tab.

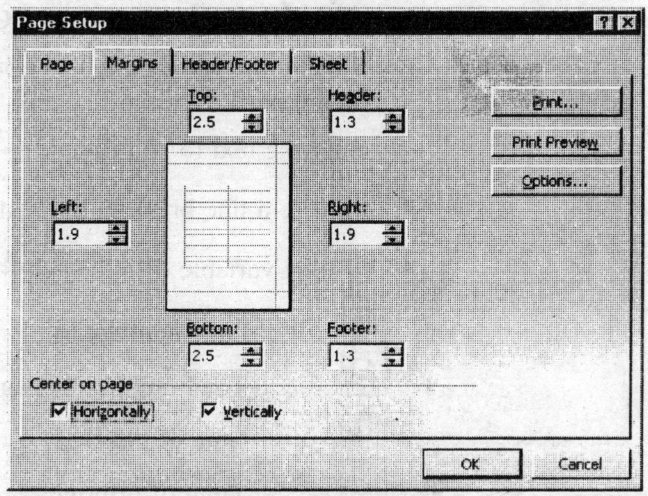

♦ Indicate the width of the various margins in the corresponding text boxes. The **Header** and **Footer** options determine the position of the header and footer in the top and bottom margins.

♦ Centre the table either **Horizontally** or **Vertically** on the page.

♦ Enter.

Creating headers and footers

The header is printed at the top of each page and the footer at the bottom of each page.

♦ Go into the page setup options.

♦ If necessary, activate the **Header/Footer** tab.

*You could also use the **View - Header and Footer** command.*

♦ If you wish, choose a pre-set **Header** and/or **Footer** from the appropriate list.

Headers and footers chosen from the list are automatically centred at the top/bottom of the page.

- If you prefer, create your own header and footer. To do this:
  - click the **Custom Header** or **Custom Footer** button.
  - activate the text box which corresponds to the required position on the page.
  - enter the text to be printed.
- To create a line break in the text, press Enter.
- To insert variable details click the appropriate buttons.

Page number

Total number of pages

Date of printing

Time of printing

Workbook name and file path

Name of the workbook

Name of the sheet

Picture

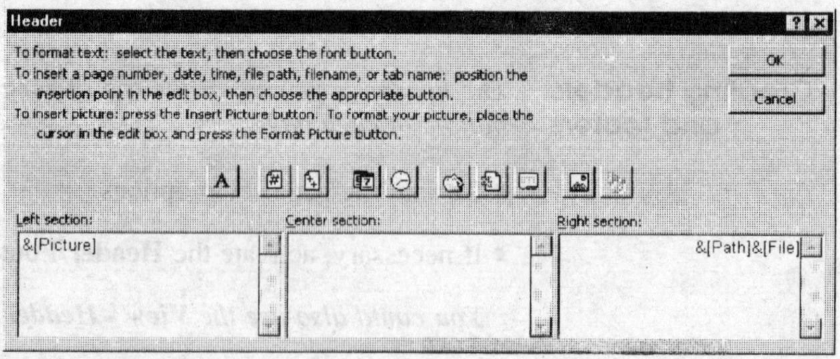

Each variable corresponds to a code placed within square brackets.

- If you wish, format the variable or the text entered by selecting that element and clicking the button.
- To format an inserted picture, click in that section and click the button.
- Click **OK**.

  Excel displays a preview of the header or footer as it will look in print.

- When you have finished defining your header and footer, click **OK**.

Using views *A view is a way of saving certain settings, such as a print area, page setup, filter settings or hidden rows/columns. When you switch to a view, the saved options are activated automatically.*

Creating a view

- Prepare the sheet for printing (page setup, print area, hiding columns, etc).
- **View**
  Custom Views
  Add
- Enter the name of the view being created.
- Indicate whether the view should include the **Print settings** and **Hidden rows, columns and filter settings.**

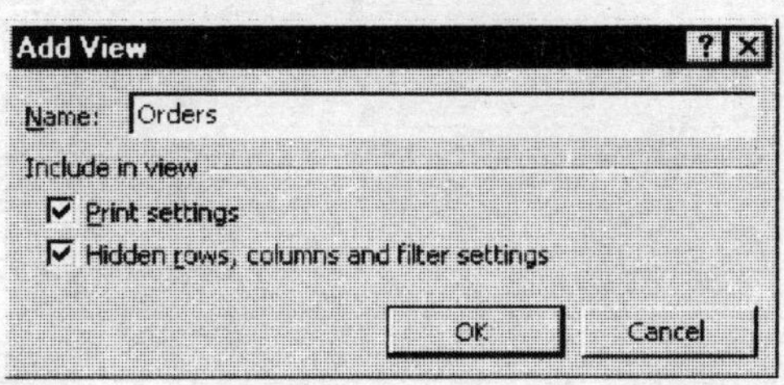

♦ Enter.

Using a view

♦ **View**
Custom Views

♦ Click the name of the view that you want to activate.

♦ Click **Show**.

❑ *The **Delete** button removes the view currently selected in the **Views** list.*

.... *Personal notes* ....

Creating a chart

♦ If the data needed for the chart is contained in a continuous block of cells, select that range.

♦ If the data for the chart is in several different ranges, select the nonadjacent ranges in the usual way (with Ctrl-clicks). So that Excel can analyse the data correctly, make sure the cell ranges selected form a coherent set each time, including blank cells if necessary.

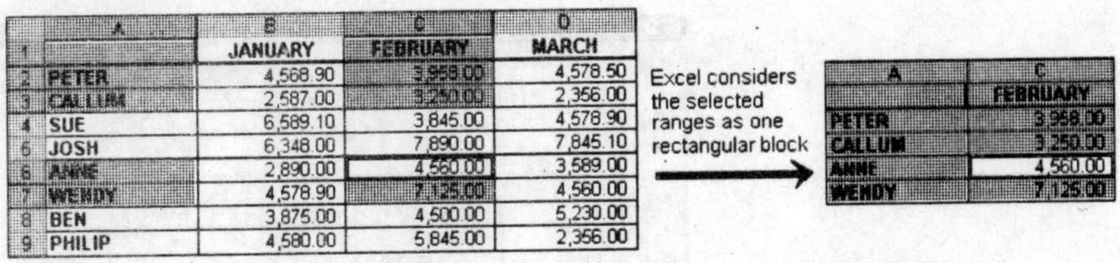

	A	B	C	D
1		JANUARY	FEBRUARY	MARCH
2	PETER	4,568.90	3,958.00	4,578.50
3	CALLUM	2,587.00	3,250.00	2,356.00
4	SUE	6,589.10	3,845.00	4,578.90
5	JOSH	6,348.00	7,890.00	7,845.10
6	ANNE	2,890.00	4,560.00	3,589.00
7	WENDY	4,578.90	7,125.00	4,560.00
8	BEN	3,875.00	4,500.00	5,230.00
9	PHILIP	4,580.00	5,845.00	2,356.00

A	C
	FEBRUARY
PETER	3,958.00
CALLUM	3,250.00
ANNE	4,560.00
WENDY	7,125.00

In the example above, the blank cell in the top left corner was included to ensure a symmetrical selection.

♦ **Insert**
Chart

♦ Select the **Chart type** and then the **Chart sub-type**.

♦ Click the **Next** button.

♦ Check the references of the selected cells in the **Data range** box and if necessary, modify the selection using the button.
Indicate whether the series are in rows or columns (**Rows** or **Columns** option).
If the chart shown does not resemble the required chart, click the **Series** tab to check the references of each series. To do that, select a **Series** in the list then check, and modify if required, its **Name** and the **Values** of the cells that make up that series. You can also verify and change, the **Category (X) axis labels**.

♦ Click **Next**.

♦ Customise your chart by giving the various chart titles on the **Titles** page. At this stage in the wizard, you can also select options from the other tabs (cf. below).

♦ Click **Next.**

♦ To create the chart on a separate chart sheet, activate the **As new sheet** option and enter the name of the sheet you are creating. Otherwise, leave the **As object in** option active and select the sheet in which to insert the chart.

♦ Click **Finish.**

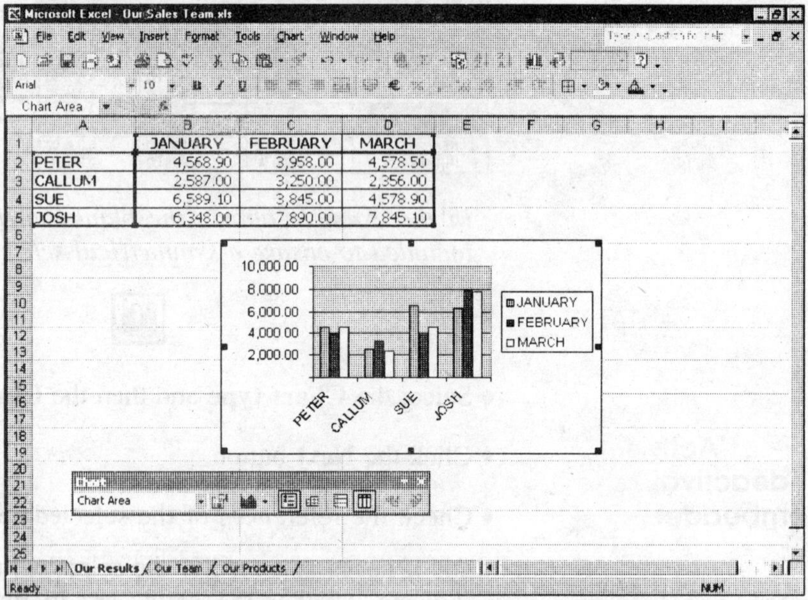

In the example above, the chart has been inserted as an object in the active worksheet.

When you insert a chart as an object in the active sheet, it appears in the workspace. It is surrounded by black squares (handles) to show it is selected.

When you select an embedded chart made from data adjacent to it on the worksheet, coloured rectangles appear around certain cell ranges. These highlight the data on the sheet that is used in the chart:

- *data series are enclosed in a green rectangle,*
- *categories are enclosed in a purple rectangle,*
- *data points are enclosed in a blue rectangle.*

♦ If necessary, move the chart as you would move any other drawing object: point to one of its edges and drag it. You can also resize the chart by dragging one of the handles.

❑ *A chart created on a worksheet is known as an **embedded chart**: it belongs to the family of drawing objects.*

❑ *In a 2D chart, each series can contain up to 32000 points and in a 3D chart, up to 4000.*

❑ *Unless you alter the default, a chart and its source data are linked and any changes to the data are carried over into the chart.*

Activating/ deactivating an embedded chart

♦ To activate an embedded chart click it once to select the whole chart object, or to select one of the chart items.

*The **Data** menu is replaced by the **Chart** menu. The chart toolbar may appear.*

♦ To deactivate an embedded chart, click a cell in the sheet, outside the chart.

♦ To display an embedded chart in a window, select it then use **View - Chart Window**. To deactivate the chart, close the window.

Selecting objects in the charts

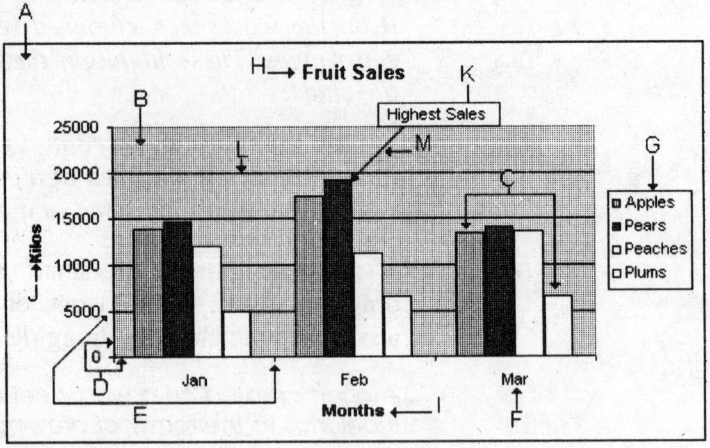

	object	to select	contents
A	Chart area	click in the chart but not in any object	all the chart object
B	Plot area	click in the plot area but not in any object	axes and data markers
C	Point	click the series then click the point.	each value in a series
	Series	click one of the data markers in the series	all the points which constitute a data series.
D	Value Axis Category axis	click one of the tick mark labels	
E	Tick marks	no selection	lines which divide up the axes
F	Tick mark labels		texts attached to tick marks

G	Legend	click the object	shows the names of the series represented in the chart and identifies the symbol or colour used for the data markers.
H	Chart title		attached text
I	Axis title		attached text
J	Axis title		attached text
K	Text boxes		unattached text
L	Gridlines	click one of the lines	lines crossing the plot area to make it easier to read the chart
M	Arrow	click the object	

❑ *When you point to a chart object, its name and if appropriate, its value appear in a ScreenTip, providing the **Show names** and **Show values** options are active in the **Options** dialog box (**Tools - Options - Chart** tab).*

❑ *To access a dialog box in which you can format a chart object, select the object then use the first command in the **Format** menu. This command name changes depending on the object. You can also double-click the selected item.*

> *Another way to select a chart object is to open the list box on the **Chart** toolbar and click its name.*

Setting up a chart for printing

♦ If you are working on an embedded chart, activate it.

♦ **File**
Page Setup

*The worksheet options are inaccessible when you are dealing with a chart. The **Sheet** tab has disappeared, replaced by a new tab: **Chart**.*

- As well as modifying the usual options, you can adjust the **Printed Chart Size** on the **Chart** tab:

Use full page	Distorts the proportions of the chart so that it fills the whole page.
Scale to fit page	Increases the size of the chart as much as the page allows, without distorting its proportions.
Custom	Prints a chart the same size as the chart on the screen.

- Click **OK**.
- Start printing.

Personal notes

Changing the chart type

♦ If necessary, activate the chart.

♦ **Chart**
Chart Type

♦ Choose the chart type.

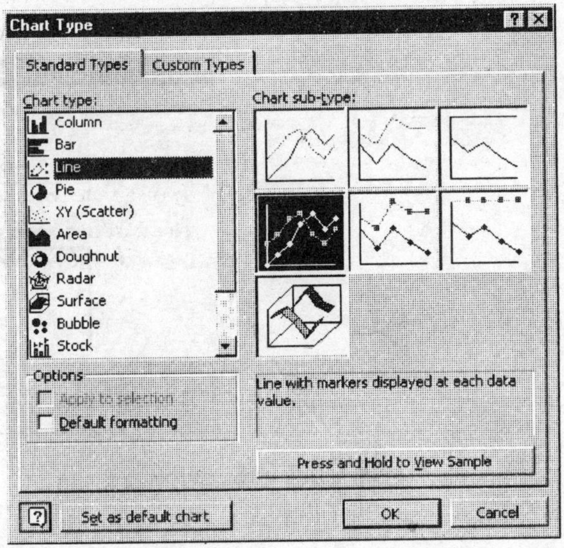

♦ Double-click the sub-type you prefer.

❑ *You can use the*  *button on the **Chart** toolbar to change the chart type but not to choose from the various sub-types.*

❑ *If you need to redefine one or more of the chart's series, take the **Source Data** option in the **Chart** menu.*

> *All the options for managing the chart can be found in **Chart - Chart Options**.*

Creating custom charts

♦ Select the chart that will be used as a model.

♦ **Chart**
Chart Type

- ♦ Activate the **Custom Types** tab, then the **User-defined** option in the **Select from** list.
- ♦ Click **Add**.
- ♦ Fill in your chart **Name** and **Description** in the corresponding text boxes.

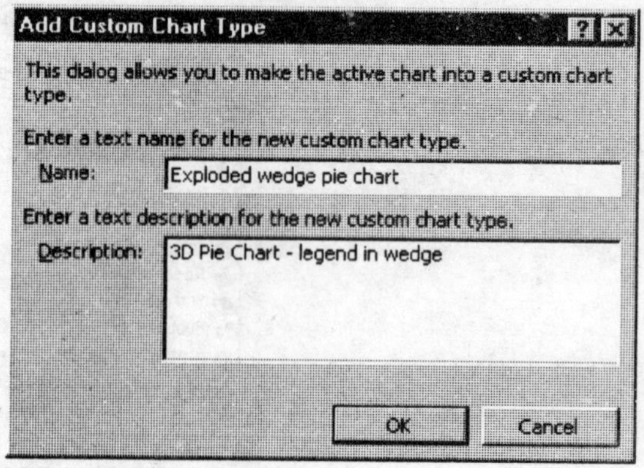

- ♦ Click **OK** twice.

Using a custom chart

- ♦ Select the range of data that you want to represent as a chart.
- ♦ **Insert Chart** 
- ♦ Click the **Custom Types** tab then activate the **User-defined** option in the **Select from** frame.
- ♦ Choose the required **Chart Type** from the list.
- ♦ Click **Next**.
- ♦ If necessary, select, or enter the range of data that you want the chart to represent in the **Data Range** box then specify if the data is in **Rows** or **Columns**.
- ♦ Click **Next**.

♦ In the **Title** tab, specify your **Chart Title** in the corresponding text box.

♦ Click **Next**.

♦ Choose where and how the chart will be placed and click **Finish**.

❑ *Using a custom chart as a model ensures that any formatting does not have to be done again.*

Displaying the data table

Under the chart, you can display the table of data on which it is based:

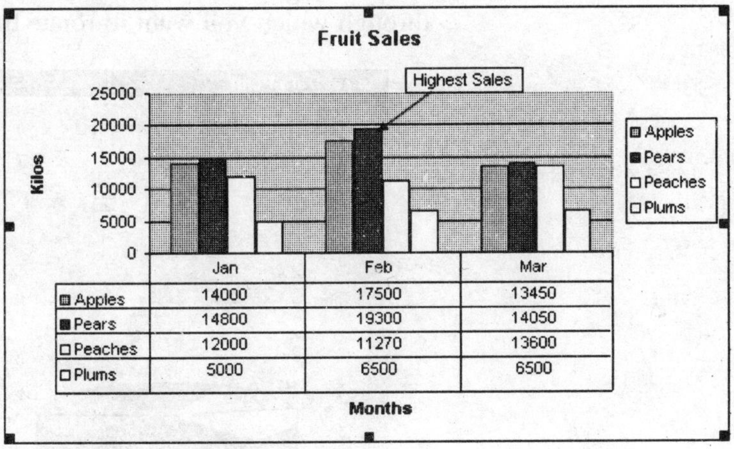

♦ Activate the chart, if necessary.

♦ **Chart**
Chart Options
Data Table tab

♦ Activate the **Show data table** option.

♦ If you wish, activate the **Show legend keys** option.

♦ Click **OK**.

You can also click the [tool button] tool button on the **Chart** toolbar.

Managing pie charts

Rotating a pie chart

♦ Select the series.

♦ **Format**
Selected Data Series
Options tab

♦ Ctrl 1

♦ In the **Angle of first slice** box enter the number of **Degrees** through which you want to rotate the chart.

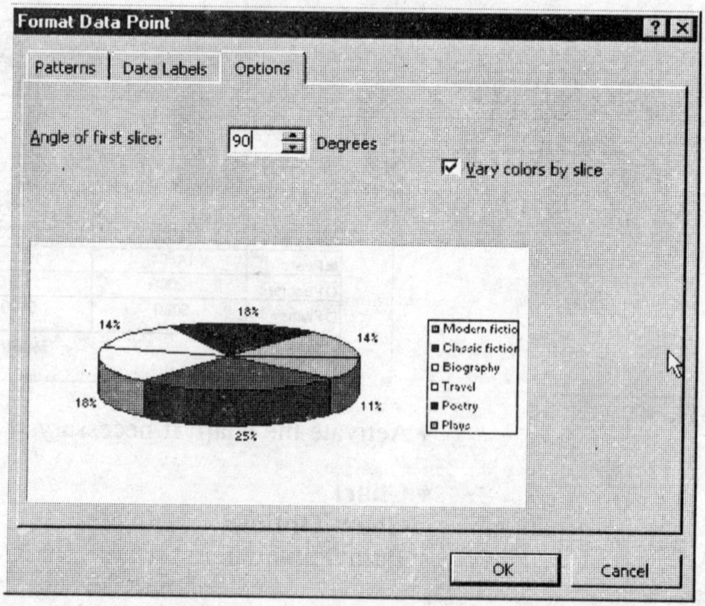

It is always the angle of the first slice that determines the rotation of a chart. Bear in mind that a full-circle rotation is 360°.

♦ Click **OK**.

Pulling out a slice

♦ Select the slice you want to pulling out.

♦ Drag it away from the rest.

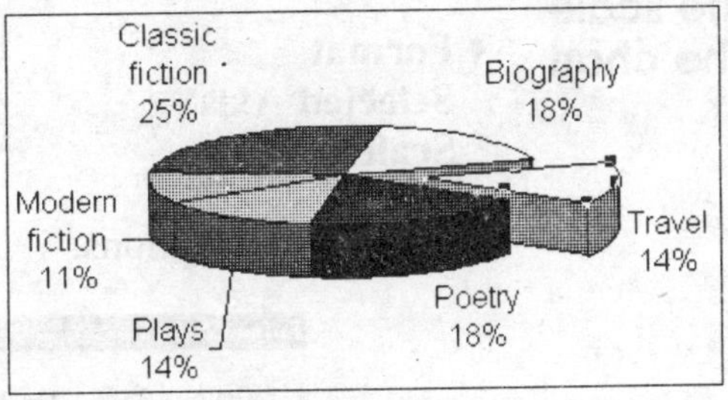

Adding gridlines to a chart

♦ Activate the chart, if necessary.

♦ **Chart**
Chart Options
Gridlines tab

♦ To add vertical gridlines to the chart, activate the options in the **Category (X) axis** frame.

♦ To add horizontal gridlines, use the options under **Value (Y) axis.**

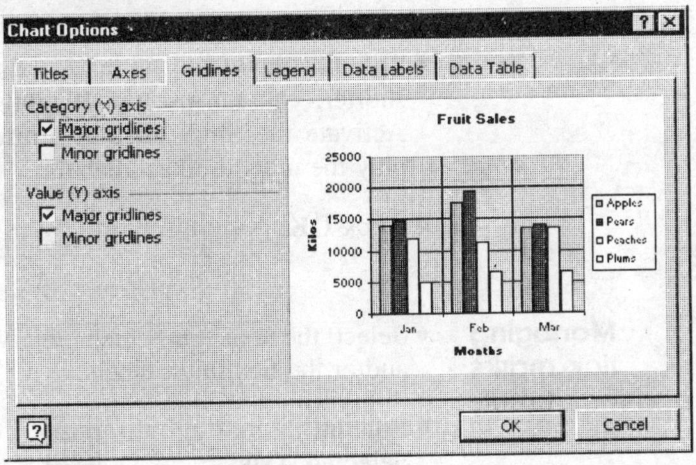

♦ Click **OK**.

Changing the scale of the chart

♦ Select the value axis.

♦ **Format**
Selected Axis
Scale tab ♦ Ctrl 1

♦ Set the scale options.

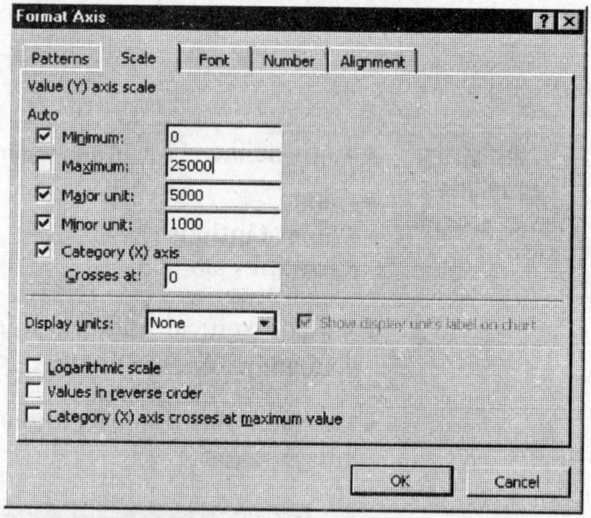

♦ To make the values on the Y-axis more readable by making them shorter, you can use the **Display units** list to modify their unit. Activate the **Show display units label on chart** option to display the units used as a label.

♦ Click **OK**.

Managing tick marks and their labels

♦ Select the axis on which you want to modify the tick marks and/or the tick mark labels.

♦ **Format**
Selected Axis ♦ Ctrl 1

♦ Use the **Font** and **Number** tabs to define the format of text and numbers in the labels.

♦ Define the position of the labels relative to the axis, using the options under the **Patterns** tab.

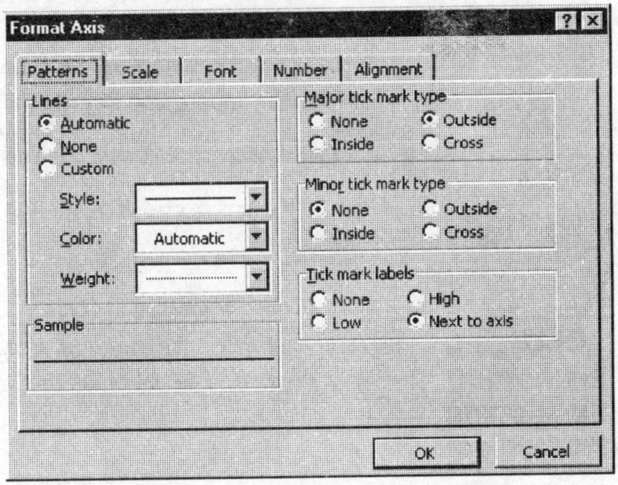

♦ On the **Alignment** page, determine the orientation of the text in the labels.

♦ Click **OK**.

❑ *With the*  *and*  *buttons on the* ***Chart*** *toolbar you can also change the orientation of the text in the labels.*

Modifying the content of the category labels

♦ Activate the chart, if necessary.

♦ **Chart**
Source Data
Series tab

♦ Change the contents of the **Category (X) labels** box.

♦ Click **OK**.

❑ *You could also select the first series in the chart, then edit the second argument of the SERIES() function, on the formula bar.*

Formatting a chart object's characters

♦ Select the drawing object which contains the text.

♦ Use the various tool buttons on the **Formatting** toolbar or, if these do not correspond to your needs, open the **Format [object]** dialog box using the **Format - [name of object]** command or the tool button and use the formatting options provided.

❑ *The format of numerical values in the chart is defined in the same way.*

Changing the border/ colour/shading of a chart object

In this example, the bars of the first series in the chart are filled with a picture. The bars in the second series are filled with a pattern.

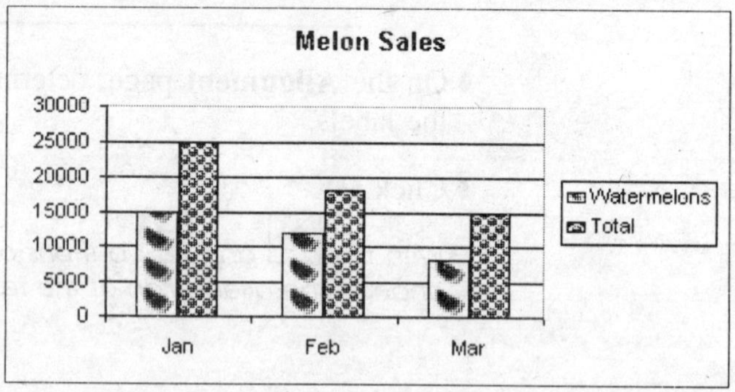

♦ Select the element you want to modify.

♦ **Format Selected[object]**	double-click the object.	♦ Ctrl 1

For unattached text, double-click one of the selection borders, which will open the ***Format "name of object"*** *dialog box.*

♦ If necessary, activate the **Patterns** tab.

♦ Use the various **Border** options to make the borders of your choice.

*Check the resulting effect in the **Sample** box.*

♦ Select a background colour for the item in the **Area** frame. To apply shading, a pattern or a texture to the item, click the **Fill Effects** button.

♦ To apply a gradient, first choose the gradient **Colors** and define the style of gradient, or choose to use a **Preset** gradient and select one from the list:

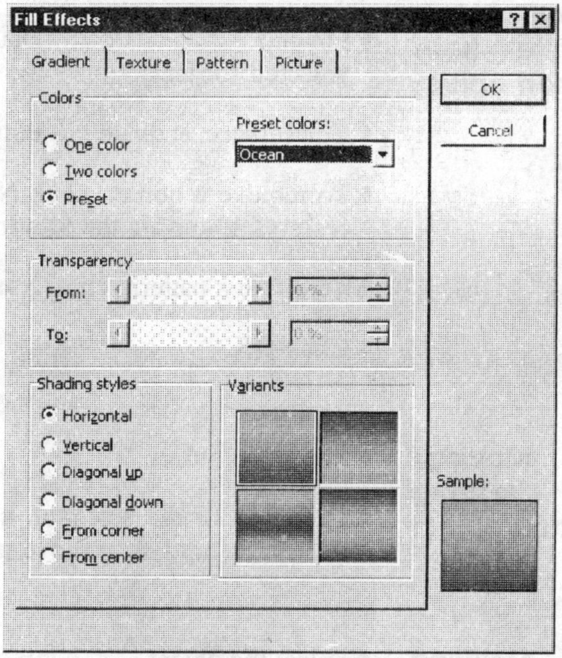

♦ To apply a texture, choose from the options under the **Texture** tab.

♦ If you prefer to fill the object with a pattern, click the **Pattern** tab then select a **Background** colour and a colour for the pattern (**Foreground**).

♦ To fill the object with a picture, click the **Picture** tab then click the **Select Picture** button to select the file which contains the picture; modify the **Format** options if required.

♦ Enter.

You can apply colour to an object by selecting that object then using the list on the [fill colour] tool button.

Deleting borders and/or a pattern from a chart object

♦ Select the object concerned.

♦ **Format Selected [object]**	Double-click the object	♦ Ctrl 1

♦ If necessary, activate the **Patterns** tab.

♦ To remove a border, click **None** in the **Border** frame and if necessary, deactivate the **Shadow** option.

♦ To delete a pattern, click **None** in the **Area** frame.

♦ Click **OK**.

Moving/ resizing a chart object

♦ Select the object.

♦ Drag one of the selection handles to change its dimensions, or one of the borders to move it.

Deleting a chart object

♦ Select the object.

Check the name of the object on the formula bar.

♦ **Edit Clear All**	♦ Del

Adding text to a chart

Adding a title

♦ **Chart**
Chart Options
Titles tab

♦ Give the various titles you need in the chart.

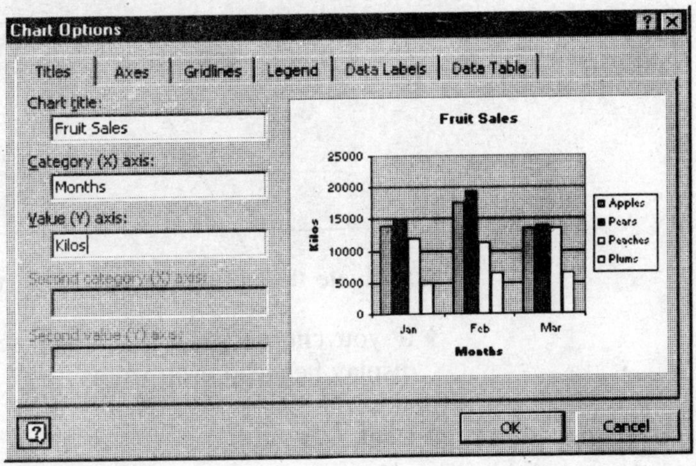

♦ Click **OK**.

Adding a text linked to a point in a series

♦ Select the point or series concerned.

♦ **Format**
Selected Data
or **Selected Data Series**

♦ Ctrl 1

♦ If necessary, activate the **Data Labels** tab.

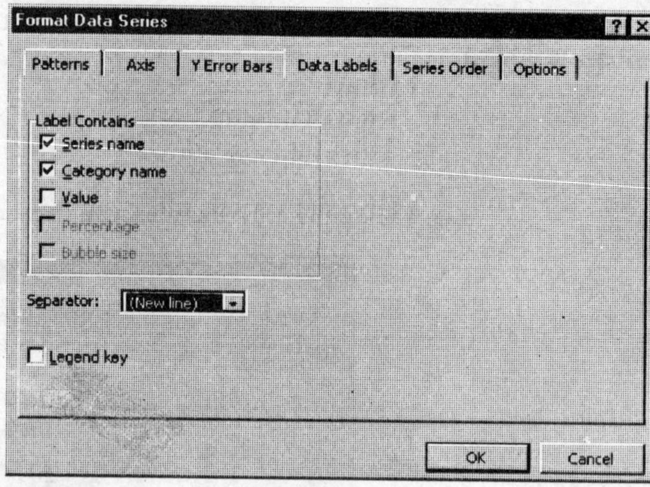

♦ Activate the options of your choice.

♦ If you choose several options, select the type of **Separator** to display between each value.

♦ Click **OK**.

Adding unattached text (text box)

♦ Make sure that you have not selected any text items.

♦ Enter the text required.

The text appears on the formula bar.

♦ Press [Enter].

This creates a drawing object called Text Box. This appears in the middle of the chart and you can drag it into place, like any drawing object.

> *When working with unattached text, press [Ctrl][Enter] each time you wish to start a new line.*

Inserting text from a worksheet

♦ Make sure that you have not selected any object in the chart containing text.

♦ Type =

♦ Select the cell(s) containing the text to be inserted.

♦ Enter.

♦ Drag the text box to where you want it.

❑ *Each time the contents of the cells from the worksheet change, this text will be updated.*

Modifying an item of text

♦ Select the object to be modified (if it is a text box, you do not need to select it).

♦ Click inside the text.

The insertion point appears.

♦ Make the necessary changes.

♦ Finish by pressing Esc.

❑ *While modifying text, use* Enter *to create a new line.*

Managing the legend

♦ If necessary, activate the chart.

♦ **Chart**
Chart Options
Legend tab

♦ To display or hide the legend, activate or deactivate the **Show legend** option.

♦ If required, choose the legend's **Placement** (position) in relation to the chart.

♦ Click **OK**.

❑ *When moved to the top or the bottom of the chart, the legend is displayed horizontally.*

❑ *You can also show or hide the legend with the*  *tool button on the* ***Chart*** *toolbar.*

> *The legend can also be dragged to its new position.*

Linking points in a chart

This option is only available for line charts.

♦ Select a series.

♦ **Format**
Selected Data Series
Options tab

♦ Ctrl 1

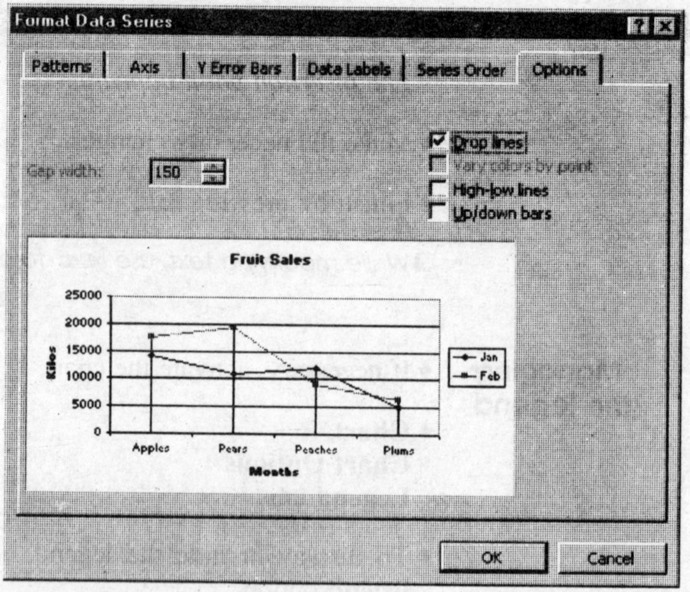

♦ Choose one of these types:

Drop lines the line starts from the highest point and finishes on the category axis.

High-low lines the line links the highest and the lowest value for each category.

Up-down bars the points are linked by bars instead of lines.

♦ Click **OK**.

Changing the depth of a 3D chart

♦ Select a series in the chart.

♦ **Format**
Selected Data Series
Options tab

♦ Ctrl 1

♦ Activate the **Chart depth** box and enter the percentage of depth in relation to width.

♦ Click **OK**.

Changing the display options for a 3D chart

♦ **Chart**
3-D View

♦ Enter your own values in the **Elevation**, **Propertive** and **Rotation** boxes or click the arrows to increase/decrease the values given.

♦ Click **Default** to return to the values proposed by Excel.

♦ Enter, or cancel by clicking **Close**.

Adding a data series to an embedded chart

<u>First method</u>

This can only be used when the series to be added is next to the series already included in the chart.

♦ Select the chart area.

On the worksheet, the cells containing the data series are enclosed in a green rectangle.

♦ Drag the handle of the green rectangle until it has encompassed the values of the new series.

Second method

♦ Select the cells containing the values corresponding to the series.

♦ Drag the selection onto the chart.

❑ *This method is very quick but can only be used for embedded charts when the source data is close by. If the chart is in a chart sheet, you can copy the source data using the clipboard.*

Third method

♦ If necessary, activate the chart.

♦ **Chart**
Source Data
Series tab

♦ Click the **Add** button.

*Excel creates a new series called **Series<n>**.*

♦ Click the **Name** box and give the name of the new series.

♦ Click the **Values** box, click the button and in the worksheet, select the cells containing the values for the new series. Click to restore the dialog box.

♦ Click **OK**.

❑ *This command can also be used to modify the cell references associated with a series.*

❑ *You can also use the **Chart - Add Data** command.*

❑ *To add a series or category to a chart sheet, select the cells that correspond to the data you wish to add, copy them with [copy icon] then activate the chart sheet and paste the cells with [paste icon].*

Modifying the chart type for a data series

♦ Select the series concerned.

♦ **Chart**
Chart Type

♦ Select the required **Chart type** and **Chart sub-type**.

♦ Make sure the **Apply to selection** option is active.

♦ Click **OK**.

♦ If you wish, modify the presentation of this series by making sure the series is still selected and using **Format - Selected Data Series.**

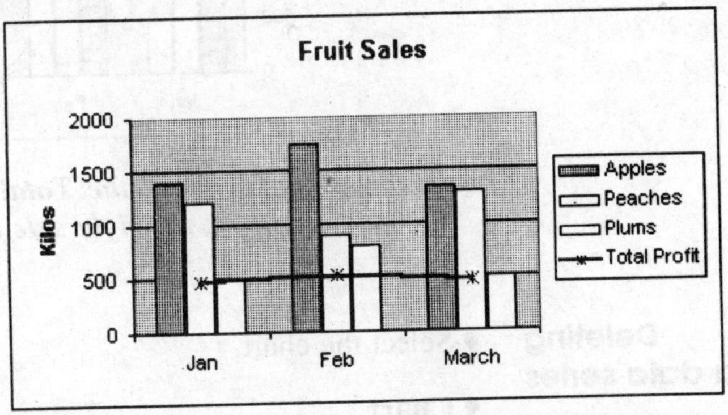

*In the example above, a **Line** chart type has been applied to the **Total Profit** series.*

Adding a secondary axis

If the values of some series vary greatly or if the series represent different types of data (such as sales and percentages) you can plot one or more series on a secondary axis.

♦ Select the series concerned.

♦ **Format**
Selected Data Series
Axis tab

♦ Activate the **Secondary axis** option.

♦ Click **OK**.

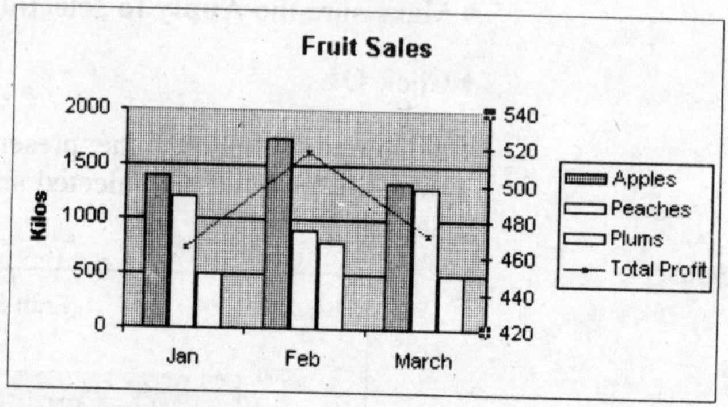

*In the example above the **Total Profit** series is attached to the secondary axis on the right side of the chart.*

Deleting a data series

♦ Select the chart.

♦ **Chart**
Source Data
Series tab

♦ In the **Series** list, select the series you want to delete.

♦ Click the **Remove** button.

♦ Click **OK**.

> *You can also delete a data series by clicking it in the chart then pressing the* Del *key.*

Changing the order of the series

- Select one of the series on the chart.
- **Format**
  Selected Data Series
  Series Order tab
- Click the series you wish to move in the **Series order** frame and click the **Move Up** or **Move Down** button as appropriate.
- Click **OK.**

❑ *When a series is selected, the SERIES() function appears in the formula bar. The last argument in this function refers to the place of that series in the order.*

Adding/deleting a category

Either the mouse or the menus can be used to add or delete a category in an embedded chart.

- Select the chart area.
- To add a new category and its corresponding data points, drag the handle of the purple rectangle until it encompasses the cells containing the new category. To delete a category, reduce the rectangle so the data in question is excluded from it.

❑ *This method can only be used in the case of an embedded chart, with the source data close by.*

❑ *If the category you wish to add is not adjacent to the existing categories, you can select the corresponding cells and drag them into the chart.*

- Select the chart area.
- **Chart**
  Add Data

♦ In the **Range** text box, give the references of the data you want to add then click **OK**.

*The **Paste Special** dialog box may appear.*

♦ If this occurs, activate the **New point(s)** option. In the **Values (Y) in** frame, indicate whether the series are in rows or columns. Activate the **Categories (X Labels) in First Column** option if the selected range contains category labels.

♦ Click **OK**.

Unlinking a chart and the worksheet

♦ For each data series:

– Select the series,

– select everything that appears in the formula bar,

– press F9,

– enter.

❑ *The arguments in the SERIES() function no longer refer to the cells in the worksheet: the chart data will no longer be updated automatically.*

Drawing an object

♦ Display the **Drawing** toolbar by clicking the tool button.

♦ Click the button that corresponds to the shape you wish to draw or click the **AutoShapes** button and choose one of the shapes given in the sub-menus.

♦ Drag to draw the shape on the workspace. Hold down the Alt key as you drag to align the object to the cell grid.

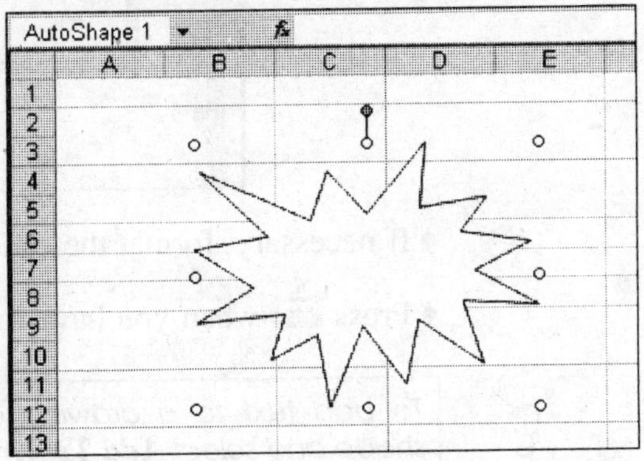

The name of the object drawn appears on the left of the formula bar.

Hold down the Shift key as you draw if you wish to make an evenly-proportioned square, circle or arc, or a perfectly horizontal, vertical or diagonal line.

Creating a text box

A text box is a drawing object that is designed to contain text.

♦ Click the tool button on the **Drawing** toolbar.

♦ Drag to draw the text box or click the place you wish to start entering the text. Use the Alt key as you drag if you wish to align the text box to the cell grid.

Once the text box has been created, an insertion point appears inside it.

♦ Enter your text, without worrying about line breaks. Use the [Enter] key when you want to start a new paragraph.

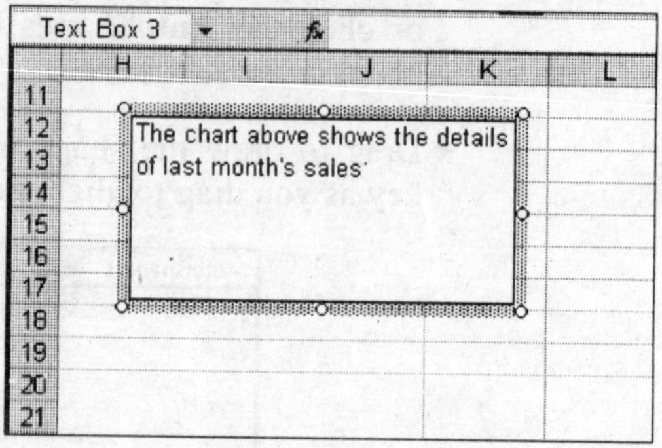

♦ If necessary, format the characters entered.

♦ Press [Esc] when you have finished your text.

> *To add text to a drawing or AutoShape, right-click the drawn shape and select **Add Text**.*

Inserting a picture, a sound or a video clip

Finding and inserting a picture, a sound or a video clip

♦ If necessary, use the **Insert - Picture - Clip Art** command to display the **Insert Clip Art** task pane.

*The **Add Clips to Organizer** dialog box may appear on the screen:*

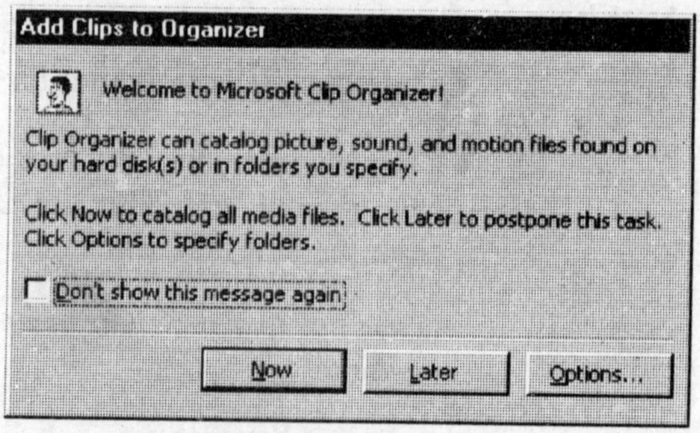

♦ If the dialog box illustrated above appears, click the **Now** button if you want to add the image, audio and video files from your hard disk into the Clip Organizer. If you do not want to do that just yet, click the **Later** button.

♦ Enter one or more key words in the **Search text** box.

♦ To define where the search should be carried out, open the **Search in** list and make a choice, following these guidelines: the plus (+) sign expands the hierarchy while the minus (-) sign collapses it. Click a check box to select (or deselect) the corresponding category: double-clicking selects (or deselects) that category and all its subcategories.

*The **Office Collections** category and its subcategories correspond to the image, sound and video elements installed with Office. The **Web Collections** category provides you with elements found on the Web (or more precisely on the Microsoft site). Excel will only take this category into account if you have an open Internet connection.*

♦ To limit the type of items being searched for (**Clip Art**, **Photographs**, **Movies** or **Sounds**), open the **Results should be** list and deselect any elements that should be excluded from the search. You can also limit the search to certain file types. To do this, click the plus (+) sign on the type of element concerned and deselect any file types that should not be included in the search.

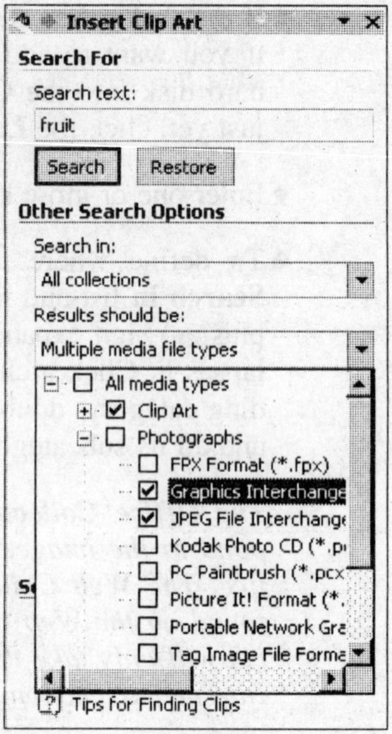

♦ Click the **Search** button.

*If you want to interrupt the search, click the **Stop** button that appears near the bottom of the pane.*

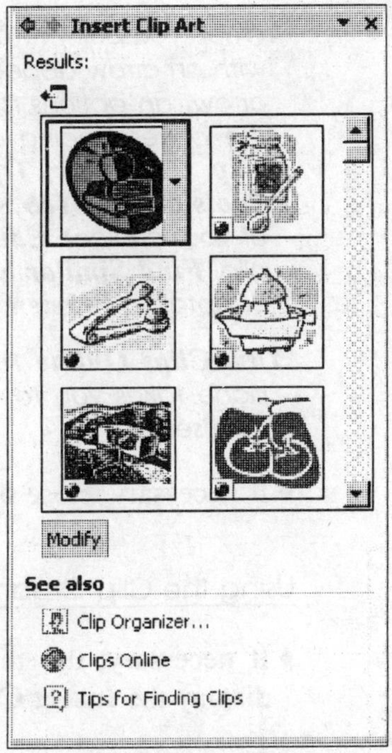

The  *icon at the bottom left of some items indicates it was found on the Web. This will only occur if you have included the Web as one of your search areas and your Internet connection is open.*

- When the search is finished or if you click the **Stop** button, the **Modify** button appears, which you can use to set up a new search.

- To insert one of the items found into your active document, select the cell where you wish to put the item then click the clip in the **Insert Clip Art** task pane.

❑ *When you point to an item in the **Insert Clip Art** task pane, a bar with an arrow appears on the right side of the clip. If you click the arrow, an options menu appears, which you can use to perform the corresponding action, such as **Copy** the item, **Delete from Clip Organizer**, **Open Clip In** another application, activate **Tools on the Web**, **Copy to Collection** (to copy to the collection of your choice), **Edit Keywords** that may be associated with that clip, **Find Similar Style** (to base the search on that style of clip) or obtain a **Preview** or the **Properties** of that clip.*

❑ *The **Clips Online** link at the bottom of the **Insert Clip Art** task pane takes you to the Microsoft site where you can make your own search.*

♦ If necessary, close the task pane by clicking its ☒ button.

Using the Clip Organizer

♦ If necessary, use the **Insert - Picture - Clip Art** command to display the **Insert Clip Art** task pane.

♦ The **Add Clips to Organizer** dialog box may appear on the screen:

♦ Click the **Now** button if you want to add the image, audio and video files from your hard disk into the Clip Organizer. If you do not want to do that just yet, click the **Later** button.

♦ Click the **Clip Organizer** link at the bottom of the task pane.

♦ To browse the collections of image sound or video items available in Office, expand the **Office Collections** hierarchy (click the + sign) then click the subcategory of your choice to display its contents in the right half of the window.

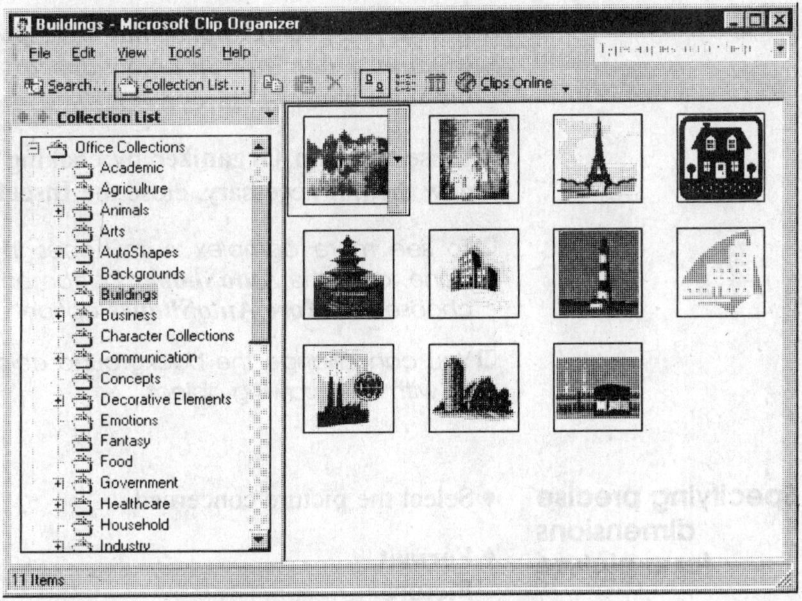

♦ In the **My Collections** collection, you can create and manage your own custom subcollections:

– To create a new collection within **My Collections**, select **My Collections** then use the **File - New Collection** command and enter the new collection's **Name**. Decide where to store this new collection then click **OK**.

– To copy a picture, sound or video clip into a subcollection of **My Collections**, look for the item in the **Office Collections** or **Web Collections** (if you are connected to the Internet) then drag the item from the right pane into the required subcollection in the left pane.

♦ You can add a picture, sound or video clip to your document from the **Microsoft Clip Organizer** window. To do this, drag the item from the right pane of the **Clip Organizer** window onto the active document. The **Clip Organizer** window disappears but is still open in the background; you can reactivate it by clicking its link on the task pane.

*If you point to a clip in the right pane of the **Clip Organizer** window, a bar with an arrow appears on the clip; this contains the same menu of options described above.*

- Close the **Clip Organizer** by clicking the button on its window then, if necessary, close the **Insert Clip Art** task pane.

❑ *To see more complex AutoShapes in the **Insert Clip Art** task pane, click the **AutoShapes** button on the **Drawing** toolbar and choose the **More AutoShapes** option.*

❑ *You can change the background colour and border of pictures, as with any drawing object.*

Specifying precise dimensions for a picture

- Select the picture concerned.
- **Format Picture** ♦ Ctrl 1

*You can also display the **Format Picture** dialog box by clicking the tool button on the **Picture** toolbar.*

- Activate the **Size** tab.
- In the **Size and rotate** frame, enter the required **Height** and **Width** then click **OK.**

Inserting a WordArt object

The WordArt application is used to apply special effects to text:

- Click the tool button in the **Drawing** toolbar.
- Select an effect then click **OK.**

♦ Type the text to which you want to apply the WordArt effect; use the Enter key when you want to create a line break.

♦ Use the **Font** and **Font Size** lists as well as the B and I tool buttons to format the text.

♦ Click **OK**.

The text appears on the worksheet as a drawing object.

❑ *When a WordArt object is selected, you can edit it using the tool buttons on the* ***WordArt*** *toolbar.*

Inserting a diagram

Here is an example of an organization chart type of diagram:

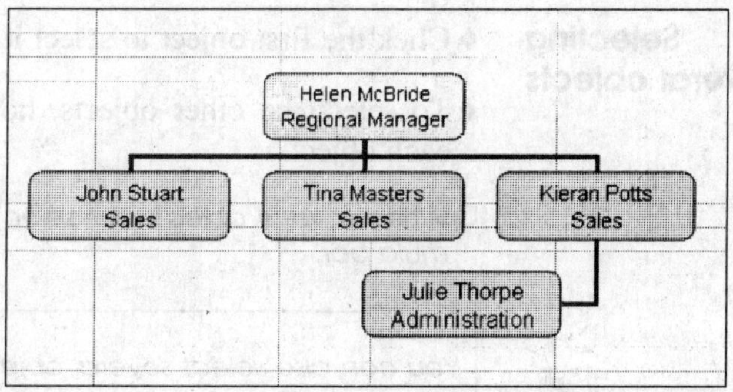

♦ Click the tool button on the **Drawing** toolbar.

♦ Select the type of diagram you wish to use then click **OK.**

The chosen type of diagram appears in a drawing canvas and the ***Organization Chart*** *toolbar appears, if you choose that type of diagram. If you choose another type, the* ***Diagram*** *toolbar appears.*

♦ Enter your text in the **Click to add text** boxes.

♦ To add another shape to an **Organization Chart**, choose the shape to which you wish to link the new one. Open the **Insert Shape** list on the **Organization Chart** toolbar and select the type of shape you wish to add. For other types of diagram, just click the **Insert Shape** button on the **Diagram** toolbar.

♦ To delete a shape from a diagram, click the edge of the shape to select it, then press Del.

❑ *The tool button on the **Organization Chart** or **Diagram** toolbar applies an automatic format to the diagram.*

❑ *To delete a diagram, click it to activate it then click its hatched border and press Del.*

Selecting several objects

♦ Click the first object to select it.

♦ To select the other objects, hold down the Shift key and click each object.

❑ *When several objects are selected, no name appears on the formula bar.*

> *You can also select several objects by selecting the tool button on the **Drawing** toolbar then dragging an invisible rectangle around them.*

Resizing/moving an object

♦ Select the drawing object concerned.

The black squares that appear around the selection are called handles. When you point to one of them, the pointer changes shape.

♦ To resize an object, drag one of these selection handles.

♦ To move an object, drag the object into its new position.

Use the Alt key as you drag to align the object with the cell grid.

Rotating an object/ a picture

♦ Select the object or picture concerned.

♦ Point to the small green circle at the top of the object or picture and drag to rotate the object.

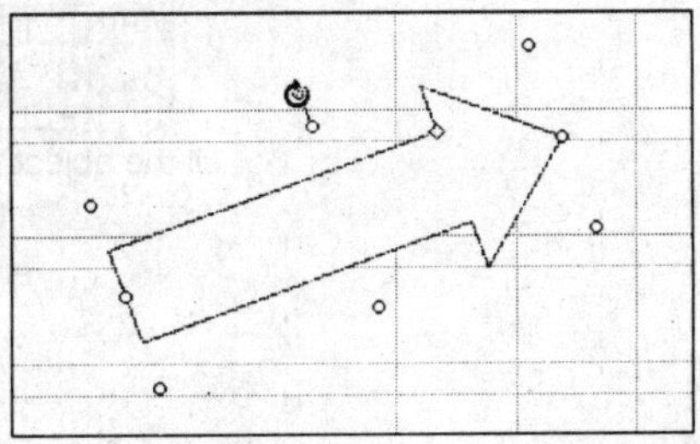

Changing an object's appearance

Changing a 2D object's appearance

♦ Select the object.

♦ Use the buttons on the **Drawing** toolbar:

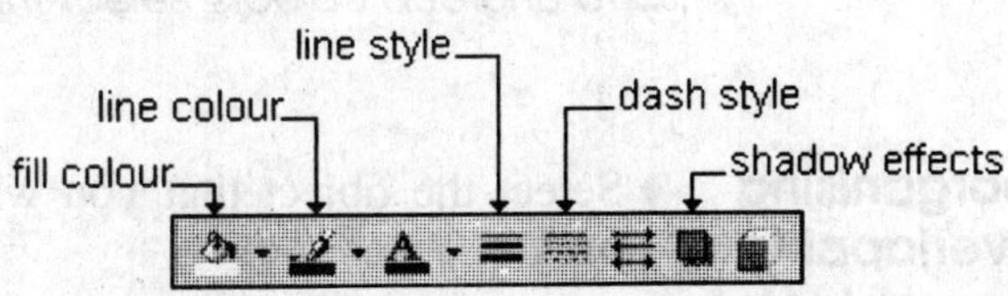

❑ *The tool button is used to define arrowheads for line objects.*

❑ *To remove an object's borders, select it then choose **Format - Text Box - Colors and Lines** tab. Go into the **Color** list and choose the **No Line** option.*

Changing a 3D object's appearance

♦ To add a 3D effect to an object, select the object then click the button on the **Drawing** toolbar to choose a preset 3D style.

♦ To customise a 3D effect, select the object, click then the **3D Settings** button.

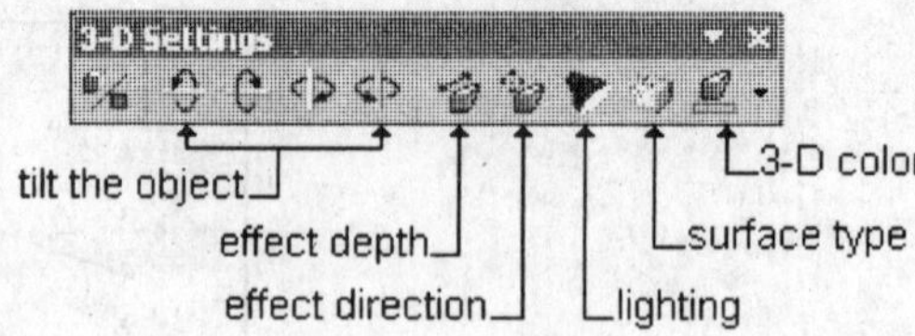

Grouping/ ungrouping several objects

♦ Select all the objects that you want to include in the group.

♦ Click the **Draw** button on the **Drawing** toolbar then click **Group**.

*You can check that the item selected is a group: **Group** should appear on the formula bar.*

❑ *To ungroup objects, select the group then use **Draw - Ungroup**.*

Reorganising overlapping objects

♦ Select the object that you want to bring forward or send further back.

♦ Click the **Draw** button then point to the **Order** option.

♦ Choose:

Bring to Front/ Send to Back	to display an object at the very front/at the very back of the stack of objects.
Bring Forward/ Send Backward	to place an object in front of the one before it/behind the one after it.

Aligning objects with one another

The bottom edges of these objects have been aligned:

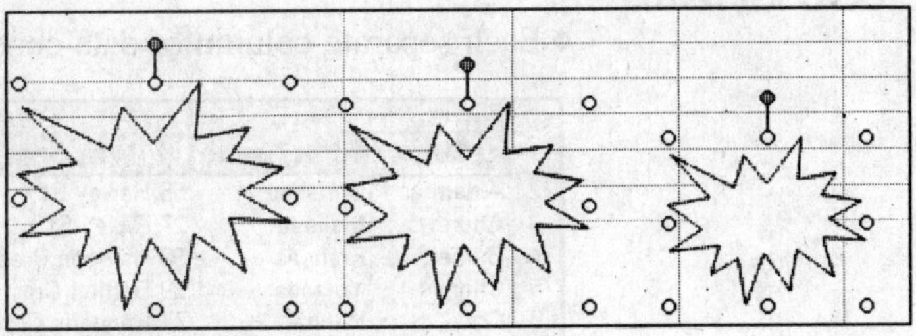

♦ Select the objects concerned.

♦ Click the **Draw** button then choose one of the first six options in the **Align or Distribute** menu.

❑ *The* ***Distribute Horizontally*** *and* ***Distribute Vertically*** *options in the same menu equalise the spaces between the selected objects.*

.... *Personal notes* ....

Defining data list terms

A list of data is commonly called a database.

♦ Each separate column of data constitutes a **FIELD**.

	A	B	C	D	E	F
1	**Name**	**First Name**	**Address**	**PC/City**	**Sex**	**Age**
2	Alderman	Christine	56 Harvey St	4100 Tewesbury	F	13
3	Andrews	Melissa	27 Ridley St	5600 St Lucia	F	15
4	Barnett	Frances	38 Harrison Cres	4500 Greerton	F	15
5	Charles	Yolanda	29 Bartlett Cres	6000 Lorton	F	14
6	Cray	Hannah	77 Kennedy Drive	5800 Rafter	F	17
7	Dell	Tammy	13 Read Road	4300 Dryden	F	16
8	Dorcas	Michelle	10 Kings Ct	5400 Fern Grove	F	16
9	Grant	Jessica	14/196 Red Sand Road	6100 Herston	F	17
10	Grey	Josephine	89 Green St	5500 Killybill	F	22
11	Greene	Louise	45 West Road	5600 St Lucia	F	25
12	Hunt	Rosemary	32 Fern Drive	5000 Gunston	F	18
13	Loxton	Marie	12/149 Grove Road	4400 Mt Gladstone	F	22
14	Marsh	Sarah	19 River Lane	6000 Lorton	F	19
15	Martingale	Joanne	9/27 Thurston Road	4500 Greerton	F	19
16	Norton	Vera	18 Quinn St	4100 Tewesbury	F	24
17	Peak	Alison	26A Pine Road	4200 New Grove	F	21
18	Peyton	Theresa	141 Mt Gladstone Road	4400 Mt Gladstone	F	25

In the example above, you can see 6 fields, corresponding to the column headings; fields for the person's surname and first name, one for his/her address, another for the postcode and town, and fields for his/her sex and age.

♦ Each field must have a column heading, which becomes its name. There are no restrictions on the name you can give but short, clear field names are easier to manage.

♦ The first row of the database contains the field names and all the other rows are **RECORDS**.

When you are creating a list of data, you can define the type of data allowed in each field by defining validation criteria.

Using the data form

The data form is used to enter records and can also be used to search for a particular record.

Accessing the form

♦ Click a cell in the table that you want to manage as a database. This table should contain the field names and at least one record:

	A	B	C	D	E	F	G	H
1	Name	First Name	Address	PC/City	Sex	Age	Subs	Paid
2	Alderman	Christine	56 Harvey St	4100 Tewesbury	F	13	2.50	Y
3	Andrews	Melissa	27 Ridley St	5600 St Lucia	F	15	3.00	Y
4								

♦ **Data**
Form

This form is made up of the following elements:

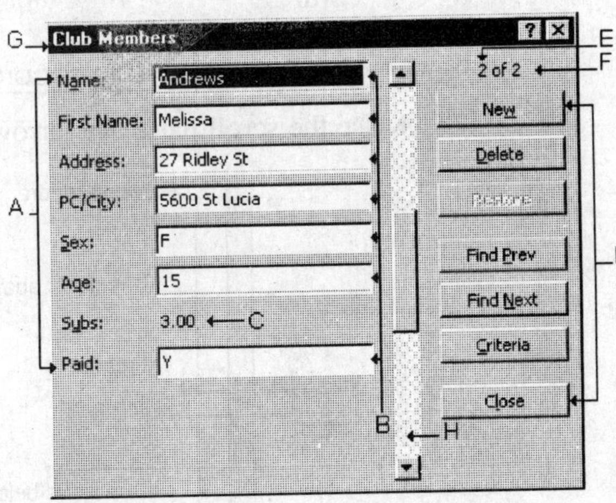

A Field names

B Edit boxes for entering field contents

C Data form fields containing computed fields

D Command buttons

E The number of the current record

F The total number of records

G Title bar

H Vertical scroll bar

Adding records

♦ To start adding a new record, click the **New** button.

♦ Fill in each new record as follows:

– press ⇆ to move to the next box, except after the last one (or ⇧Shift ⇆ if you want to go back to the previous box).

– to confirm the data entered, press Enter after the last piece of information is entered; you will go immediately into a new record.

Moving from record to record

♦ Use the scroll bar or the arrow keys, as shown below:

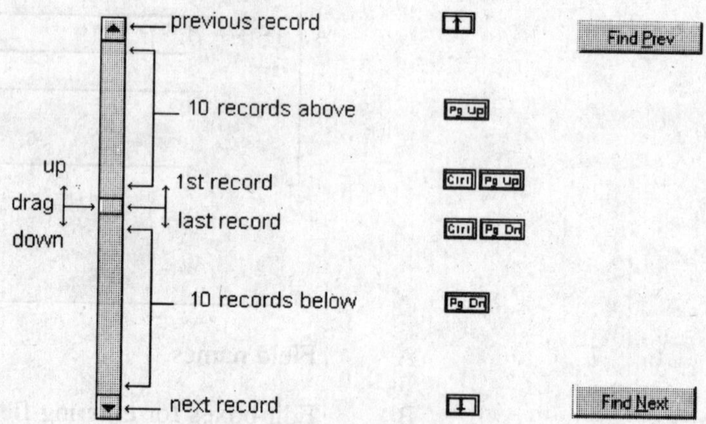

The last form displayed is always a new form ready to be filled in.

Finding a particular record

♦ Go into either the first or last record.

♦ Click the **Criteria** button.

*The record number indicator is replaced by the word **Criteria**, the calculated fields become text boxes and the **Criteria** button is replaced by a **Form** button.*

♦ Set your search conditions as if you were filling in a record but do not press Enter. For example:

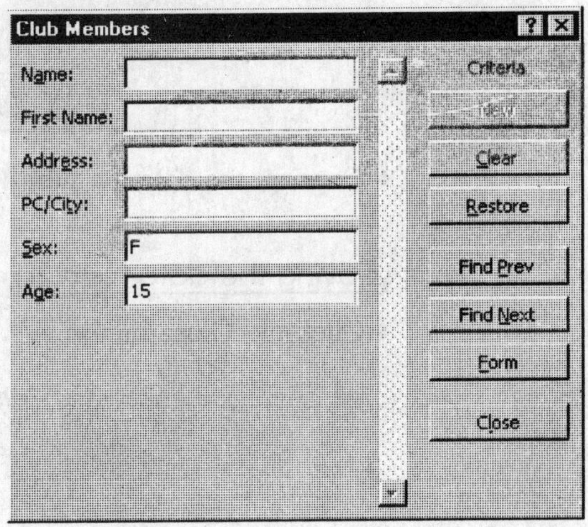

♦ If you started from the first record, click the **Find Next** button to begin searching. If you started at the last record, start searching with the **Find Prev** button.

♦ Continue your search using the **Find Next** or **Find Prev** buttons.

Modifying a record

♦ Go to the record you want to modify.

♦ Make your corrections then press Enter to confirm them.

> *If you change your mind about the changes you make, click the **Restore** button (before pressing Enter) to go back to the previous values.*

Deleting a record

- Go to the record you want to delete.
- Click the **Delete** button.

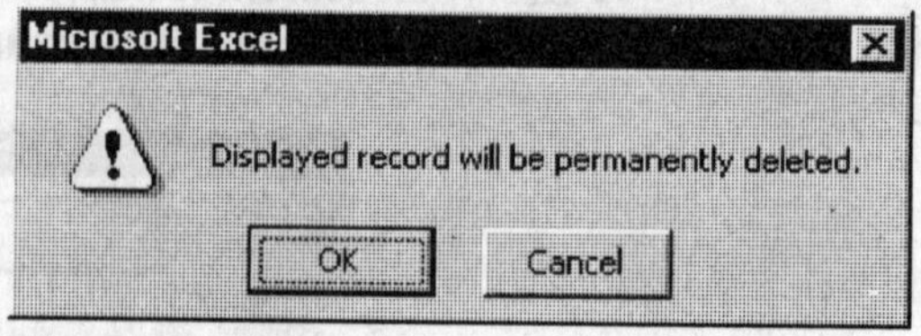

- Confirm the deletion with **OK.**

Leaving the data form

- Click the **Close** button.

.... *Personal notes* ....

Creating and using a simple filter

A filter is used to select records that correspond to a set criterion.

Activating Autofilter

♦ Activate one of cells in the list of data.

♦ **Data**
Filter
AutoFilter

Each field becomes a drop-down list that can be opened by clicking the down arrow to the right of the field name.

Filtering by one of the values listed

♦ Open the list associated with the field concerned.

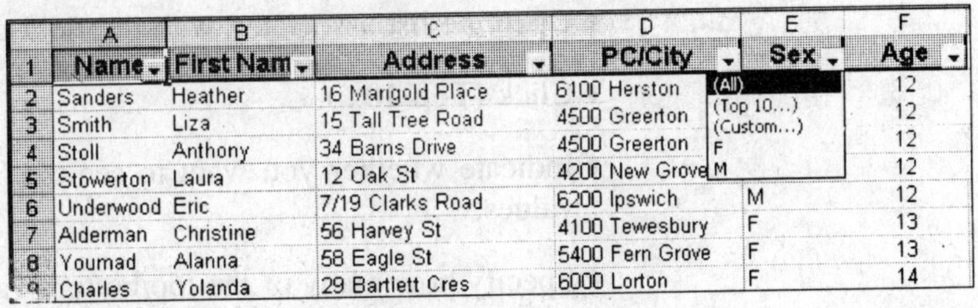

	A	B	C	D	E	F
1	Name	First Nam	Address	PC/City	Sex	Age
2	Sanders	Heather	16 Marigold Place	6100 Herston	(All)	12
3	Smith	Liza	15 Tall Tree Road	4500 Greerton	(Top 10...)	12
4	Stoll	Anthony	34 Barns Drive	4500 Greerton	(Custom...) F	12
5	Stowerton	Laura	12 Oak St	4200 New Grove	M	12
6	Underwood	Eric	7/19 Clarks Road	6200 Ipswich	M	12
7	Alderman	Christine	56 Harvey St	4100 Tewesbury	F	13
8	Youmad	Alanna	58 Eagle St	5400 Fern Grove	F	13
9	Charles	Yolanda	29 Bartlett Cres	6000 Lorton	F	14

Each list includes all the values in the field.

♦ Click the value that interests you.

All the records that do not concern the selected value are hidden automatically. The row numbers of the records displayed change colour.

Filtering by a specific criterion

♦ Open the list associated with the field concerned.

♦ Click **Custom**.

♦ In the first list box, select a comparison operator.

♦ Activate the text box next to it and enter the compare value.

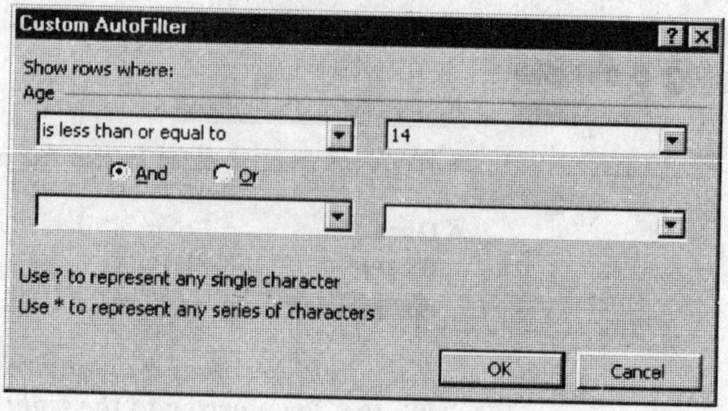

♦ Click **OK**.

Filtering the highest and lowest values

♦ Open the list associated with the field concerned.

♦ Click (**Top 10**...).

♦ Indicate whether you want to see the **Top** values or the **Bottom** values.

♦ Specify how many of the top/bottom values you want to see.

♦ Choose **Items** to filter all the records corresponding to the criteria (top or bottom) or **Percent** to filter a number of rows corresponding to a percentage of the total number of values in the list.

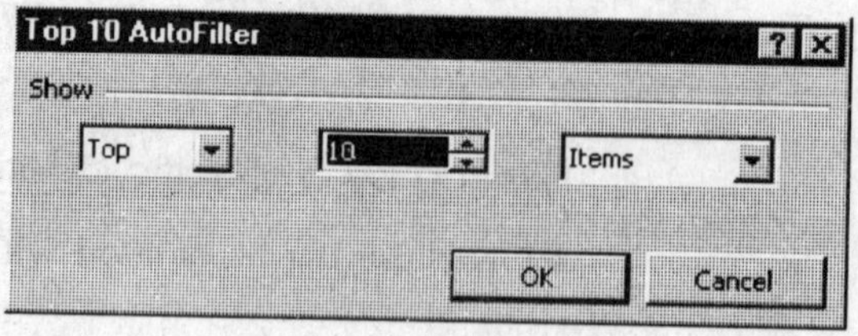

♦ Click **OK**.

Filtering by several criteria

Two criteria for the same field

♦ Activate the **AutoFilter.**

♦ Open the list for the field concerned.

♦ Click **Custom**.

♦ Define the first filter criterion.

♦ Indicate how the two criteria are to be combined:

– if both must be satisfied together, choose **And**,

– if either one or the other must be satisfied, choose **Or**.

♦ Enter your second condition.

♦ Click **OK**.

Criteria concerning several fields combined with "and"

♦ Activate **AutoFilter.**

♦ Set the conditions in each field concerned.

Displaying all records again

♦ If only one filter is active, open the list on the filtered field and click **(All)**.

♦ If several filters are active, use:

Data
Filter
Show All

Creating a complex filter

Creating a criteria range

♦ You first need to locate an empty space of a few columns and a few rows on the sheet (typically next to the list of data).

♦ In one of the empty rows, enter the field names on which to set the criteria.

♦ In the rows below, enter the criteria that should be met, paying attention to the following rules:

Combination	Method
OR	the criteria are entered in several rows
AND	the criteria are entered in several columns
OR and AND	the criteria are entered in several rows and several columns

Look at these examples to undestand better the use of AND and OR when setting criteria:

Requirements	Criteria ranges	
Records for members named: BARNETT OR SANDERS OR KELSEY	NAME	
	BARNET	
	SANDERS	
	KELSEY	
Records for 18 year-old girls: 18 AND F	AGE	SEX
	18	F
Records for boys aged 13 OR 15 OR 17 years	SEX	AGE
	M	13
	M	15
	M	17

Using a criteria range

♦ Click the data list.

♦ **Data**
Filter
Advanced Filter

The ***Filter the list, in-place*** *option is active by default.*

♦ Click the **Criteria range** box, use the to collapse the dialog box and select the criteria range previously created on the worksheet. Click to restore the dialog box:

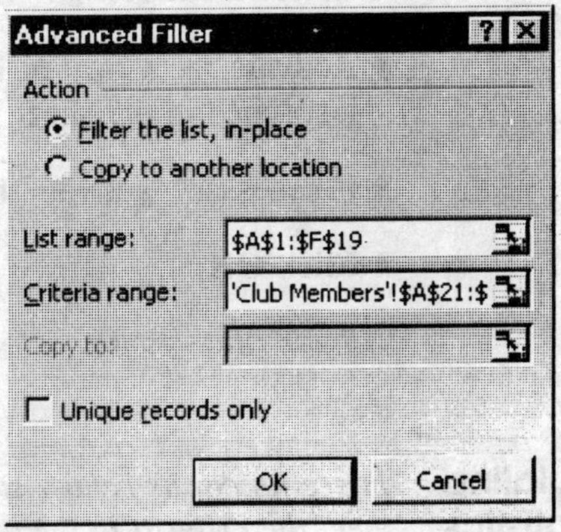

♦ If necessary, activate the **Unique records only** option to filter out any duplicate records.

♦ Click **OK.**

Only the records that meet the criteria are displayed. To display all the records again use the ***Data - Filter - Show All*** *command.*

The cells in the criteria range are now called ***Criteria****.*

Copying records that meet filter criteria

♦ In another place on the sheet, enter a row of the field headings whose contents you wish to filter and extract.

♦ Create a criteria range.

♦ **Data**
Filter
Advanced Filter

♦ In the **Action** frame, activate the **Copy to another location** option.

*The **Copy to** box becomes available.*

♦ If necessary, indicate the location of the criteria range in **Criteria range.**

♦ Activate the **Copy to** box and select the row of names you have just typed in the sheet.

♦ If necessary, activate the **Unique records only** option.

♦ Click **OK.**

❑ *If you change the criteria range, run the filter again.*

Calculating statistics from the records

These functions return statistics based on the records whose values meet the criteria in the criteria range.

♦ Create the appropriate criteria range.

♦ Use the following functions:

Function	Effect
=DCOUNT(database,field,criteria)	counts the cells
=DSUM(database,field,criteria)	totals the values of the field
=DAVERAGE(database,field,criteria)	calculates the average for the field
=DMAX(database,field,criteria)	extracts the maximal value in the field
=DMIN(database,field,criteria)	extracts the minimal value in the field

Replace:

– **database** with the reference of the cells containing the list of records (including column headings),

– **field** with the column heading,

- **criteria** with the references of the cells containing the criteria range: if you have created a complex filter, type the word "criteria".

❑ *As soon as you change anything in the criteria range, the statistics are automatically updated.*

.... *Personal notes* ....

Creating a pivot table

A pivot table allows you to synthesise and analyse data from a list or an existing table:

	A	B	C	D	E	F	G
1	***Average wages in group by age/region***						
2	**Maintenance Technician**						
3							
4	Company	(All)					
5							
6	Average of Gross Wage	Region					
7	Age	East	North	South	West	Grand Total	
8	18-24		998.45	963.25	965.84	975.8466667	
9	25-31	1035.13	988.98	1188.97	1053.375	1055.702	
10	32-38	1003.763333	1081.555	1100.48	1058.36	1059.355556	
11	39-45	1047.195	999.75	1125.85	1023.475	1039.23625	
12	46-52		1010.52			1010.52	
13	Grand Total	1026.38375	1017.34625	1109.782857	1028.10625	1043.328065	
14							

This table calculates the average gross wage by age and by region.

♦ Click in the list of data.

♦ **Data**
PivotTable and PivotChart Report

*The **PivotTable Wizard** takes over.*

♦ Indicate the source of the data for the pivot table. If the source is an Excel database, leave the first option active.

♦ If necessary, click **PivotTable** in the **What kind of report do you want to create?** frame.

♦ Click **Next >**.

♦ Check and if necessary, select the **Range** of cells containing the data used to fill in the table.

♦ Click **Next >**.

♦ Click the **Layout** button then define the table's design by dragging the field buttons from the list into the appropriate areas (**PAGE, ROW, COLUMN, DATA**).

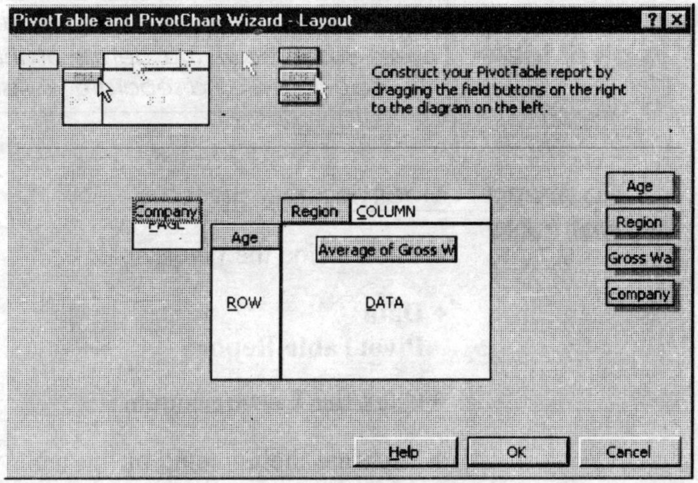

*The **DATA** area can only contain elements that Excel can use in its calculations.*

♦ If necessary, customise the fields included in the table by double-clicking the corresponding field button. For example, to change the function to something other than sum, double-click the sum button in the DATA box then choose another function.

♦ Click **OK**.

♦ In **Where do you want to put the PivotTable** indicate whether to create it on a new sheet or in an existing sheet.

♦ Click **Finish**.

❑ *You can also define the layout of a pivot table directly on the worksheet. To do this, when you arrive at the third step in the **PivotTable and PivotChart Wizard**, do not click the **Layout** button; select where the pivot table will go and click the **Finish** button. The **PivotTable Field List** window appears. Drag the fields from it onto the labelled areas on the worksheet. If the **PivotTable Field List** window does not appear, you can display it by clicking the*  *tool button on the **PivotTable** toolbar.*

❑ *Although a pivot table is linked to the data list from which it was created, it is not updated automatically.*

> *If you double-click one of the result values in a pivot table's data area, Excel shows the details of the source data used to make the calculation on a separate worksheet.*

Modifying a pivot table

Modifying the contents

♦ Click inside the pivot table.

♦ **Data**
PivotTable Report

♦ Click the **Layout** button.

♦ Redefine the contents of the table, in the same way as when you created it.

❑ *A field can also be added by dragging the corresponding field from the* ***PivotTable Field List*** *window onto the pivot table.*

❑ *To delete a field, drag the field concerned out of the pivot table.*

Updating and recalculating

♦ **Data**
Refresh Data

Changing the presentation

	A	B	C
1	Average of Gross Wage	Region	
2	Age	East	North
3	18-24		998.4
4	25-31	1035.13	988.9

click to open the list of groups generated by Excel and activate or deactivate the values you want to show or hide

♦ Format the selected cells, in the same way as you would format cells in a worksheet (you can apply an AutoFormat to the whole table using **Format - AutoFormat**).

Grouping pivot table rows and columns

You may wish to group data in your table, for example, grouping a date field by month, or ages by age groups.

♦ Click the header of the field whose data you wish to group.

♦ **Data**
Group and Outline
Group

♦ Define how the data should be grouped.

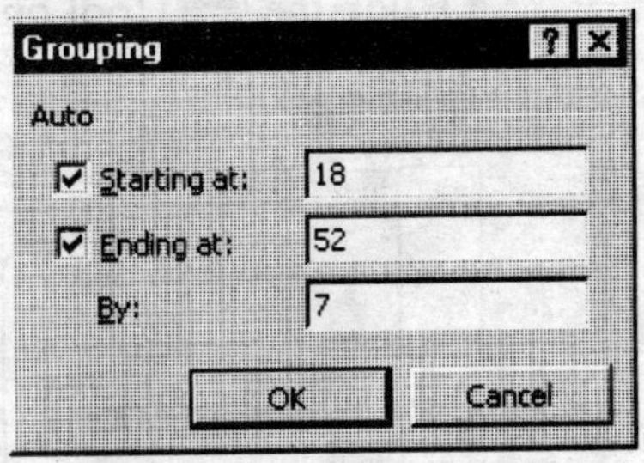

Excel generally proposes the start and end (or maximum and minimum) of the data used and suggests an interval for each group.

♦ Click **OK**.

❑ *To undo groups, use the **Data - Group and Outline - Ungroup** command.*

Creating a pivot chart

A pivot chart is always created in conjunction with A pivot table. This means that any modifications made to the table will be automatically made to the chart, and vice versa.

There are several methods you can use to create a pivot chart and the one you choose will depend on the source data you are using. In this case, a pivot table has been used as the data source.

♦ Access the pivot table you wish to use for the chart.

♦ Click the  tool on the **PivotTable** toolbar.

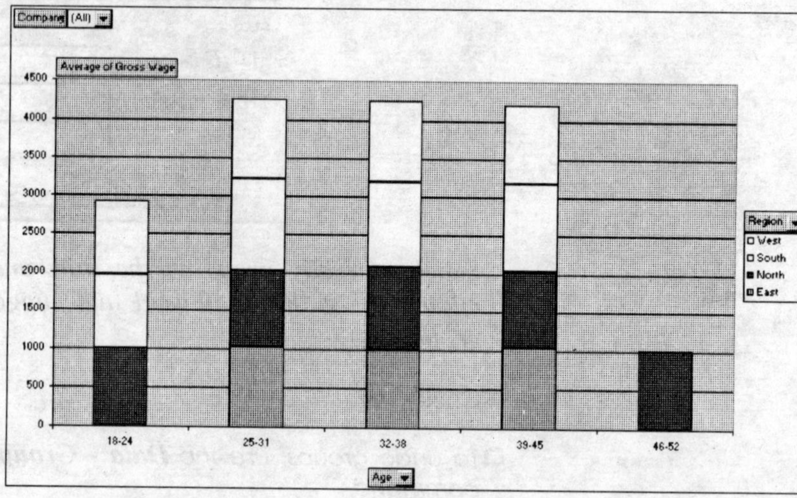

A stacked column chart appears on a separate chart sheet (stacked column is the default chart type).
The row data from the pivot table become the X-axis categories and the column data become the series.

❑ *The **PivotChart (with PivotTable)** option in the **Data - PivotTable and PivotChart Report** menu will create a pivot chart using an Excel, Access or OLAP database, or simply a range of Excel cells, as its source data. In this case, a pivot table will be created simultaneously with the pivot chart.*

❑ *To move a pivot chart's legend, use **Chart - Chart Options - Legend** tab then choose the desired position. You cannot use the mouse to move or resize a legend.*

❑ *The pivot chart's title and its axes cannot be moved but you can make them appear larger or smaller by changing the font size used for the text.*

Hiding/showing pivot chart data

Hiding/showing certain values

♦ Open the list attached to the field in question, then deactivate or activate the option which corresponds to the data you want to hide or show.

♦ Click **OK**.

The chart changes, as does the corresponding pivot table.

Adding/removing a field in a pivot chart

♦ Drag the field button out of the chart to remove the corresponding field. To add a field, drag it from the **PivotTable Field List** onto the chart.

*If the **PivotTable Field List** window does not appear, you can display it by clicking the tool button on the **PivotTable** toolbar.*

Changing chart type

♦ Select the chart area.

♦ **Chart**
Chart Type

♦ Select a new type and sub-type for the chart.

♦ Click **OK**.

*The **Scatter**, **Bubble** and **Stock** chart types cannot be used on pivot charts.*

Moving a pivot chart

♦ Activate the worksheet containing the chart.

♦ **Chart**
Location

♦ Click the **As object in** option and give the name of the sheet to which you want to move the chart.

♦ Click **OK**.

When it is moved, the pivot chart may lose some formatting and the original chart sheet will be deleted.

.... *Personal notes* ....

Protecting a workbook

You can protect a workbook by setting a password which will be required each time the workbook is opened or saved.

♦ **File**
Save As

♦ If necessary, enter the name of the document, and specify the folder in which to save it.

♦ **Tools**
General Options

♦ To restrict access to a document, type a password in **Password to open.**
To allow access but prevent unauthorised modification of the document, type a password in the **Password to modify** box.

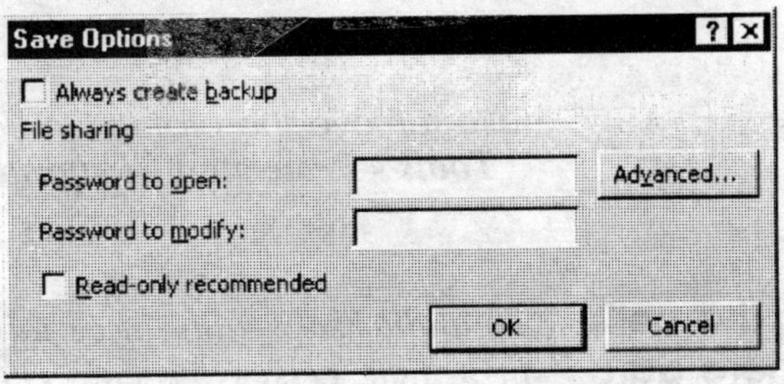

Each character of the password is replaced by an asterisk. Excel registers the difference between capital and lower case letters: be careful which you use.

♦ Click **OK**.

♦ Type the password again, to ensure against error, and enter.

❑ *A password is required as soon as a user tries to open a document. If a **Password to modify** has been set, a user who cannot give the password can still have access to the document by clicking the **Read Only** button. However in this case, if the user attempts to modify the document, Excel refuses to save the modifications.*

❑ *To delete a password, clear the corresponding text box in the **Save Options** dialog box.*

Protecting sheets

By protecting the structure of a workbook, you can for example prevent sheets from being deleted or moved, or new ones from being added.

♦ **Tools**
Protect
Protect Workbook

♦ Check that the **Structure** option is active.

♦ Activate the **Window** option to prevent the workbook window from being moved, resized, hidden or closed.

♦ If you wish, set a password (up to 255 characters long).

♦ Click **OK**.

♦ If you are setting a password, enter it again then click **OK**.

❑ *To remove the protection from the workbook, use the command* ***Tools - Protection - Unprotect Workbook****.*

Limiting the cells where data can be entered by any user

To authorise writing in certain cells only, you should first indicate in which cells you can enter data, then apply protection by password to the whole sheet.

Unlocking selected cells

♦ Select the cells where writing is allowed.

♦ **Format**
Cells

♦ Ctrl 1

♦ Deactivate **Locked** under the **Protection** tab.

♦ Enter.

Protecting the sheet

♦ **Tools**
Protection
Protect Sheet

♦ Make sure the **Protect worksheet and contents of locked cells** option is active.

♦ As necessary, activate or deactivate the actions that users can perform in the **Allow all users of this worksheet to** list.

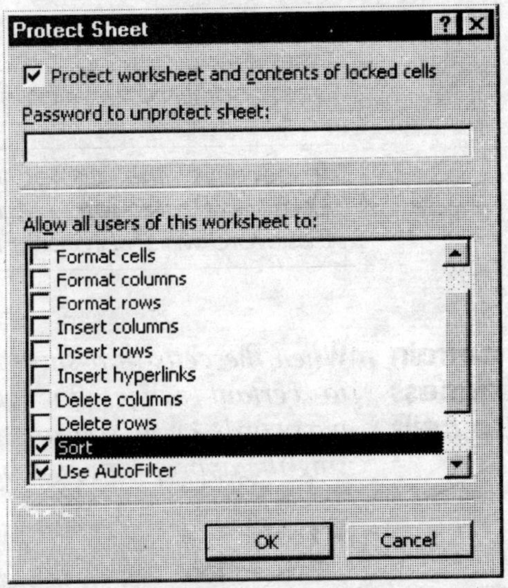

♦ Enter a password or, if you are not using a password, click **OK**.

A password can have up to 255 characters. Be careful, as Excel distinguishes between upper and lower case letters and the characters entered are always masked on the screen.

♦ Confirm your password (if you are using one) by entering it again then click **OK**.

If you try to enter data in a protected cell, the following error message appears:

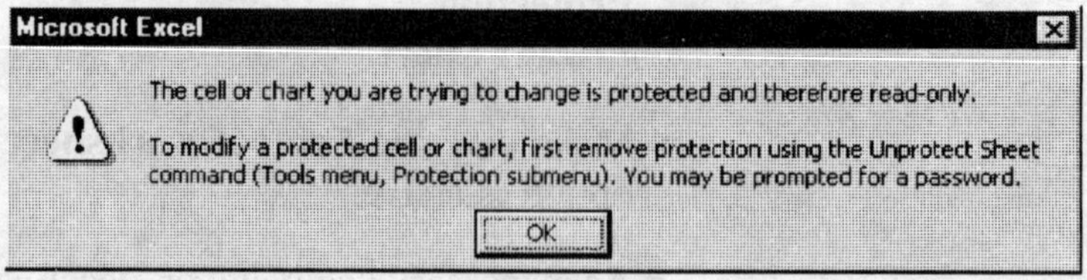

♦ Click **OK** to close this message.

❑ *Depending on the user's permissions, certain options on the Format menu may not be available on the protected sheet (the corresponding option names will be grey).*

To remove the protection from a sheet, use the command ***Tools - Protection - Unprotect Sheet****. If necessary give the password which protects the sheet, then enter.*

Giving certain users access to cells

When the cells in a sheet are protected, you can still grant access to certain ranges for certain users by either using different passwords or, if you are working under Windows 2000, by choosing the appropriate user names.

♦ **Tools**
Protection
Allow Users to Edit Ranges

♦ Click the **New** button.

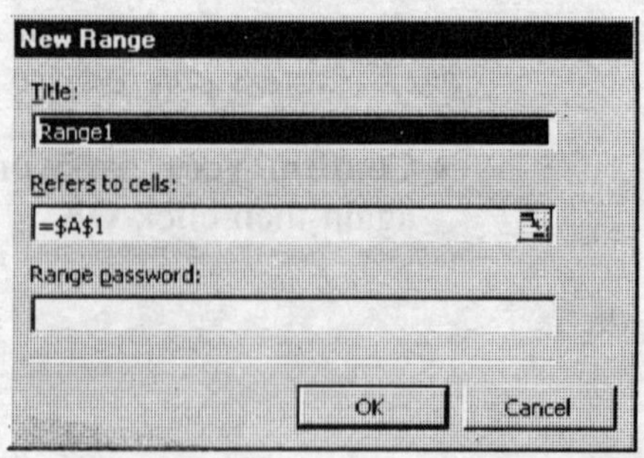

♦ If required, change the **Title** for the range of cells.

♦ Click in the **Refers to cells** box, select the cells concerned in the worksheet and click to return to the **New Range** dialog box.

You can use the Ctrl *key to select nonadjacent cells.*

♦ In the **Range password** box, enter the password that users will have to enter to be able to modify that range. Click **OK**, re-enter the password to confirm then click **OK** again.

♦ If you wish to define another range of cells controlled by a password, click the **New** button again and define further ranges.

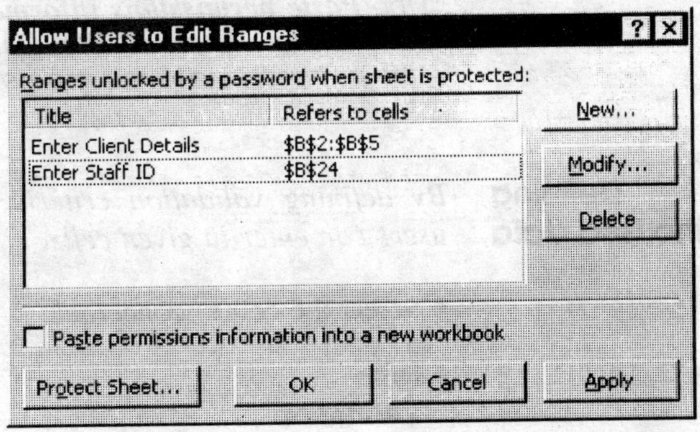

A ***Permissions*** *button appears if you are using Windows 2000. This button provides you with a list of users so you can define who can modify the range selected previously in the dialog box. This dispenses with the use of passwords.*

♦ Click the **Protect Sheet** button, make sure the **Protect worksheet and contents of locked cells** option is active and if necessary, tick any options required in the **Allow all users of this worksheet to** list.

♦ Click **OK**.

If you try to enter data in a cell within a range that is write-protected by a password (and if you are under Windows 2000 and you do not have permission to use that range without a password), Excel will open a dialog box and ask you for a password:

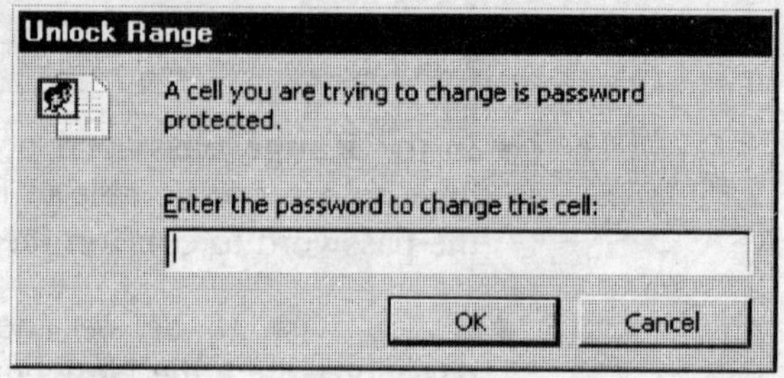

❑ *The **Paste permissions information into a new workbook** option in the **Allow Users to Edit Ranges** dialog box makes a report of the permissions defined in a new workbook.*

Defining authorised data

By defining validation criteria, you can limit what information users can enter in given cells.

♦ Select the cell(s) concerned.

♦ **Data**
Validation
Settings tab

♦ Open the **Allow** list and choose the type of data you wish to authorise.

Any value	no restrictions.
Whole number	the cell must contain an integer.
Decimal	the cell must contain a number or a fraction.
List	this option allows you to list cell references containing authorised data.

Date the cell must contain a date.

Time the cell must contain a time.

Text length this option allows you to specify the number of characters authorised in the cell.

Custom this option allows you to enter a formula to limit the data which the cell will accept.

♦ If you have selected **Whole number**, **Decimal**, **Date** or **Time** from the list, choose a comparison operator from the **Data** list and give values for comparison.

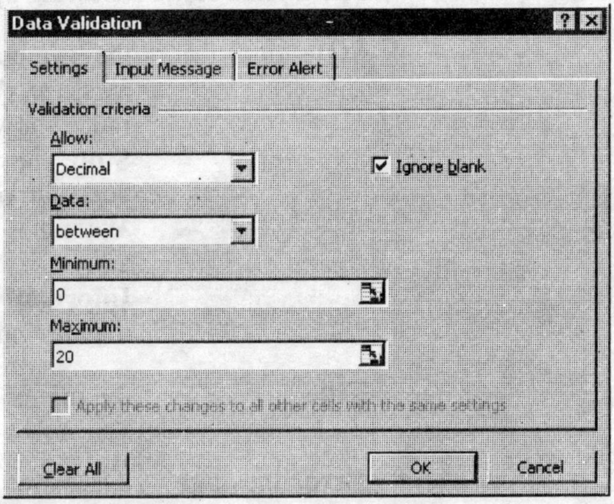

These validation criteria allow you to enter whole numbers or decimals between 0 and 20.

♦ If you have chosen **Text length**, select the **equal to** operator, then give the authorised number of characters in the **Length** box.

♦ If you have chosen **List** enter the references of the cells containing authorised data in the **Source** box.
To add a drop down list of authorised data to the cells concerned, activate the **In-cell dropdown** option.

*In the **Source** option, you can give a named range of cells, preceded by an = sign (e.g. = stafflist).*

- If you have chosen **Custom** enter your **Formula**, starting with an equal sign (=). The formula must be of the type which returns TRUE or FALSE.
- Whatever the type of data specified, activate **Ignore blank** if you authorise the cell to remain empty.
- Click the **Error Alert** tab to enter a message to display when the data entered do not meet the validation criteria.
- Leave the **Show error alert after invalid data is entered** option active and set the following options:

Style — the symbol that should appear in the error message dialog box and the degree of tolerance shown to unauthorised data:
Stop: the user is strictly limited to what has been authorised.
Warning: the user can force an unauthorised entry.
Information: the user is simply informed that they are entering an unauthorised value.

Title — the title of the error message dialog box.

Error message — the text of the error message.

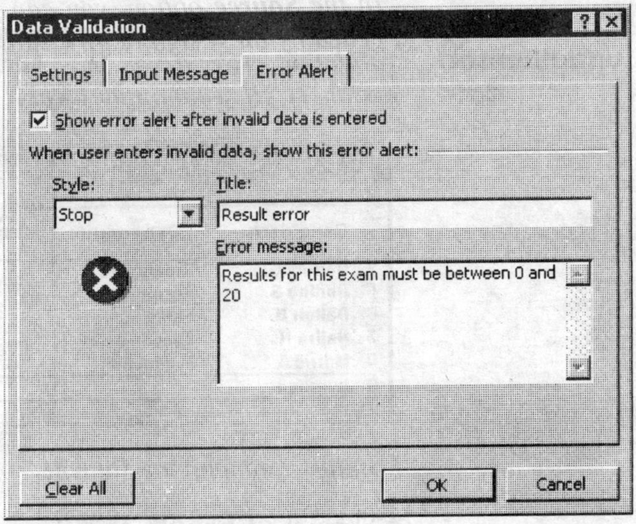

♦ Click **OK**.

If you enter any data that does not correspond to the validation criteria, an error message will appear:

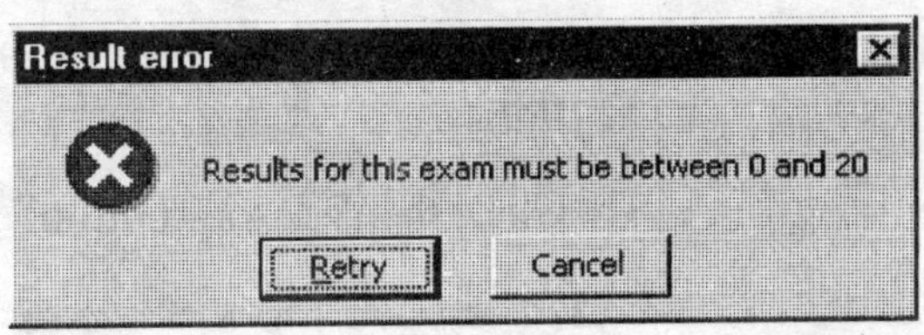

*The buttons that appear on the error message differ depending on the **Style** used for the **Error Alert**. These may or may not allow you to force unauthorised data.*

❑ *Data entered before the criteria were set are not tested. There is, however, an option in Excel which will find any data that do not meet the criteria. (cf. below: Tracing unauthorised data).*

❑ *The options on the **Input Message** page of the **Data - Validation** dialog box make it possible to display a message in a ScreenTip when the mouse pointer is on the cell.*

Tracing unauthorised data

This is a technique for finding cells whose values do not meet any validation criteria you may have set using the ***Data - Validation*** *options. Cells containing invalid data are circled in red.*

	A	B	C	D	E	F
2						
3	**Candidate**	**Department**	*Marketing*	*Commercial law*	*Tax law*	*Financial management*
4	**Barnes G.**	**Production**	13	14.5	24	15
5	**Bonino S.**	**Accounts**	15	14	14	12
6	**Dalton B.**	**Sales**	12.5	8.5	11	7
7	**Hajira N.**	**Accounts**	12	13	14	15
8	**Morris A.**	**Production**	11	11	26	14
9	**Average**					
10						

In this example, the students' marks should be between 0 and 20.

♦ Show the **Formula Auditing** toolbar:

Tools
Formula Auditing
Show Formula Auditing Toolbar

You can also right-click any toolbar and choose ***Formula Auditing****.*

♦ Click the  tool button.

❑ *To remove the red circles, click the*  *tool button on the* ***Formula Auditing*** *toolbar.*

Managing shared workbooks

Several users can work on, and modify a shared workbook at the same time. A shared workbook must be stored in a folder that is accessible to all its users.

Sharing a workbook

♦ **Tools**
Share Workbook
Editing tab

♦ Tick the **Allow changes by more than one user...** option.

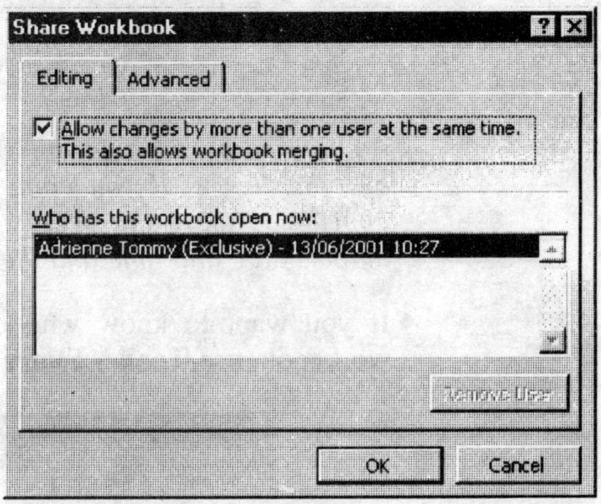

♦ Click **OK**.

♦ Confirm the message that offers to save the workbook.

The term "[Shared]" appears after the workbook's name on the title bar.

Using a shared workbook

♦ Open the shared workbook.

The term "[Shared]" on the title bar indicates that you are using a shared workbook.

♦ Make your changes.

Some actions cannot be performed on shared workbooks. For example, you cannot merge cells, create charts or drawing objects, insert pictures or create subtotals or pivot table.

- Save the shared workbook to update the changes made and saved by other users. If another user has saved changes to the shared workbook and there is no conflict in the changes made, the following message appears:

A coloured border appears around cells that have been modified by other users. If you point to one of these cells, a ScreenTip appears relating the details of the changes made, such as the author, date and time and the type of changes.

- If you want to know who currently is working on the shared workbook, use **Tools - Share Workbook - Editing** tab.

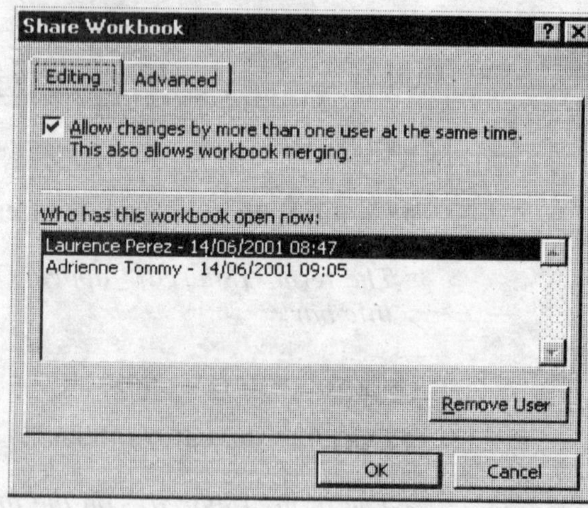

Excel shows the names of the users who are working on the shared workbook, as well as the date and time they opened it.

❑ *If you would prefer other users' changes to be updated at regular intervals rather that each time the workbook is saved, go into **Tools - Share Workbook - Advanced** tab. In the **Update changes** frame, tick the **Automatically every** option and specify a time interval in minutes. This option can be modified independently by each user.*

Resolving modification conflicts

If you modify the same cells as another user and try to save those changes, a conflict occurs. Excel displays a dialog box that allows you to choose which changes are saved.

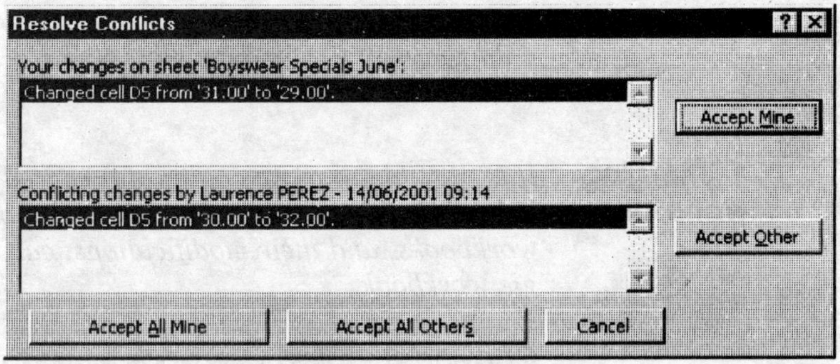

♦ To examine each conflicting change one by one, click **Accept Mine** or **Accept Other** to confirm respectively your own modification or that of the other user and go on to the next modification.

♦ To accept all your changes or all those made by the other user, click **Accept All Mine** or **Accept All Others** as required.

❑ *If you wish to give your changes priority over those made by other users, which means that the **Resolve Conflicts** dialog box will no longer appear, activate the **The changes being saved win** option (**Tools - Share Workbook - Advanced** tab - **Conflicting changes between users** frame).*

Unsharing a workbook

♦ When you no longer wish to share your workbook, make sure you are the only person currently using it (**Tools - Share Workbook - Editing** tab). If other users are using it, they will lose any work that they have not saved.

♦ **Tools**
Share Workbook
Editing tab

♦ Deactivate the **Allow changes by more than one user** option.

♦ Click **Yes** on the dialog box that asks if you are sure you no longer want to share the workbook.

Merging workbooks

It is possible to make copies of a shared workbook, with each copy being modified by a different user independently. The copied workbooks, and their modifications, can then be merged into a single workbook.

Copying a shared workbook

♦ A little preparation is required before you make copies of your shared workbook. Start by opening the **Tools - Share Workbook** menu and clicking the **Editing** tab.

♦ If the workbook is not yet shared, tick the **Allow changes by more than one user** option.

♦ Click the **Advanced** tab.

♦ Check that the **Keep change history for** option is active in the **Track changes** frame. If necessary, modify the number of days during which the other users can change or add comments to the copies of the shared workbook.

You will not be able to merge the copies of the workbook once this reviewing date is passed. If you are unsure about the amount of time required, enter a high number such as 1000 days.

♦ Click **OK**.

♦ If necessary, confirm saving the workbook.

♦ To make the copies of the workbook, use the **File - Save As** command and give each copy a different name.

Merging two or more workbooks

The workbook copies must be merged before the specified change history date has expired (this date is specified in the ***Advanced*** *tab of the* ***Share Workbook*** *dialog box).*

♦ Open the shared workbook in which you wish to merge modifications made to all the copies.

♦ **Tools**
Compare and Merge Workbooks

♦ If necessary, confirm saving the workbook.

♦ In the **Select Files to Merge into Current Workbook** dialog box, select the copy or copies of the shared workbook whose changes you wish to merge.

To select several files, use [Shift] *to select adjacent files or* [Ctrl] *to select nonadjacent ones.*

♦ Click **OK** to start the merge.

❑ *If you do not wish to merge several copies of the shared workbook at the same time, use the* ***Tools - Compare and Merge Workbooks*** *option several times.*

Tracking changes

Tracking the changes in a shared workbook

When you activate tracking, certain changes made to the workbook are highlighted as you work.

♦ Open the shared workbook.

♦ **Tools**
Track Changes
Highlight Changes

♦ Activate the **Highlight changes while editing** option.

When this option is active, the options in the ***Highlight which changes*** *frame become available, enabling you to choose exactly what type of changes you want to make stand out.*

♦ Activate the **When** option to see the changes made in relation to the time interval chosen in the list box:

Since I last saved	highlights only the changes made since the last time the workbook was saved.
All	highlights all the changes made.
Not yet reviewed	highlights those changes which have not been accepted or rejected.
Since date	highlights the changes made after the date entered in the **When** text box.

♦ Activate the **Who** option to choose whose changes should be highlighted (yours or those of another user), using the names in the list box.

♦ If you wish to highlight the changes in a specific range of cells, activate the **Where** option and select the cells in the workbook.

If none of the three ***Highlight which changes*** *options are active, Excel will pick out all the changes made by all the users of the shared workbook, including your own.*

♦ Tick the **Highlight changes on screen** check box to see the changes directly emphasised in the cells.

When you choose this option, Excel highlights the modified areas, using a different colour for each user. If you point to one of these cells, details of the changes made appear as a comment.

♦ To **List changes on a new sheet**, tick the corresponding option.

When you choose this option, Excel shows all the changes as a list in a new sheet called ***History****. This list can be filtered.*

♦ Click **OK**.

❑ *By default, the history of tracked changes is kept for 30 days. You can alter this value by changing the number of days in the* ***Keep change history for*** *option in* ***Tools - Share Workbook - Advanced*** *tab.*

Accepting or rejecting changes in a shared workbook

The changes made to a workbook shared by several different users can be accepted or rejected.

♦ Open the shared workbook.

♦ **Tools**
Track Changes
Accept or Reject Changes

♦ If Excel offers to save the workbook, click **OK**.

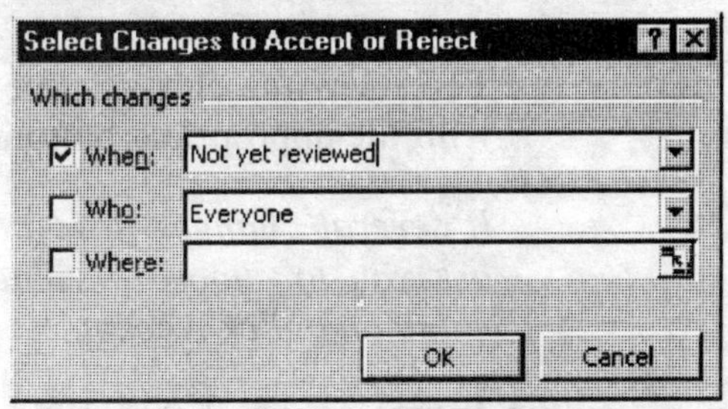

♦ If necessary, modify the time interval involved in the **When** list box.

Not yet reviewed	selects all the changes you have not yet examined.
Since date	examines the changes made to the workbook since the date you specify in the **When** box.

♦ Activate the **Who** option to choose whose changes should be reviewed, selecting the names in the list box.

♦ If you wish to review the changes made to a specific range of cells, activate the **Where** option and select the cells in the workbook.

If none of these three options are active, Excel reviews all the changes made to the shared workbook.

♦ Click **OK**.

*The modification details appear in the **Accept or Reject Changes** dialog box and the first modification is highlighted in the workbook.*

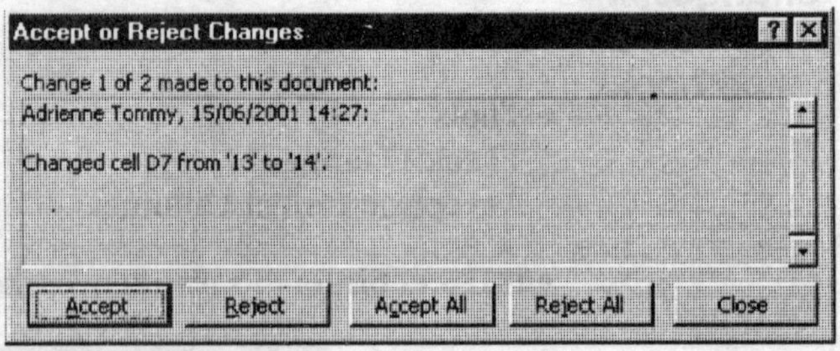

♦ To review the changes one at a time, choose to **Accept** or **Reject** with the appropriate buttons. Excel will go on to the next change.

*If several changes have been made to the same cell, Excel will ask you to choose a value. If this happens, choose the correct value and click **Accept**.*

♦ To act upon all the changes at once, use the buttons to **Accept All** the changes or **Reject All** of them.

Protecting a shared workbook

Protecting a shared workbook prevents other users from "unsharing" it and deleting the history of changes made. You should activate this protection before sharing the workbook.

♦ Open the workbook that is not currently shared.

- ♦ **Tools**
  Protection
  Protect and Share Workbook

- ♦ Tick the **Sharing with track changes** option.

- ♦ To prevent other users removing the protection, enter a password and click **OK.**

- ♦ Enter the password again to confirm it and click **OK** again.

- ♦ Confirm saving the workbook.

*The workbook is shared automatically. The **Allow changes by more than one user** options under the **Editing** tab and the **Track changes** option under the **Advanced** tab (**Tools - Share Workbook**) are no longer available.*

❑ *To remove the protection, and stop the workbook from being shared, use the **Tools - Protection - Unprotect Shared Workbook** command, enter the password if necessary and confirm the message that asks if you no longer wish to share the workbook.*

Sending a workbook for review

If you want one or more colleagues to review a workbook, you can send them a link to the workbook saved on a network or send them a copy of it. This command can only be used if you have Outlook 2002.

- Open the workbook you wish to send for review.
- **File**
  Send To
  Mail Recipient (for Review)
- If the workbook you wish to send is saved on a network, a message appears asking if you would like to send a copy of the file as well as a link to it. Click **Yes** or **No** depending on what you require.
- If the workbook you wish to send is saved on your hard disk, Excel may prompt you to saved a shared version of the workbook. If you want to track changes or merge changes at a later time, click **Yes** and indicate where to save the copy, otherwise click **No.**

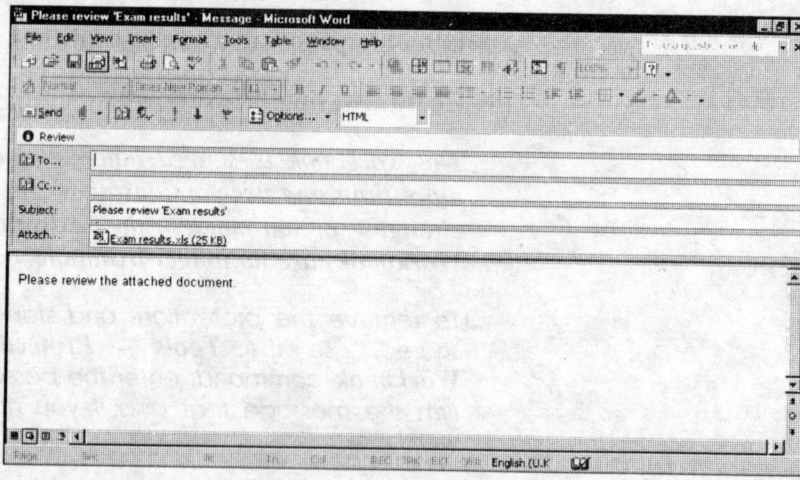

- In the **To** and **Cc** boxes, indicate to whom you wish to send the file, or a carbon copy.

♦ If necessary, change the message **Subject** and enter any further comments in the main message pane.

♦ Click **Send**.

❑ *The recipient receives a message containing (depending on the options chosen as you prepared it) an attached workbook file and/or a link to the file on a network. The recipient can make changes to the workbook and return it to the sender by using the* ***File - Send To - Original Sender*** *command. This message can be modified in the usual ways and sent using the* ***Send*** *button.*

.... *Personal notes* ....

What is a smart tag?

*Sometimes, when you have entered data into an Excel cell, a purple triangle may appear in the top corner of the cell. This indicator means that there is a **smart tag** associated with that cell.*

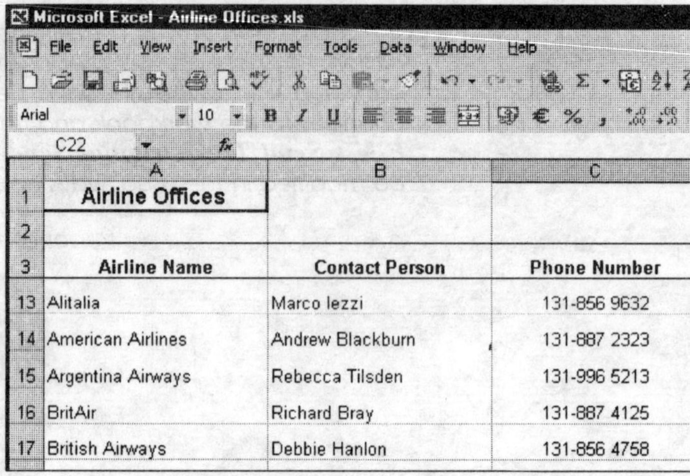

*A smart tag indicator has appeared next to the name **Andrew Blackburn**.*

Smart tags can be used to perform certain actions usually performed by other applications within Excel. The actions proposed depend on the type of data that Excel recognises. For example, Sandra Reid (or Sandra REID) may be recognised by Excel as a "recent mail recipient" smart tag. The associated actions enable you to open that person's contact file, if there is one, send that person an e-mail if he/she has an e-mail address, set up a meeting, add that person's name to your contacts or even insert that person's address in your Excel workbook, if it can be found in your list of contacts!

Other smart tags may appear; for example, if you enter a financial symbol into a cell, a smart tag will enable you to obtain information about that company, such as stock prices.

You must activate the smart tag feature before you can use them.

Activating smart tags

- ♦ **Tools**
  AutoCorrect Options

- ♦ Click the **Smart Tags** tab.

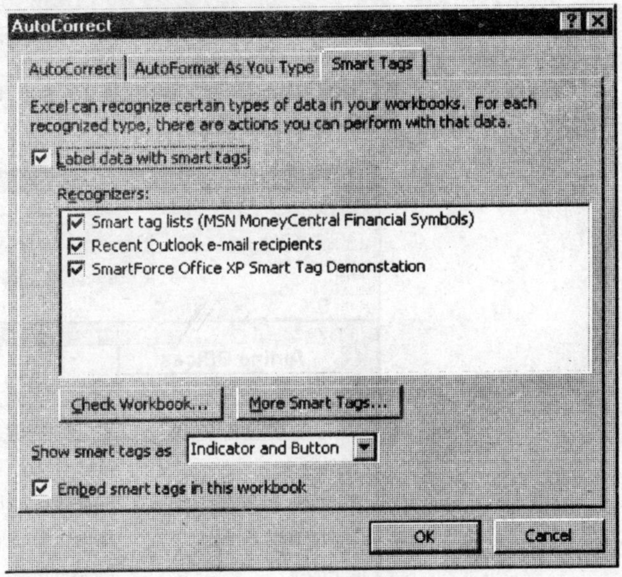

- ♦ To activate smart tags, tick the **Label data with smart tags** option.

- ♦ To choose what type of data Excel should recognise and label with smart tags, activate or deactivate the options in the **Recognizers** list.

*The **Check Workbook** button checks the content of the current workbook according to the options you have defined in the dialog box.*

- ♦ Use the **Show smart tags as** list box to specify whether smart tags should be displayed with a cell indicator (the triangle in the corner) and/or the **Smart Tag Actions** button .

- ♦ To save the smart tags when you save the workbook, activate the **Embed smart tags in this workbook** option.

♦ Click **OK.**

Using smart tags

♦ Point to the smart tag indicator in the corner of the cell to make the **Smart Tag Actions** button appear.

♦ Click the button to see the list of actions associated with this type of data.

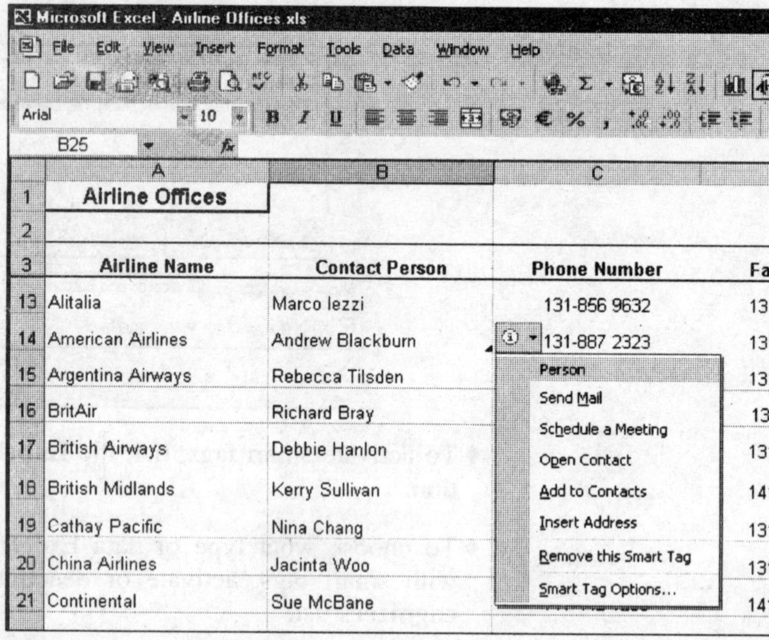

Excel recognises the data as a person's name, and that you have recently sent a message to that person. The actions given allow you to send a message, add that person to your contacts, open the contact file and so on.

♦ Click the name of the action you wish to carry out.

❑ *If Excel does not recognise the names of recent mail recipients, you may need to close Outlook then Excel and reopen Excel so it can update the information received from Outlook.*

Downloading new smart tags

You can download new smart tags from Web sites to add to those already installed with the Microsoft Excel application. Other smart tags may be created by Microsoft but mainly by other IT companies and technicians.
New smart tags are being developed constantly so you can download new smart tags regularly, if you wish.

♦ **Tools**
AutoCorrect Options

♦ Click the **Smart Tags** tab.

♦ Click the **More Smart Tags** option.

A page from the Microsoft Web site appears in your Web browser window, showing the categories into which the smart tags are organised.

♦ Click the link that corresponds to the category that interests you then click the link to download the required smart tag application.

Deleting smart tags

♦ To delete a smart tag, point to the cell until the **Smart Tag Actions** button  appears, click the  button and choose the **Remove this Smart Tag** option.

♦ To remove all the smart tags from the current workbook, deactivate the **Label text with smart tags** and the **Embed smart tags in this workbook** options in the **AutoCorrect Options** dialog box (**Tools - AutoCorrect Options, Smart Tags** tab).

♦ Click **OK**.

♦ Close then open the workbook again to make these changes take effect.

❑ You can deactivate specific types of smart tags by deactivating the corresponding option in the ***Recognizers*** list and the ***Embed smart tags in this workbook*** option. Save the workbook, close it then open it again.

Importing data from a text file

You can use this technique to import data into Excel from a text file; this method allows the data to be updated.

♦ Activate a cell outside a range of imported data.

♦ **Data**
Import External Data
Import Data

♦ In the **Files of type** list box, choose **Text Files**.

♦ Select the drive then the folder in which the text file is stored.

♦ Select the text file you wish to import and click the **Open** button.

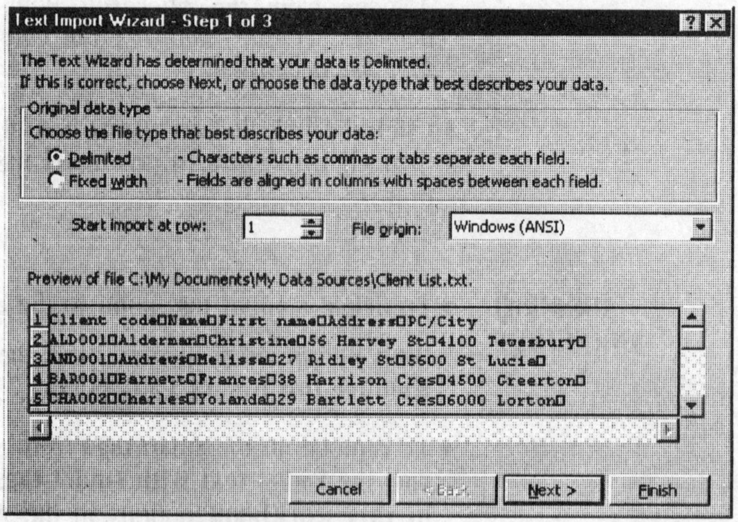

The wizard will interpret the data as having either a ***Delimited*** *style (the data is separated by commas or tabs) or a* ***Fixed width*** *(separated by spaces).*

♦ If necessary, modify the **Original data type** in the corresponding frame.

♦ If you do not want to import the data from the first row in the file, select or enter the required row number in the **Start import at row** text box.

♦ Click the **Next** button to go on to the next step.

♦ Select the delimiters contained in data that are **Delimited** or choose the field widths following the instructions in the first frame of the window, if they are of **Fixed width**.

♦ Click **Next** to go on to the next step.

♦ For each column, select the data format. Do this by clicking the column then choosing one of the options in the **Column data format** frame.

*The **Advanced** button enables you to check, and possibly modify numerical data settings on the imported data such as the decimal and thousands separators.*

♦ To insert the table in an **Existing worksheet**, activate this option then click the button. Access the worksheet then click the first destination cell for the external data. Click the button again to restore the dialog box.

♦ To insert the table into a **New worksheet**, activate the corresponding option.

*The **Properties** button displays options for refreshing data and layout options (cf. Updating imported data).*

♦ Click **OK**.

❑ *You can change the source file by activating an item of imported data and using the **Data - Import External Data - Edit Text Import** command or clicking the tool button on the **External Data** toolbar.*

❑ *The **File - Open** command can be used to import a text file. Excel then guides you in importing the data with the **Text Import Wizard**. However, if you use this method you cannot update the data.*

Copying data from another application into Excel

- Open the application then the file in which the data you want to copy are stored.
- Select the data you want to copy.
- If you are copying text that is not separated by a delimiter (for example, a tab stop), it will be pasted into a single cell in the Excel sheet.
- Copy the data, using the appropriate command. For Office applications, use **Edit - Copy** or [Copy button] or Ctrl **C**.
- Open the Excel application, if necessary, then the workbook in which you want to paste the copied data.
- Activate the first destination cell for the copy.
- To paste the data, without creating a link, use **Edit - Paste** or [Paste button] or Ctrl **V**.
- To paste data with a link, so any changes to the source data are carried over into the Excel worksheet, use **Edit - Paste Special**. Activate the **Paste link** option and in the **As** list, choose the format the pasted data should take then click **OK**.

Importing data from a Web page

Using a Web query

A Web query enables you to import data from a Web page, originating from one or more tables; this data can be updated.

- Activate a cell outside a range of imported data.
- **Data**
  Import External Data
  New Web Query
- In the **Address** box, enter the URL of the Web page from which you wish to import data or expand the list to choose a recently visited **Address** then click **OK**.

*The Web page appears in the **New Web Query** dialog box and the information it contains is divided into a series of tables, each indicated by a small yellow box with an arrow in it.*

♦ Click the to the top left of any table(s) you wish to import or click the symbol in the upper left corner of the page to import the data from the whole page.

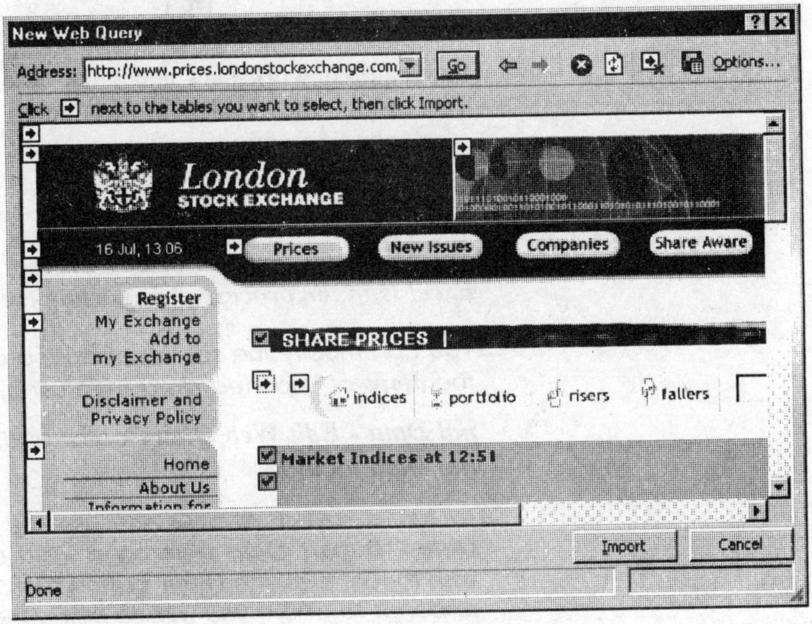

The symbol is transformed into .

*If you cannot see any icons on the Web page, click the button on the **New Web Query** window.*

*The **Options** button displays the default options for formatting and importing Web data, which you can modify.*

♦ If you wish to be able to extract the query data into other workbooks or share the query with other users, you should save that query. Click , select the file in which to save and enter the **File name** then click **Save**.

A Web query is saved as a file with an .iqy extension. If you do not save the Web query as a separate file, it will be saved as part of your workbook and can only be run from that workbook.

♦ Click the **Import** button.

♦ In the **Import Data** dialog box, specify where to place the imported data. To insert them in an **Existing worksheet**, click this option then click the button, go to the first destination cell in the required worksheet and click to restore the dialog box. To insert the table in a **New worksheet**, activate the corresponding option.

♦ Click **OK**.

The icon appears briefly on the status bar, indicating that Excel is in the process of importing the data.

❑ *You can modify the source of a Web query by activating one of the items of imported data then using the* ***Data - Import External Data - Edit Web Query*** *command or click on the* ***External Data*** *toolbar.*

❑ *To run a saved Web Query, use the* ***Data - Import External Data - Import Data*** *command. Find and select the query you wish to run, click the* ***Open*** *button then select the option that corresponds to where you wish to place the imported data. Click* ***OK*** *to finish.*

Copying data from a Web page

This method can be used to copy data using the Internet Explorer Web browser (4.1 or later).

♦ In the browser, select the data you wish to copy.

♦ **Edit**
Copy

♦ Go into Excel and activate the first destination cell for the copied data.

♦ **Edit**
Paste

♦ To change the way Excel pastes the data, click the icon at the bottom right of the range of pasted cells and choose to **Keep Source Formatting**, or to **Match Destination Formatting.** The **Create Refreshable Web Query** option will create a query based on the Web page from which you copied the data.

Importing data via MS Query

*It is possible to import data from a **Relational** database such as Microsoft Access 2002 or from an **OLAP** database, such as Microsoft SQL Server OLAP, or from a **Text file**. You can import this information directly into an Excel worksheet by using the Microsoft Query application.*
The principle of Microsoft Query is to create a query that will copy data from an external database into an Excel workbook and simultaneously sort and filter the imported data. One advantage of this technique is that you can exclude data that you do not require. Microsoft Query is a Microsoft Excel option, which by default is only installed on your computer the first time you try to extract external data with Excel.
*During this chapter you will see the import procedure for an (existing) Access 2002 database, which is a **relational** database.*

♦ Activate a cell outside a range of imported data.

♦ **Data**
Import External Data
New Database Query
Databases tab

*You may see a message informing you that the required component is not installed: if this occurs, insert the Office XP or Excel 2002 CD-ROM and click **Yes** to install the component.*

♦ In the list, select **MS Access Database** as the source of the data you wish to extract.

♦ Make sure the **Use the Query Wizard to create/edit queries** option is active.

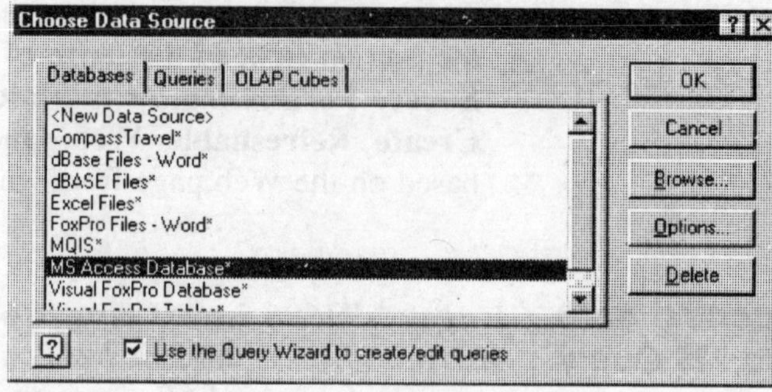

♦ Click **OK**.

♦ In the **Drives** list, choose the disk drive where the database is stored then, in **Directories**, choose its folder.

♦ Click to select the database that contains the information you want to extract then click **OK**.

*The **Query Wizard - Choose Columns** dialog box appears on the screen. The first step is to choose the columns (fields) to include in the query. To display all the columns in a table, click the plus sign (+) which appears to the left of the table's name in the **Available tables and columns** list.*

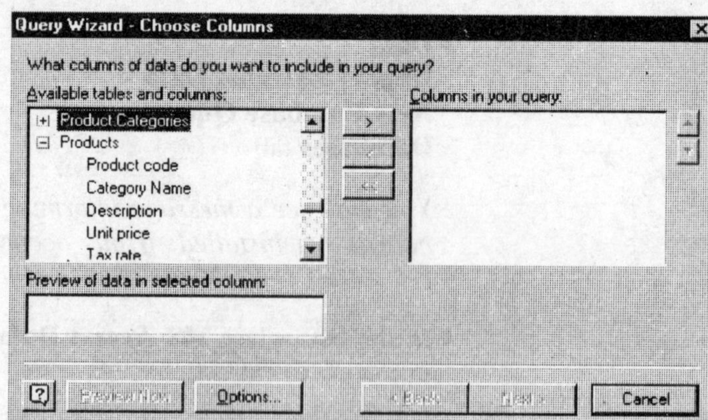

♦ For each complete table or column you want to add to the **Columns in your query** list, click the element to be added in the **Available table and columns** list then click the > button.

♦ Click the **Next** button.

If you add columns from different tables, these tables must have at least one column in common. If not, you will see a message asking you to create a manual link between the tables.

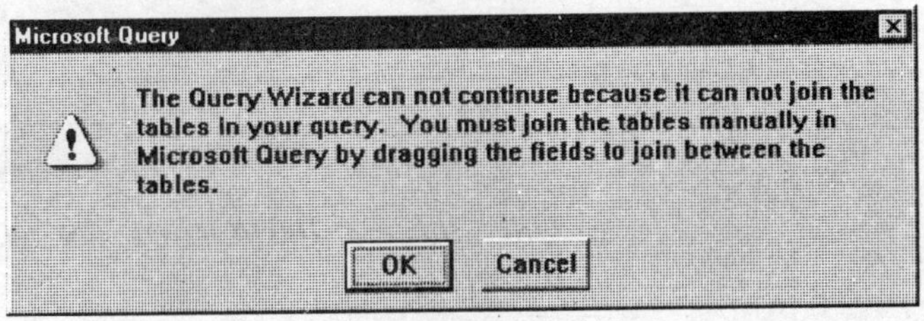

*The **Query Wizard - Filter Data** dialog box allows you to set filter criteria per column (field) in order to limit which data is imported. If no criteria are present, all the data in the column concerned will be imported.*

♦ For each column to be filtered:

– Select in the **Column to filter** list the name of the column to which the filter should be applied.

– Select the comparison operator of and the compare value in the **Include only rows where** boxes.

*To delete a criterion, open the list of operators for the criterion concerned then click the empty space above the **equals** operator.*

♦ Activate the **And** or **Or** option to define one or more further filter criteria based on the same column: when the **And** option is active, all of the conditions set must be met simultaneously, and when the **Or** option is active, only one condition needs to be met.

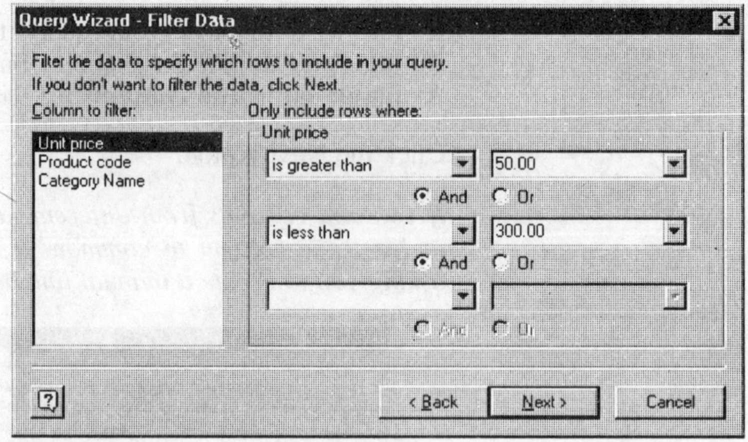

Only three criteria rows are visible but you can define many more.

♦ Click the **Next** button.

♦ If you wish, specify how Excel should sort the data. In the **Sort by** list, select the name of the column by which Excel must sort the data and request a sort in **Ascending** or **Descending** order. If the first column contains duplicate values, you can sort by a second column selected in the **Then by** list, then a third column in the next list and so on.

♦ Click **Next**.

♦ Make sure the **Return Data to Microsoft Excel** option is active in the **Query Wizard - Finish** dialog box.

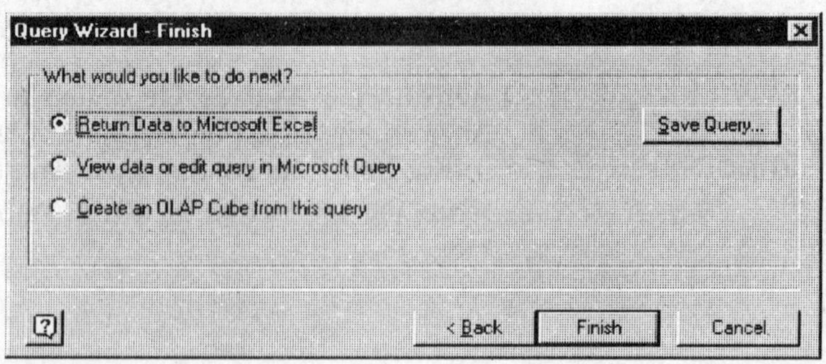

♦ If you wish to save your query to use it later, or in other workbooks, click the **Save Query** button, select a location for the file and enter a **File name** then click the **Save** button.

♦ Click the **Finish** button to close the application and retrieve the data in Microsoft Excel.

♦ To insert the data in an **Existing worksheet**, activate this option. The text box on this option contains the reference of the cell that was active when the import procedure first started. If you want to modify the active cell, click the button to collapse the dialog box (if necessary) and click the first destination cell for the external data. Restore the dialog box by clicking .

♦ To insert the data in a **New worksheet**, activate the corresponding option.

*The **Properties** button displays settings for refreshing data, which you can modify (cf. Updating imported data).*

*The **Create a PivotTable report** link opens the **PivotTable and PivotChart Wizard** so you can analyse the imported data in a pivot table.*

♦ Click **OK**.

❑ *You can modify the source of a query by activating one of the items of imported data then using the **Data - Import External Data - Edit Query** command or click on the **External Data** toolbar.*

Updating imported data

After you have imported data from a text file, a Web page or with Microsoft Query (see previous sections), you can update this data from Excel and modify the update settings.

Updating data

♦ Activate one of the cells containing imported data.

*When you activate a cell containing imported data, Excel displays the **External Data** toolbar, which contains data update buttons. If this toolbar does not appear, you can display it using **View - Toolbars - External Data**.*

♦ **Data**
Refresh Data (on the **External Data** toolbar)

Depending on the type of data you are refreshing and the current update settings, Excel may ask you to select the source file or enter a password.

Modifying the update settings

♦ Activate one of the cells containing imported data.

♦ **Data**
Import External Data
Data Range Properties (on the **External Data** toolbar)

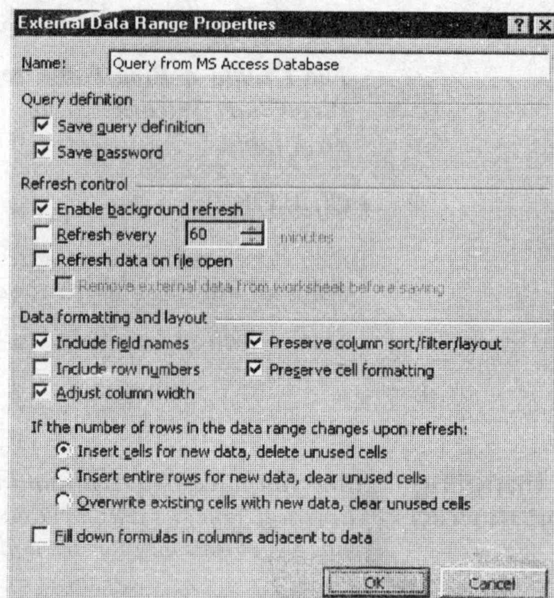

♦ Keep the **Save query definition** option active if you want to be able to update the imported data.

♦ The **Save password** option enables you to save a password entered once, so Excel does not ask for it each time you update the data (whether or not this option appears depends on the type of data).

♦ Use the **Refresh control** options to choose how Excel should update and how often.

♦ Select formatting options for the imported data under **Data formatting and layout**.

♦ Indicate how Excel should react **If the number of rows in the data range changes upon refresh**.

♦ The **Fill down formulas in columns adjacent to data** option allows for the automatic copying of formulas that you may add after having imported the data.

♦ Click **OK**.

♦ Depending on the type of data imported, some of the options in the **External Data Range Properties** dialog box may be unavailable.

.... *Personal notes* ....

Creating a macro

♦ If necessary, open the workbook concerned by the macro.

♦ **Tools**
Macros
Record New Macro

♦ Give the macro a name.

♦ Do not put any spaces in a macro name.

♦ If you wish, specify a shortcut key which will run the macro.

♦ Indicate where the macro is to be stored: in **This Workbook** or a **New Workbook.** If you want the macro to be permanently accessible, choose **Personal Macro Workbook.**

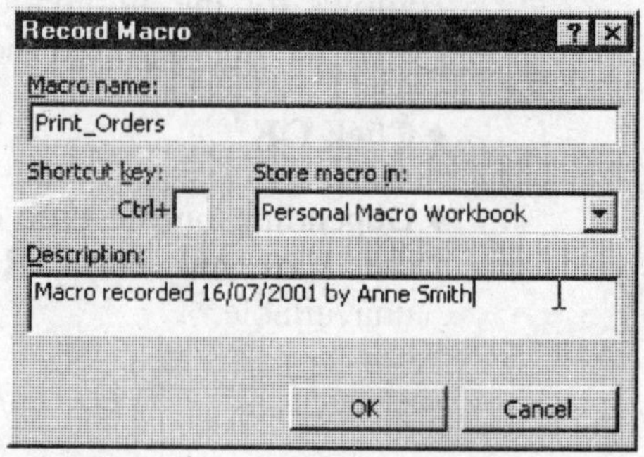

♦ Click **OK.**

*The **Stop Rec.** bar appears, and the word **Recording** appears on the status bar (you should check this).*

♦ Go through all the actions to be automated in the macro.

♦ When all the actions have been recorded, click the button on the **Stop Rec.** bar (or use **Tools - Macro - Stop Recording**).

❑ *Macros recorded in this way are created in a file called PERSONAL.XLS, where all personal macros are stored.*

❑ *This type of macro is always accessible as the PERSONAL workbook is automatically opened and hidden when Excel is started.*

Running a macro

- If a macro has been created in a workbook other than PERSONAL.XLS, open it.
- **Tools**
  Macro
  Macros

  ♦ Alt F8
- In the **Macros in** list, indicate where the macro you require is stored.
- Double-click the macro you want to run.

> *If the macro is stored in a workbook which is open or in PERSONAL.XLS, you can also run it by pressing the shortcut key defined when the macro was created.*

Viewing the contents of a macro

- If the macro is stored in PERSONAL.XLS, use the command **Window - Unhide** to display it, as you would for any other hidden workbook.
- **Tools**
  Macro
  Macros

  ♦ Alt F8
- Select the macro, then click **Edit**.

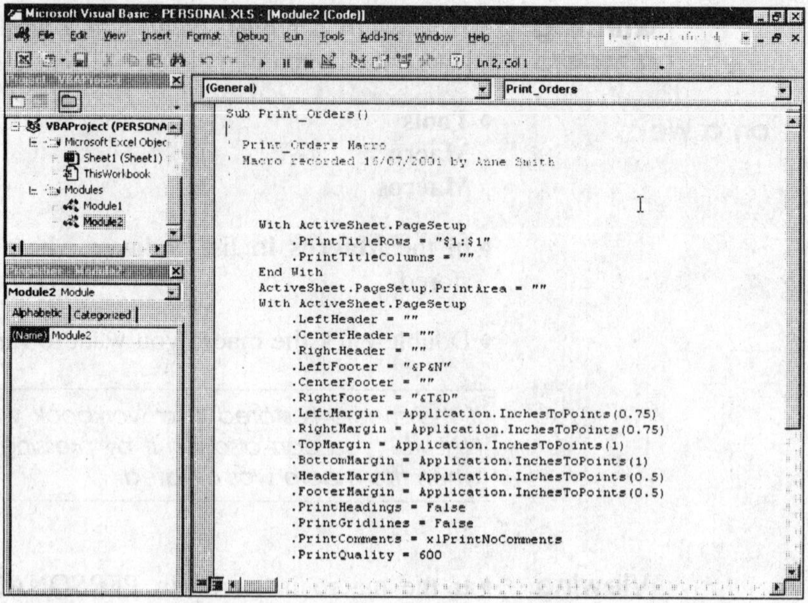

The contents of the macro appear in a Microsoft Visual Basic window.

- Close the Visual Basic window.

*If you have displayed the Personal.xls workbook, remember to hide it with the **Window - Hide** command.*

Deleting a macro

- **Tools**
  Macro
  Macros

- Alt F8

- In the **Macros in** list, indicate where the undesired macro is.
- Select the macro.
- Click the **Delete** button.
- Click **Yes** to confirm deleting the macro.

Creating a shortcut to a folder on a Web server

If you want to publish your Web page in an existing folder on a Web server, you should create a shortcut to that folder before you start work.

- If necessary, open the task pane with the **View - Task Pane** command, then open the drop-down list on the pane's title bar with the ▼ arrow and click the **New Workbook** option.
- If you are working under Windows 2000 or Windows Me, click the **Add Network Place** link in the task pane then activate the **Create a shortcut to an existing Network Place** option in the **Add Network Place Wizard** dialog box.
  If you are working under Windows NT 4.0 or Windows 98, click the **Add Web Folder** link in the task pane then activate the **Create a shortcut to an existing Web Folder** option.
- Click the **Next** button.
- In the **Location** text box, enter the complete URL of the Web server to which the shortcut should lead.
- Enter the **Shortcut name**.

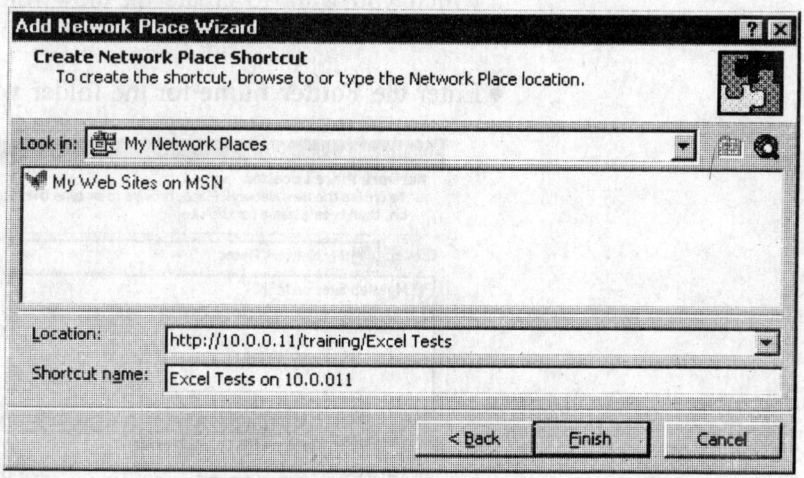

- Click the **Finish** button.

Creating a folder and its shortcut on a Web server

Before you publish a Web page on a Web server, you should first create a Web folder on the server as well as a shortcut to make it easier to access that folder. You must have the appropriate permissions from your systems administrator or your Internet Service Provider to be able to do this.

♦ If necessary, open the task pane with the **View - Task Pane** command, then open the drop-down list on the pane's title bar with the arrow and click the **New Workbook** option.

♦ If you are working under Windows 2000 or Windows Me, click the **Add Network Place** link in the task pane then activate the **Create a new Network Place** option in the **Add Network Place Wizard** dialog box.

♦ If you are working under Windows NT 4.0 or Windows 98, click the **Add Web Folder** link in the task pane then activate the **Create a new Web Folder** option.

♦ Click the **Next** button.

♦ In the **Folder location** text box, enter the URL for the server on which you want to create the new folder (your administrator or ISP will have to supply you with the corresponding URL).

♦ Enter the **Folder name** for the folder you are creating.

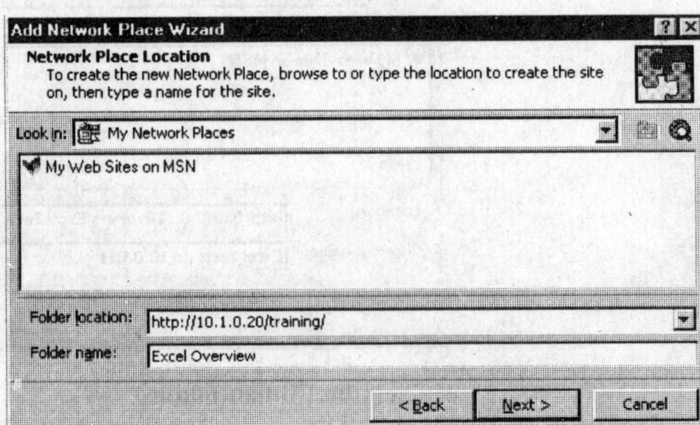

♦ Click the **Next** button.

♦ Click the **Finish** button to create the new folder on the Web server and the corresponding shortcut in **My Network Places.**

Publishing a non-interactive Web page

*A **non-interactive Web page** contains information that can be consulted by users visiting your Internet/intranet site but cannot be modified. You can publish a selection of cells, a worksheet or a whole Excel 2002 workbook as a non-interactive Web page.*

♦ Create or open the workbook (in xls or htm format) that you want to publish.

♦ If necessary, select the data you wish to publish, or if you want to publish a whole sheet or workbook, do not make any selection.

♦ **File**
Save As Web Page

♦ Select the location in which you want to publish your Web page, using the **Save in** list or the **Places Bar**. Depending on your version of Windows, the **Places Bar** can take you rapidly to one of the previously created **Web Folders** (in Windows NT 4.0/98) or to the existing **My Network Places** (in Windows 2000/Me) (cf. previous sections).

It is a good idea to test your Web page before publishing it on a Web server. To do this, first publish the Web page on your hard disk, test it, make any necessary changes then when you are satisfied with the results, go ahead and publish it on the Web server, where any authorised user can access it (cf. Previewing a non-interactive Web page). The publication procedure is identical, whether you are publishing on your own workstation or on a Web server; the only thing that differs is the place chosen to publish the page.

♦ Use the **Web Options** in the **Tools** menu to modify the settings for the Web page you are publishing.

- Specify whether you are saving the **Entire Workbook** or just a **Selection** by activating the appropriate option.
- Make sure the **Add interactivity** option is not active.
- If you wish, click the **Change Title** button and enter the text that will appear on the browser's title bar when the Web page is opened, then click **OK**.
- If necessary, change the proposed **File name**.

  You should avoid putting spaces and characters with accents in file names as they are not always managed correctly by Web servers.

- To save the Web page, without accessing the publication options, click the **Save** button.

  The Web page appears in htm format and the original file closes automatically. Along with the Web page, Excel generates a folder that contains all the components of the Web page, which are called "supporting files"; this separate folder only appears when you save, not publish, a Web page. This folder is called ***[Web page name]_files****; the supporting files folder and the Web page are indissociable. Your Web page is now saved.*

- To publish your Web page, choosing more advanced options if you wish, click the **Publish** button.

A new dialog box appears:

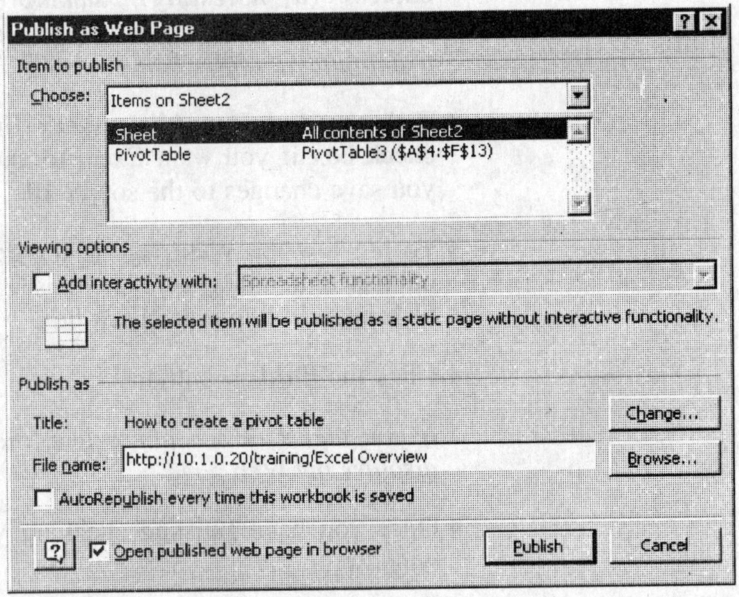

♦ In the **Choose** list, select the element you want to publish.

What appears in this list depends on the contents of the Web page.

♦ Make sure the **Add interactivity with** option is not active.

♦ Click the **Change** button if you want to modify the name entered for the page during the previous step.

♦ By default the place of publication followed by the file name defined in the previous step appear in the **File name** text box. If you are publishing the Web page on your own computer, modify this address (if necessary), making sure you use this syntax: *drive:\folder\file.htm* (for example, c:\training\excel2002\pivot_tables.htm). Typing in this kind of information can be tedious, so you may prefer to click the **Browse** button and select the folder (and its subfolders, if necessary) in your computer's file hierarchy then complete the address with the required file name.

If you are publishing the Web page on a Web server, modify this address (if necessary), making sure you use this syntax: *http://server_address/file.htm (for example http://10.1.0.20/excel training/pivot tables.htm.*

♦ Tick the **AutoRepublish every time this workbook is saved** check box if you want Excel to update the Web page each time you save changes to the source file.

♦ To preview the Web page in the default browser once you have published it, make sure there is a tick in the **Open published web page in browser** check box.

♦ Click the **Publish** button.

If you chose to see a preview, the default browser opens and displays the Web page.

♦ Once you have finished checking your page, close the browser window.

❑ *If you published your Web page on your own workstation, you can check the result by viewing the file in your Web browser. If necessary, modify the original workbook you used to create the Web page then when you are satisfied with the result, publish the Web page again using the same procedure but replace the address of your own computer by the address of the Web server concerned.*

❑ *If you saved (not published) a whole workbook as a non-interactive Web page, you can still preview the page without publishing it. To do this, open the htm file in question then use the* ***Web Page Preview*** *command in the* ***File*** *menu.*

Publishing an interactive Web page

A visitor to an interactive Web page can modify the page, but he/she must have Internet Explorer (4.01 or later) installed on his/her computer and also have the appropriate Microsoft Office licence to use worksheets, charts and pivot table lists published exclusively from Microsoft Excel.

- Create or open the worksheet (in xls or htm format) that you want to publish.

  It is possible to publish an entire workbook but some features may then be unavailable to Web users.

- **File**
  Save As Web Page

- Select the location in which you want to publish your Web page, using the **Save in** list or the **Places Bar**. Depending on your version of Windows, the **Places Bar** can take you rapidly to one of the previously created **Web Folders** (in Windows NT 4.0/98) or to the existing **My Network Places** (in Windows 2000/Me) (cf. previous sections).

- Use the **Web Options in the Tools** menu to modify the settings for the Web page you are publishing.

- Select the **Selection: sheet** option and tick the **Add Interactivity** check box.

- If necessary, click the **Change Title** button to enter the text that will appear in the browser's title bar when you open the Web page then click **OK**.

- If you wish, modify the suggested **File name**.

  You should avoid putting spaces and characters with accents in file names as they are not always managed correctly by Web servers.

- To save the Web page, without accessing the publication options, click the **Save** button.

  The Web page appears in htm format and the original file closes automatically. For an interactive Web page, Excel does not generate a supporting files folder. You have finished saving your Web page.

- To publish your Web page, choosing more advanced options if you wish, click the **Publish** button.

A new dialog box appears:

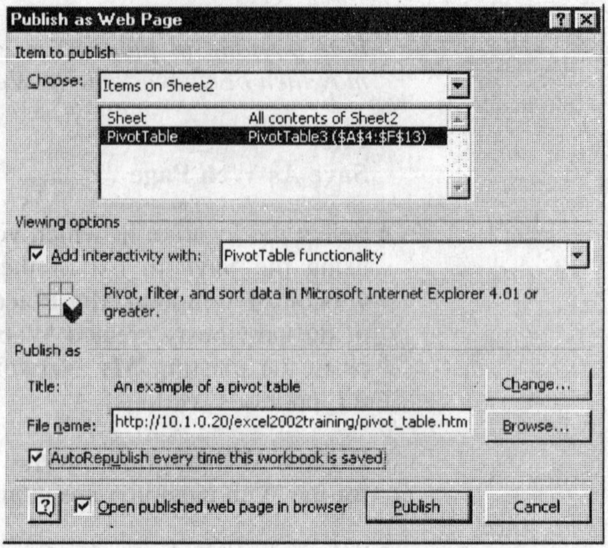

♦ In the **Choose** list, select the element you want to publish.

What appears in this list depends on the contents of the Web page.

♦ Make sure the **Add interactivity with** check box is still ticked and if necessary, open the attached drop-down list to choose which Excel functionality you want to make available to users of the page. This depends on what type of interactive element you are publishing (you can offer spreadsheet, chart or pivot table functionality).

♦ Click the **Change** button if you want to modify the name entered for the page during the previous step.

♦ By default the place of publication, followed by the file name defined in the previous step, appear in the **File name** text box.

If you are publishing the Web page on your own computer, modify this address (if necessary), making sure you use this syntax: *drive:\folder\file.htm* (for example, c:\training\excel2002\pivot_tables.htm). Typing in this kind of information can be tedious, so you may prefer to click the **Browse** button and select the folder (and its subfolders, if necessary) in your computer's file hierarchy then complete the address with the required file name.

If you are publishing the Web page on a web server, modify this address (if necessary), making sure you use this syntax: *http://server_address/file.htm (for example http://10.1.0.20/excel training/pivot tables.htm.*

♦ Tick the **AutoRepublish every time this workbook is saved** check box if you want Excel to update the Web page each time you save changes to the source file.

♦ To preview the Web page in the default browser once you have published it, make sure there is a tick in the **Open published web page in browser** check box.

♦ Click the **Publish** button.

If you are publishing a pivot table, your browser may inform you that the source data for your table is located in another domain.

♦ In this case, click **Yes** to continue.

Excel publishes the Web page in htm format in the chosen place (on your workstation or on a Web server) but the source file, in xls format, remains on your hard disk in its original location.

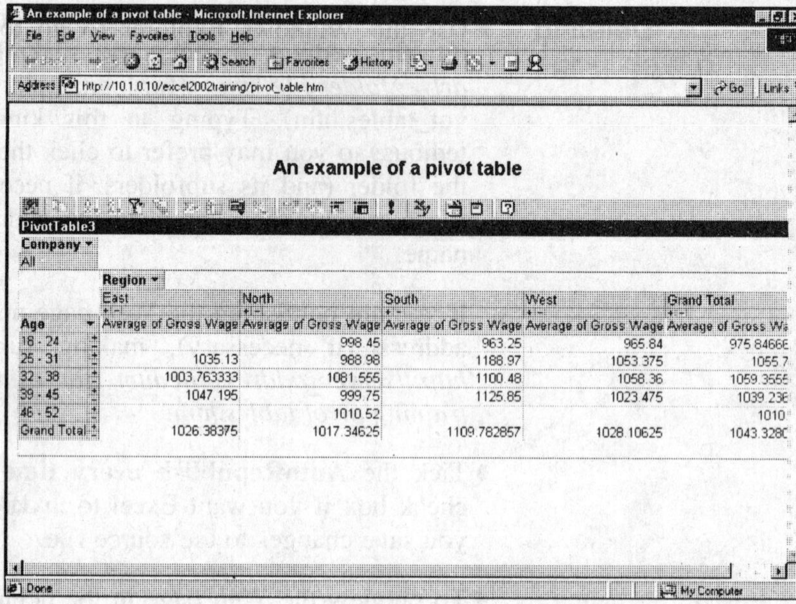

An example of a pivot table

PivotTable3

Company: All

Age	East Average of Gross Wage	North Average of Gross Wage	South Average of Gross Wage	West Average of Gross Wage	Grand Total Average of Gross Wa
18 - 24		998.45	963.25	965.84	975.84666
25 - 31	1035.13	988.98	1188.97	1053.375	1055.7
32 - 38	1003.763333	1081.555	1100.48	1058.36	1059.3555
39 - 45	1047.195	999.75	1125.85	1023.475	1039.238
46 - 52		1010.52			1010
Grand Total	1026.38375	1017.34625	1109.782857	1028.10625	1043.3280

You can see that in the example above, which is a pivot table, each field has its own drop-down list, containing the details of that field. You can modify the table by activating or deactivating one or more of these detail items. A user visiting this page can change the table as he/she likes, without needing the Microsoft Excel application, as the changes are made directly in the Web browser (the user does however need the appropriate Microsoft Office licence to use the Excel functionalities).

- ♦ When you have finished your work, close the browser window.
- ♦ If you wish, close the Excel file.

Deleting a Web page

- Use the Windows Explorer to go to the server and/or folder where the Web page is located.
- Select the Web page ([filename].htm) and its supporting files folder ([filename]_files), if you are deleting a saved (not published) non-interactive Web page.
- Press the Del key.
- Click **Yes** to confirm the file deletion.

.... *Personal notes* ....

WORKING WITH MENUS AND OPTIONS

Keys	Command
Shift F10	Display shortcut menu
	File
Ctrl N	New
Ctrl O	Open
Ctrl S	Save
F12	Save As
Ctrl P	Print
Alt F4	Exit
	Edit
Ctrl Z	Undo
Ctrl Y	Repeat
Ctrl X	Cut
Ctrl C	Copy
Ctrl V	Paste
Ctrl D	Fill down
Ctrl R	Fill right
Suppr	Clear contents
Ctrl -	Delete
Ctrl F	Find
Shift F4	Find next
Ctrl Shift F4	Find previous
Ctrl H	Replace
F5 or Ctrl G	Go To
	Insert
Ctrl + (numeric keyboard)	Cells, Rows, Columns
Shift F11	Worksheet
	Chart
F11	As New Sheet
	Name
Ctrl F3	Define
F3	Paste
Ctrl Shift F3	Create
Shift F2	Cell comment
Ctrl K	Hyperlink

Keys	Command
	Format
Ctrl 1	Cells, Object
	Row
Ctrl 9	Hide
Ctrl ⇧Shift 9	Unhide
	Column
Ctrl 0	Hide
Ctrl ⇧Shift 0	Unhide
Alt '	Style
	Tools
F7	Spelling
	Macro
Alt F8	Macros
Alt F11	Visual Basic Editor
Alt ⇧Shift F4	Microsoft Script Editor
	Calculation
F9	Calculate Now
⇧Shift F9	Calculate worksheet
	Data
	Group and Outline
Alt ⇧Shift →	Group
Alt ⇧Shift ←	Ungroup
	Help
F1	Microsoft Excel Help
⇧Shift F1	What's This?

OTHER KEY COMBINATIONS

Keys	Command
	Entering data
Ctrl ;	Enter the current date
Ctrl ⇧Shift :	Enter the current time
Alt Gr 4	Euro symbol
Ctrl '	Insert same formula/value as cell above
Ctrl ⇧Shift "	Insert value only from cell above
Alt =	Insert Autosum

Keys	Action
Del	Clear selection of formulas/data
Ctrl ⇄	Tab within a text box

Working in the Formula Bar

Keys	Action
F2	Activate Edit mode in cell and formula bar
=	Start a formula
Ctrl Del	Delete from insertion point to the end of line
Alt Enter	Insert a line break
Esc	Cancel unconfirmed entry
Enter	Confirm cell entry
Ctrl Enter	Fill selected range with the current entry
F4	Create relative/absolute renferences
Ctrl A	After a function has been entered, displays the formula palette
Ctrl ⇧ Shift A	After a function has been entered, displays function arguments

Formatting cells

Keys	Action
Ctrl ⇧ Shift &	Apply an outline border
Ctrl ⇧ Shift -	Remove all borders
Ctrl B	Apply or remove bold type
Ctrl I	Apply or remove italic type
Ctrl U	Apply or remove an underline

Formatting numbers and dates

Keys	Action
Ctrl ⇧ Shift ~	Apply General number format
Ctrl ⇧ Shift !	Thousands, two decimal places plus separator
Ctrl ⇧ Shift $	Currency format, two decimal places
Ctrl ⇧ Shift ^	Exponential number format, two decimal places

Moving in worksheets

Keys	Action
↖	Beginning of current row
Ctrl ↖	A1 on current sheet
Ctrl End	Cell at intersection of column used furthest to the right and row used furthest down
Ctrl F6 or Ctrl ⇄	Next window
Ctrl ⇧ Shift F6 or Ctrl ⇧ Shift ⇄	Previous window
Ctrl Pg Dn	Next sheet in the workbook
Ctrl Pg Up	Previous sheet in the workbook
F6	Next pane in a split worksheet
⇧ Shift F6	Previous pane in a split worksheet

Keys	Action
	Selecting
Ctrl A	Whole sheet
Ctrl space	Whole column
Shift space	Whole row
F8	Activates/deactivates extend mode
Shift F8	Add a range of cells to current selection
	Selecting of individual cells
Ctrl Shift O	Cells containing comments
Ctrl Shift *	Rectangular range of cells surrounding the active cell
Ctrl /	The entire array to which the cell belongs
Ctrl [	Only cells to which the formulas in the selection make direct reference.
Ctrl Shift [	All cells to which formulas in the selection make direct or indirect reference.
Ctrl]	Only cells with formulas that refer directly to the active cell.
Ctrl Shift]	All cells with formulas that refer directly or indirectly to the active cell.
Alt ;	Only visible cells in the current selection.
Ctrl \	Select cells in a selected row whose contents are different from the active cell.
Ctrl Shift \	Select cells in a selected column whose contents are different from the comparison cell in each column; for each column the comparison cell.

A

B

C

M

N

O

ISBN	TITLE	AUTHOR	PRICE	PAGES
8170084512	The Power of Oracle 9i	Rajiv Parida	Rs. 475.00	1100

DOEACC 'O' LEVEL

ISBN	TITLE	AUTHOR	PRICE	PAGES
8170085640	Programming and Problem Solving Through "C" Language	Harsha Priya, R. Ranjeet	Rs. 95.00	306
8170084474	IT Tools and Applications	Ramesh Bangia	Rs. 145.00	392
8170085594	Business Systems	Ramesh Bangia	Rs. 145.00	441
8170085454	Internet & Web Design	Ramesh Bangia	Rs. 120.00	321

DOEACC, BCA, MCA, IGNOU, ENGINEERING

ISBN	TITLE	AUTHOR	PRICE	PAGES
8170086140	Data Structure for 'C' Programming	Ajay Kumar	Rs. 145.00	290
817008363X	Practical Project Management	Ivan Bayross	Rs. 195.00	342
8170082102	Numerical Methods in 'C'	J.G. Kori	Rs. 50.00	168
8170083834	Comprehensive Compiler Design	O.G. Kakde	Rs. 125.00	346
8170081858	Comprehensive Computer Graphics (Including C++)	V.K. Pachgare	Rs. 80.00	224
8170082145	Comprehensive Discrete Mathematics and Structures	Satinder Bal Gupta	Rs. 90.00	256
8170083559	Comprehensive Computer & Languages	Ashok Arora & Shefali Bansal	Rs. 175.00	590
8170082110	Comprehensive C++ Programming	Nishant Kundalia	Rs. 75.00	168
8170084407	Comprehensive Theory of Automata and Formal Languages	Anand Sharma	Rs. 145.00	352
8170085276	Fundamentals of Computer Programming and Information Technology	J.B. Dixit & Sangeeta Dixit	Rs. 175.00	558

EMBEDDED SYSTEMS/ARCHITECTURE

ISBN	TITLE	AUTHOR	PRICE	PAGES
8170083435	Practical Linux Programming : Device Drivers, Embedded Systems, and the Internet	Ashfaq A. Khan	Rs. 295.00	420
8170083575	TCP/IP Application Layer Protocols for Embedded Systems	M. Tim Jones	Rs. 295.00	350
8170086264	Grid Computing : A Practical Guide to Technology and Applications	Ahmar Abbas	Rs. 295.00	408

INTERNET & WEB

ISBN	TITLE	AUTHOR	PRICE	PAGES
8170083206	The Internet Hand Book for Writers, Students & Teachers	Mary McGuire, Linda Stillborne	Rs. 195.00	288
8170083400	Professional Web Design (Techniques and Templates)	Clint Eccher	Rs. 295.00	425
8170083524	Marketing in The Cyber Age	Kurt Rohner	Rs. 295.00	250

Please write for a free color Firewall Media Catalog for details on the above books.

ISBN	TITLE	AUTHOR	PRICE	PAGES
8170083583	**FrontPage 2000 for Visual Learners**	Chris Charuhas	Rs. 95.00	200
8170083591	**HTML & JavaScript for Visual Learners**	Chris Charuhas	Rs. 95.00	200
8170083605	**The Visual Learner's Guide to Managing Web Projects**	Chris Charuhas	Rs. 95.00	130
8170083613	**Dreamweaver 4 for Visual Learners**	Chris Charuhas	Rs. 95.00	200
8170084768	**IT Resource-Implementing XML : Managing and Formatting Data**	Johnny Brochard	Rs. 125.00	279
8170084776	**Way in-Internet Getting Started**	Elizabeth Bramire	Rs. 95.00	165
8170085470	**Design Your Web World**	Sunil Jalota	Rs. 45.00	103
8170085497	**Electronic Commerce**	Pete Loshin, John Vacca	Rs. 295.00	472
	KEEPING AHEAD SERIES			
8170084652	**Keeping Ahead—Exchange 2002 Server**	Phillippe Levesque	Rs. 145.00	285
8170084660	**Keeping Ahead—Windows 2000 Professional**	Jose Dardoigne	Rs. 175.00	388
8170084679	**Keeping Ahead—Windows 2000 Server**	Phillippe Mathon	Rs. 175.00	360
8170084687	**Keeping Ahead—Linux Administration Kernel Version 2.0 to 2.2**	Bruno Guerin	Rs. 125.00	240
8170084695	**Keeping Ahead—Using Linux Kernel Version 2.0 to 2.2**	Bruno Guerin	Rs. 125.00	258
8170084709	**Keeping Ahead—Java 2**	Benjamin Aumaille	Rs. 145.00	284
8170084717	**Keeping Ahead—SQL Server 7**	Joelle Mosset	Rs. 145.00	329
8170084725	**Keeping Ahead—Java Script and VB Script**	Benjamin Aumaille	Rs. 145.00	313
8170084733	**Keeping Ahead—C++ Programming Language**	Bruno Dubois	Rs. 125.00	234
8170084741	**Keeping Ahead—TCP/IP in the NT Environment**	Bruno Ferec	Rs. 125.00	230
	MCSE			
817008489X	**MCSE-Administering SQL Server 7.0**	Jerome Gabillaud	Rs. 295.00	580
8170084903	**MCSE-Networking Essentials**	Jose Dordoigne	Rs. 245.00	453
8170084911	**MCSE-Windows 2000 Professional**	Jose Dordoigne	Rs. 325.00	665
817008492X	**MCSE-Windows 2000 Server**	Phillippe Mathon	Rs. 345.00	712
	MULTIMEDIA			
8170082439	**Multimedia Basics-Technology (Vol. I)**	Andreas Holzinger	Rs. 195.00	285
8170082447	**Multimedia Basics-Learning (Vol. II)**	Andreas Holzinger	Rs. 195.00	300
8170082455	**Multimedia Basics-Design (Vol. III)**	Andreas Holzinger	Rs. 195.00	280
8170083532	**Maya Feature Creature Creations**	Todd Palamar	Rs. 295.00	450
8170083540	**Sound Forge Power**	Scott R. Garrigus	Rs. 195.00	250
8170086205	**Building A Digital Human**	Ken Brilliant	Rs. 295.00	380

Please write for a free color Firewall Media Catalog for details on the above books.

ISBN	TITLE	AUTHOR	PRICE	PAGES
8170086213	**Making Digital Videos**	Ben Lang	Rs. 295.00	284
8170086116	**Multimedia and Web Technology**	Ramesh Bangia	Rs. 295.00	706

NETWORKING

ISBN	TITLE	AUTHOR	PRICE	PAGES
817008203X	**Telecom & Networking Glossary**	Robert Mastin	Rs. 300.00	250
8170082048	**Data Networking Made Easy**	Karen Patten	Rs. 360.00	350
8170082056	**Digital Convergence**	Andy Covell	Rs. 300.00	250

ON YOUR SIDE SERIES

ISBN	TITLE	AUTHOR	PRICE	PAGES
8170084830	**On your side-Powerpoint 2002**	Andrew Blackburn	Rs. 145.00	282
8170084849	**On your side-Excel 2002**	Adrienne Tommy	Rs. 125.00	275
8170084857	**On your side-Word 2002**	Adrienne Tommy	Rs. 125.00	289
8170084865	**On your side-Access 2002**	Adrienne Tommy	Rs. 125.00	303
8170084873	**On your side-Frontpage 2002**	Andrew Blackburn	Rs. 95.00	245
8170084881	**On your side-Windows XP**	Adrienne Tommy	Rs. 125.00	310

OPERATING SYSTEMS

ISBN	TITLE	AUTHOR	PRICE	PAGES
8170083427	**The MS-Windows XP Professional Handbook**	Louis Columbus	Rs. 295.00	330
8170084784	**Way in-Windows XP Home Edition**	Andrew Blackburn	Rs. 95.00	183
8170086221	**Operating System Fundamentals**	D. Irtegov	Rs. 295.00	498

PROGRAMMING

ISBN	TITLE	AUTHOR	PRICE	PAGES
817008623X	**Cyber Rookies—C++ Programming Fundamentals**	Chuck Easttan	Rs. 295.00	417
8170083648	**Mastering C++ Programs**	J.B. Dixit	Rs. 295.00	614
8170082889	**Basics of C++ Programming**	Nishant Kundalia	Rs. 95.00	168
8170083443	**Learning Computer Programming : It's not about Languages**	Mary Farrell	Rs. 295.00	375
8170083702	**The Power of C#**	Rajiv Parida	Rs. 295.00	592
8170085632	**Mastering Graphics Programming in C**	Sudhir Dawra	Rs. 145.00	286
8170086248	**Prevantative Programming Techniques : Avoid and Correct Common Mistakes**	Brain Hawkins	Rs. 295.00	322
8170086256	**Object-Oriented Programming From Problem Solving to Java**	Jose M. Garrido	Rs. 295.00	360

SECURITY

ISBN	TITLE	AUTHOR	PRICE	PAGES
3826607546	**Firewall Systems**	Norbert Pohlmann	Rs. 1,630.00	600
8170083419	**Computer Forensics : Computer Crime Scene Investigation**	John Vacca	Rs. 445.00	600
8170083494	**Firewall Architecture for the Enterprise**	Norbert Pohlmann, Tim Crothers	Rs. 295.00	480

Please write for a free color Firewall Media Catalog for details on the above books.

ISBN	TITLE	AUTHOR	PRICE	PAGES
8170086272	**Net Spies**	Andrew Gauntlett	Rs. 195.00	210

STRAIGHT TO THE POINT SERIES

ISBN	TITLE	AUTHOR	PRICE	PAGES
8170084601	**Straight to the Point : Word 2002**	Corinne Hervo	Rs. 45.00	154
817008461X	**Straight to the Point : Excel 2002**	Corinne Hervo	Rs. 45.00	153
8170084628	**Straight to the Point : Dreamweaver 4**	Corinne Hervo	Rs. 45.00	135
8170084636	**Straight to the Point : Flash 5**	Corinne Hervo	Rs. 45.00	126
8170084644	**Straight to the Point : Photoshop 6**	Corinne Hervo	Rs. 45.00	152
8170084482	**Straight to the Point : MS Office 2000**	Dinesh Maidisani	Rs. 95.00	300
8170086100	**Straight to the Point : MS Office 2003**	Dinesh Maidisani	Rs. 145.00	288

STUDIO FACTORY

ISBN	TITLE	AUTHOR	PRICE	PAGES
8170084792	**Studio Factory-Photoshop 6**	Christophe Aubry	Rs. 175.00	364
8170084806	**Studio Factory-Flash 5**	Sami Ben Yahiya	Rs. 145.00	314
8170084814	**Studio Factory-Dreamweaver Ultradev 4**	Phillippe Chatellier	Rs. 95.00	240
8170084822	**Studio Factory-Dreamweaver 4**	Christophe Aubry	Rs. 175.00	373

LAXMI PUBLICATIONS (P) LTD.

22 Golden House Daryaganj, New Delhi-110002

Phones : **23 26 23 68 ; 23 26 23 70**

Faxes : **011-23 25 25 72 ; 011-23 26 22 79**

http:/www.laxmipublications.com

BRANCHES

- 129/1, IIIrd Main Road, IX Cross Chamrajpet, **Bangalore** (*Phone* : 080-661 15 61)
- 26, Damodaran Street, T. Nagar, **Chennai** (*Phone* : 044-2434 47 26)
- St. Benedict's Road, **Cochin** (*Phone* : 0484-239 70 04)
- Pan Bazar, Rani Bari, **Guwahati** (*Phones* : 0361-254 36 69, 251 38 81)
- 4-2-453, Ist Floor, Ramkote, **Hyderabad** (*Phone* : 040-2475 02 47)
- Adda Tanda, **Jalandhar City** (*Phone* : 0181-222 12 72)
- 37-G, Bondel Road, **Kolkata** (*Phones* : 033-22 80 29 31, 22 80 90 19)
- 18, Madan Mohan Malviya Marg, **Lucknow** (*Phone* : 0522-220 95 78)
- 128A, Block 3, First Floor, Noorani Building, L.J. Road, **Mumbai** (*Phone* : 022-24 46 39 98)
- Radha Govind Street, Tharpagna, **Ranchi** (*Phone* : 0651-230 77 64)

Please write for a free color Firewall Media Catalog for details on the above books.

ORDER FORM

LAXMI PUBLICATIONS (P) LTD.

7/19, Ansari Road, Daryaganj, New Delhi-110002
Phones : 23262368, 23262370 ; *Faxes* : 011-2325 25 72, 2326 22 79
Email : colaxmi@hotmail.com
Website : www.laxmipublications.com

Please send me the following books by V.P.P. I have sent Rs. .... by M.O./Draft on Date ....

☐ ______________________________

☐ ______________________________

☐ ______________________________

☐ ______________________________

☐ ______________________________

☐ ______________________________

☐ ______________________________

(Please use separate sheet if you need more books)

Fill in this coupon in BLOCK letters only.

Name ______________________________

Address ______________________________

____

P.O. ________________ Distt. ________________

State ________________ Pin Code ☐☐☐☐☐☐

Phone ________________ Email ________________

Please do not refuse to accept the V.P.P. Honour it and write to us if there is any complaint. We shall set right your complaint, if any.

Our books are available at all leading bookshops.

Please mention Name of Books, clearly.

It is necessary to send Rs. 50.00 per book as an advance. Without advance order will not be sent.

Terms and Conditions for the supply of Books by V.P. Parcels to Students

1. Mention your name, address and nearest post office, with Pin Code No., in capital block letters for quick compliance of your order.
2. You can also send complete payment in advance by Money Order.
3. V.P. Parcels are detained by the Postal Authorities for only 5 days. Hence the same should be honoured on receiving intimation to avoid legal action against the defaulter.
4. Half Postage free.
5. All disputes will be settled in Delhi Courts only.
6. V.P. Parcels are not accepted for stations served by A.P.O. 56 and A.P.O. 99. While ordering for our Books from these stations, please ascertain and send the amount in full, in advance, on receipt of which, the books will be sent by registered post.
7. (*i*) V.P.P. Orders should be accompanied with advance of Rs. 50.00 per book. Without advance, ordered book(s) will not be sent.

   (*ii*) While sending advance by money order, please write your requirements on the last part of money order (space for communication). On its reverse side write your complete name and address.

   (*iii*) **Please note that the upper part of the money order form here you have written your address, remains with post office. So it is necessary to write your address again on last part of the M.O. form.**
8. Order placed will not be cancelled.
9. For books which are not supplied to you due to their being out of stock, please write again after 30 days with 25% advance.
10. Requests for our Books from students who did not honour their previous order will not be considered unless they send us full advance payment plus the postage charges for the returned parcel.
11. Prices are subject to change without notice.

Please write your letters to :

LAXMI PUBLICATIONS (P) LTD.

7/19, Ansari Road, Daryaganj, New Delhi-110002

Phones : 23262368, 23262370 ; *Faxes* : 011-2325 25 72, 2326 22 79

Email : colaxmi@hotmail.com

Website : www.laxmipublications.com